DEVELOPMENT AND THE CHALLENGE OF GLOBALIZATION

DEVELOPMENT AND THE CHALLENGE OF GLOBALIZATION

Edited by Peter Newell, Shirin M. Rai and Andrew Scott

ITDG
PUBLISHING

Published by ITDG Publishing
103–105 Southampton Row, London WC1B 4HL, UK
www.itdgpublishing.org.uk

© ITDG Publishing 2002
© The individual contributors 2002

First published in 2002

ISBN 1 85339 492 0

ITDG Publishing is the publishing arm of the Intermediate Technology Development
Group. Our mission is to build the skills and capacity of people in developing countries
through the dissemination of information in all forms, enabling them to improve the
quality of their lives and that of future generations.

Index by Indexing Specialists (UK) Ltd, Hove, E. Sussex
Typeset by Dorwyn Ltd, Rowlands Castle, Hants
Printed in Great Britain by Bell & Bain Ltd., Glasgow

Contents

Acknowledgements

THE EDITORS WOULD like to thank the Centre for the Study of Globalisation and Regionalisation (CSGR), University of Warwick, and the Intermediate Technology Development Group (ITDG) for the resources provided to bring together the scholars whose work is represented in this book. The seminars were organized under the theme of Globalization and Development. The aim was to bring together the community of scholars/activists to engage their mutual interests in this area. Thanks are due to those of our contributors who were present at the seminars and also to those who accepted our invitation to contribute to the project at a later date. In particular we would like to thank all our contributors for their patience, as this volume has taken longer to produce than we first anticipated, but we do think it is a stronger volume for that.

Peter Newell would like to thank John Wiley and Sons for permitting him to reproduce his journal article 'Managing multinationals: the governance of investment for the environment' from the *Journal of International Development* (vol. 13, 2001, pp. 907–19) as a chapter in this book, and Neil Adger for helpful comments on an earlier draft of the paper. We would also like to thank the Institute of Development Studies, University of Sussex, for allowing us to use some material that first appeared in the *IDS Bulletin*, vol. 30(3), 1999 in the environmental papers in this book. Finally, we would like to thank the referees for each of the chapters in the book as well as the anonymous referees who took the time to read the manuscript and provide positive and thoughtful feedback.

Contributors

Stephanie Barrientos is a fellow of the Institute of Development Studies. She has carried out research on gender and export horticulture in Chile and South Africa, globalization and ethical trade. Her publications include: *Women and Agribusiness: working miracles in Chilean fruit export sector* (with A. Bee, A. Matear and I. Vogel), (Macmillan, 1999); and *Women, Globalisation and Fragmentation in the Developing World* (ed. H. Afshar) (Macmillan, 1999).

Sharmishta Barwa studied at Presidency College and Calcutta University. She joined the Indian Administrative Service in 1975 and resigned in 1999. During her career she represented the World Bank as an advisor on small-scale industries to the Government of Ghana between 1992 and 1995. Since then she has worked as a consultant for several international organizations, including the ILO, UNDP, IFAD and the Commonwealth Secretariat, and served as an advisor to the governments of several African countries. Her research interests include: globalization, microenterprise and microcredit, gender issues in development and the protection of migrant workers. At the time of contributing to this volume, she was an Associate Fellow at the Centre for Women's Studies and the Centre for Regionalisation and Globalisation at the University of Warwick and an independent consultant.

Marilyn Carr is senior economic advisor with the United Nations Development Fund for Women (UNIFEM) and director of the Global Markets Programme, Women in Informal Employment: Globalizing and Organizing (WIEGO). She is currently based at the Institute of Development Studies, University of Sussex.

Charlie Dannreuther is a lecturer in European Political Economy at the University of Leeds, where he runs the postgraduate courses in European Politics for the Institute of Politics and International Studies. He has published on SME policy in the EU and the UK and more recently on the political economy of risk and its relationship with globalization.

Peter Dauvergne is a senior lecturer in the discipline of government and international relations at the University of Sydney. His most recent book is *Loggers and Degradation in the Asia-Pacific: corporations and environmental management* (Cambridge University Press, 2001). He is the founding and current editor of the journal *Global Environmental Politics*.

Jonathan Dawson has been a consultant for 15 years, specializing in the design and delivery of business development services for small-scale producers in Africa and Asia. He is also involved as a teacher and consultant in the promotion of sustainable community development in the industrialized world and is an advisor to the Global Ecovillage Network (GEN) – Europe.

Sudeshna Dey and **Biswajit Dhar** belong to the Research and Information System for the Non-Aligned and Other Developing Countries, a policy research institute based in New Delhi. They have been involved in the extensive debate on India's response to deliberations taking place in the World Trade Organization, particularly in key sectors like agriculture.

Matthias Finger holds PhDs in both political science and adult education. He is currently professor and director of the Management of Public Enterprises Unit at the Swiss Graduate School of Public Administration in Lausanne, Switzerland, and visiting professor at the Graduate Institute for Development Studies, Geneva. He is well known for his work in the area of social and organizational change, mainly within a public context, as well as for his contributions on international environmental policy. Among his publications are the co-authored books *Environmental NGOs in World Politics* and *The Earth Brokers*, both published by Routledge, and *Water Privatisation*, published by SPON Press.

Philip Mulligan is co-director for VSO Indonesia. His recent work at the Graduate Centre for Culture, Development and Environment, at the University of Sussex has focused on how globalization impacts on the land rights of indigenous peoples and biodiversity.

Peter Newell is a research fellow at the Institute of Development Studies. Prior to holding this position he was a lecturer in international political economy at the University of Warwick and worked with environmental NGOs in Brussels and London. He has published widely on the international politics of the environment, including the books *Climate for Change: non state actors and the global politics of the greenhouse* and *The Effectiveness of EU Environmental Policy* (co-authored). He currently works on the politics of crop biotechnology regulation and issues of corporate accountability and regulation.

Shirin M. Rai studied at the University of Delhi (India) and Cambridge University (UK). She is currently reader in politics at the University of Warwick. Her research interests are in the area of feminist politics, democratization, globalization and development studies. She has written extensively on issues of gender, governance and democratization. Author of several books, she has recently published *Gender and the Political Economy of Development: from nationalism to globalisation* (Polity Press). She has edited

International Perspectives on Gender and Democratisation (2000), *Global Social Movements* (with Robin Cohen, 2000). She is the series editor (with Wyn Grant) for the book series *Perspectives on Democratization* (Manchester University Press) and a member of the editorial boards of *Democratization* and *International Feminist Journal of Politics.* Her current research focuses on gender and political economy, as well as on citizenship and human rights.

Andrew Scott is international programmes and policy director for ITDG, responsible for overall direction of the Group's policy research and advocacy programmes, the development of ITDG's knowledge management systems and oversight of the organization's strategies. His educational background is in economics, but he has worked across the social sciences (and has even acquired a bit of technological knowledge). He has a particular interest in questions concerning small enterprises and the environment, concepts relating to technology and development, and the development impacts of modern information and communication technologies. He has worked in Botswana, Kenya, Zimbabwe, Tanzania, Malawi, Sri Lanka, India, Nepal and Peru.

Ines Smyth has a PhD in social anthropology from University College London. She has been a lecturer and researcher in various academic institutions, including the Institute of Social Studies (The Hague) and the London School of Economics. Presently she is a policy advisor for Oxfam Great Britain. Her research interests are: gender and development, industrialization and social policy, with particular concern for East Asia.

Ludivine Tamiotti worked at the United Nations International Court of Justice in The Hague, at the Institute of Advanced Studies in Public Administration in Lausanne, and at the Environment Unit of the United Nations High Commissioner for Refugees in Geneva. She is a PhD candidate at the Graduate Institute of International Studies (IUHEI-Geneva) and she holds an LLM from New York University School of Law, a Masters in International Relations from the Graduate Institute of International Studies (IUHEI-Geneva) and a Masters in International Law from the Faculty of Law of the University of Aix-en-Provence. She has published widely on environment, trade and international law issues.

Acronyms and abbreviations

AGM	annual general meeting
AIE	Analysis and Information Exchange
AMS	Aggregate Measurement of Support
AoA	Agreement on Agriculture
ASEAN	Association of South East Asian Countries
ATO	alternative trading organization
AusAID	Australian Agency for International Development
CBD	Convention on Biodiversity
CCA	Compliance Cost Assessment
CERES	Coalition for Environmentally Responsible Economies
CFC	chlorofluorocarbon
CIDA	Canadian International Development Agency
CoA	Committee on Agriculture
DEVCO	ISO Policy Committee on Developing Country Matters
DFID	Department for International Development
EA&RI	Environmental Auditing & Related Investigations
EDU	Enterprise and Deregulation Unit
EL	Environmental Labels and Declarations
EMS	Environmental Management Systems
EPE	Environmental Performance Evaluation
EPZ	Export Processing Zone
ETI	Ethical Trading Initiative
EU	European Union
FDI	foreign direct investment
FDL	foreign direct liability
FSC	Forestry Stewardship Council
GATT	General Agreement on Tariffs and Trade
GDP	gross domestic product
GEF	Global Environment Facility
GMO	genetically modified organism
GNP	gross national product
ICT	information and communications technology
IEC	International Electrotechnical Commission
ILO	International Labour Organisation
IMF	International Monetary Fund
ISO	International Organization for Standardization
IT	information technology
ITTO	International Tropical Timber Organization
LCA	Life Cycle Assessment
LDCs	less-developed countries
MAI	Multilateral Agreement on Investment
MFA	Multilateral Fibre Arrangement
MFN	Most Favoured Nation
MNC	multinational corporation

NAFTA	North American Free Trade Agreement
NFIDC	the net food-importing developing country
NGO	non-governmental organization
NTAE	non-traditional agricultural exports
NTB	non-tariff barrier
NTC	non-trade concern
NTFP	non-timber forest products
OECD	Organisation for Economic Co-operation and Development
PRA	participatory rural appraisal
REDS	Rural Enterprise Development Services
RIA	radioimmunoassay
RIIA	Royal Institute of International Affairs
RRA	rapid rural appraisal
S&D	special and differential
SAGE	Strategic Advisory Group on Environment
SAP	structural adjustment policy
SBLT	Small Business Litmus Test
SEWA	Self-Employed Women's Association
SGS	Société Générale de Surveillance
SMEs	small and medium-sized enterprises
SSG	special safeguard
STE	State Trading Enterprise
T&D	Terms and Definitions
TBT	technical barriers to trade
TC	technical committee
TCFUA	Textile, Clothing and Footwear Union
TNC	transnational corporation
TRIPS	Trade-Related Intellectual Property Rights
TRQ	tariff rate quota
UN	United Nations
UNCED	United Nations Conference on Environment and Development
UNCTC	United Nations Centre on Transnational Corporations
UNCTAD	United Nations Conference on Trade and Development
UNDP	United Nations Development Programme
UNEP	United Nations Environment Programme
UNICED	United Nations Conference on Environment and Development
UNICEF	United Nations Children's Fund
UNIFEM	United Nations Development Fund for Women
UNRISD	United Nations Research Institute on Social Development
USTPO	United States Patent and Trade Mark Office
WDM	World Development Movement
WEDO	Women Environment and Development Organization
WHO	World Health Organization
WIEGO	Women in Informal Employment: Globalizing and Organizing
WIPO	World Intellectual Property Organization
WTO	World Trade Organization
WWF	World Wide Fund for Nature

Introduction: Development and the challenge of globalization

PETER NEWELL, SHIRIN M. RAI and ANDREW SCOTT

IN THE BRITISH government's White Paper on international development (DFID, 2000), the challenge for development was outlined as follows: 'the reduction of abject poverty in the world … As a first step toward the complete elimination of poverty, the targets include a reduction by one half in the proportion of people living in extreme poverty by 2015' (p. 12).[1] However, as the World Development Report 2000/2001 points out:

> At the start of a new century, poverty remains a global problem of huge proportions. Of the world's 6 billion people, 2.8 billion live on less than $2 a day and 1.2 billion on less than $1 a day. Eight out of every 100 infants do not live to see their fifth birthday. Nine of every 100 boys and 14 of every 100 girls who reach school age do not attend school. Poverty is also evident in poor people's lack of political power and voice and in their extreme vulnerability to ill health, economic dislocation, personal violence and natural disasters. And the scourge of HIV/AIDS, the frequency and brutality of civil conflicts, and rising disparities between rich countries and the developing world have increased the sense of deprivation and injustice for many (World Bank, 2000).

After more than 50 years of international development cooperation, elimination of poverty remains the challenge.

The context of development, however, has changed and continues to shift rapidly under globalization. This is increasingly being recognized by key actors in the development debate. But there remains a need to assess in what ways this new context poses challenges for development. How do processes of globalization transform, undermine or reinforce existing patterns of inequality and injustice? What new configurations of power emerge in globalized society and what are their implications for the poor? The aim of this book is to take a critical look at the trends we associate with globalization and assess what they mean for traditional practices of development. Going beyond attempts to quantify the pros and cons of globalization and the ideological tenor of much of the polemical debate, our approach here is to focus on the actors, institutions and processes by which the relationship between globalization and poverty is mediated. Emphasizing agency and structure in this debate is important in establishing who the winners and losers from globalization are likely to be, given the current political and economic constraints under which we operate. Such an approach helps to clarify the sense of the obstacles and opportunities that will shape any attempt to promote poverty elimination in a context of globalization.

Reviewing debates on globalization

Few phenomena have so rapidly gained popular currency as 'globalization'. The term is often taken as a byword for any activity that extends beyond sovereign borders in the economic, political, social or cultural domain. Two sets of debates have dominated the field of globalization studies. The first focused on whether globalization is a new phenomenon or whether the uniqueness attached to this new phase of development is misplaced. Hirst and Thompson (1996) suggest, for instance, that there has merely been an extension of the trend towards 'internationalization', which has waxed and waned over many centuries, rather than a quantifiable break with previous eras of economic integration. Others, such as Giddens, have argued that many elements of contemporary globalization are unique and therefore we need a new analytical framework to understand our world (Giddens, 1990; Held *et al.*, 1999).[2] Hence the very language we use to describe the nature of the contemporary global political economy is contested. Different accounts of the changes taking place have been used to sustain conflicting claims such as:

○ the state is in retreat (Strange, 1996)
○ that the notion of a powerless state is a 'myth' (Weiss, 1998)
○ that 'corporations rule the world' (Korten, 1995)
○ that the idea of a global corporation is a myth (Doremus *et al.*, 1998)
○ or that, in fact, the language of globalization is a useful device for neoliberals to advance the process they claim merely to describe.

At the centre of these debates is the changing relationship between national states and global markets, and the shifts in the processes and institutions that regulate this relationship. These concerns about the relationship between the state and the market are the focus of the second set of debates – about the consequences of globalization. It is in this growing area of scholarship that most of the current debates about globalization and development are taking shape (Held *et al.*, 1999; Scholte, 2000; Marchand and Runyan, 2000), and where we hope this volume will make a contribution.

The consequences of globalization have been mapped in two areas.[3] First, the consequences of global convergence for the nation state. It is often claimed that the world capitalist economy is posing a threat to national sovereignty and a threat to national culture in the form of 'westernization', which, in turn, supports dominant forms of global capitalism. Second, competing explanations of globalization also focus on the consequences of globalization for issues of security, governance and equity. In the following section, we examine some of these debates to provide a context for the issues examined in the book as a whole.

Converging cultures and markets

Among the liberal political theorists of the immediate post-Cold War period, three articulations, in particular, have been extremely influential: Fukuyama's 'end of history' thesis (Fukuyama, 1993), Huntington's vision of the victory of the Christian liberal ethic over Islam in a clash of civilizations (Huntington, 1996), and Barber's lament against global capitalism and Islamic (and other) fundamentalisms that undermine democracy and evocation of a revitalized liberal democracy within the national state structure (Barber, 1996). In each of these three envisionings of the world in the twenty-first century, liberal values triumph over others; aspects of Western civilization predominate over other cultures and modernity's concerns are resolved through these triumphs. Struggles to reform cultures, religions and ideologies from within are, according to these narratives, doomed to failure. The logical conclusion then is that the Western liberal world is the only future that we can 'rationally' look forward to if we wish to live civilized, non-violent and democratic lives (Rai, 1998: 2). Already, however, this certitude seems untenable. With the Asian Economic Crisis of 1997 on the one hand, and the Seattle protests against the World Trade Organization (WTO) on the other, the liberal economic and cultural certainty that such accounts provide seems to be fracturing. Getting away from these meta-narratives of globality, others have tried to pin down its meanings by examining its component features.

For some, like Albrow, while the nation state was firmly tied to modernity, the promise of a global age is based on the future of post-modernity: 'Fundamentally the Global Age involves the supplanting of modernity with globality and this means an overall change in the basis of action and social organization for individuals and social groups' (Albrow, 1996: 4). For Giddens, on the other hand, globalization is about 'late modernity', where technological developments have brought about a new reflexivity about the world in which we live. He describes a time–space distantiation which is irreversible and indeed worthy of celebration as it allows human kind to move towards a cosmopolitanism based on a true melding of cultures (Giddens, 1990). In this reading, reflexivity of a new kind underpins globalization, which allows us to be concerned about the 'global village', about future generations and their access to resources, and about the interaction of the individual with governance mechanisms, not only at the local but at the global level. John Gray, on the other hand, finds late modernity besieged by the forces of globalization which, for him, are essentially forces of the free market, which in turn is dominated by the concerns of the major player in the market – the United States (Gray, 1998). The free market, for Gray, is where the false dawn rises, as it is not free at all, except for a minority, and indeed its operations erode communities and cultures everywhere. While Gray's analysis of globalization is largely a normative one, other scholars have examined this phenomenon from a political economy perspective.

Picciotto, for example, has argued that the core of globalization is 'The Market, or at least ideologies of free trade and open markets ... What seems to be more important is the increased *potential* for such flows [of international market transactions], resulting from the reduction or elimination of national and local barriers to all kinds of trade and investment' (Picciotto, 1996: 3). This focus on elimination of state boundaries has been constructed in different ways too. For Strange, the breaking down of boundaries has been seen in terms of the erosion of state power in the face of the globalization of markets (Strange, 1996). From another perspective, Robert Cox argues that from being bulwarks against global intrusions into national economies, today's states are facilitating the adaptation of their societies to new realities within the global political economy. Evidence of this is most apparent in the rejection of Keynesian welfarist economics. To perform this changed role, state managers have reconfigured the power structures of government, giving far more emphasis to ministries responsible for finance and trade rather than industry and labour, for example. The state's role, therefore, becomes one of helping to adjust the domestic economy to the requirements of the world economy (Cox, 1996). The disciplinary power of mobile capital and the potential of credit-rating agencies to destabilize economies provide the necessary incentives to ensure compliance and deter those governments tempted to deviate from the rule of the market (Gill, 1995). Thus governance under globalization, while retaining the state as a crucial actor, has also expanded to include other social and economic actors across public and private fora and at all levels of political activity. These trends are described more fully below in the section on governance and globalization.

Differential effects: who gains?

The distribution of the effects of globalization between countries has been very uneven, with the North benefiting much more than the South in general terms. Even among and within countries of the South, processes of integration and marginalization co-exist as wealthier countries are benefiting more than those most in need of economic development (Hoogvelt, 1997). Ten countries, for example, receive about 75 per cent of the foreign direct investment in the South (World Bank, 2000) with areas of sub-Saharan Africa neglected altogether. The impacts of economic dislocation and programmes of reform invariably fall on the poorest, those least able to adapt to change and with fewer resources to create alternative livelihoods. While members of the élite, both North and South, have benefited from the greater availability of foreign goods, cheaper travel and increased incomes, the social costs have been borne by the poor, in terms of increased insecurity, withdrawal of welfare provisions and exposure to market forces over which they have no control. In this sense, processes of globalization should be seen as deriving from a conscious set of decisions and non-decisions by those with power to intervene or not intervene on behalf of the poor (Newell, 2001). It should not be surprising then that many of the trends we associate with globalization have served to consolidate and extend the power of the already powerful. This has inevitably generated new inequalities and consolidated ownership of key resources in the hands of the wealthy. For example, when 95 per cent of the world's patents are held in the North, it is clear that the concentration of ownership of intellectual property is likely to lead to a transfer of income from the less-developed countries to the more-developed countries and widen the income disparities between them (see Chapter 2).

As with every period of large-scale economic restructuring at the global level, globalization introduces new shocks and vulnerabilities. Increased openness of trade brings increased instability to many countries, and to vulnerable groups within countries. Though economic gains might be achieved (measured in terms of gross national product (GNP) or total employment) through openness, it is important to recognize that the poor can become even more marginalized under volatile conditions (as evidenced in the Asian crisis). While there is a role for the state and civil society to ensure social protection for these vulnerable sectors, this is difficult to provide when the ability of the state to create and maintain effective safety nets is undermined by squeezes on state spending on public services under structural adjustment programmes. In addition, when subsidies are removed, protection withdrawn, services privatized and user charges introduced, it will be those with fewer resources to adapt and innovate who will be hit hardest. Protests over water privatization in Bolivia and the quadrupling of water charges suggest that imposed changes of this nature will not be passively accepted. The debate in India over the pace at which quantitative restrictions are lifted as part of India's obligations under the WTO, outlined by Biswajit Dhar and Sudeshna Dey in Chapter 4, lends further weight to this concern. In comprehending the discriminating effects of global change on different social groups, we confront the gendered nature of globalization processes. Crises brought about by financial volatility or market collapse affect the poor, but there is evidence that poor women are disproportionately the losers (DAW, 1999; Truong, 2000). Similarly, patterns of export-oriented production are generating negative effects that are often more visible in women's lives. As Carr notes in Chapter 8, ' . . . although tea producing households have higher income than those which do not produce tea, they have higher levels of malnutrition because women have little or no control over income in the former'.

With 2 billion people continuing to live in absolute poverty, the policy challenge is whether and, if so, how, globalization can be harnessed to contribute to reducing or even eliminating poverty. What then are the challenges to the objective of poverty reduction implied by globalization? These operate at a number of levels. Here we will focus on two key themes central to understanding the implications of global economic change and the patterns of political power that are created: governance and production.

Governance and globalization

The principal aim of this book is to explore how the relationship between globalization and poverty is mediated by the institutions and actors that govern social and economic interactions at every level of society. This means critically examining key actors, their changing roles and the discourses they use to sustain their position in development debates. This is in sharp contrast to one of the most common representations of globalization as a process which is not guided, a driver-less machine beyond anyone's control, where anonymous flows of trade and finance move around the globe with consequences we can neither anticipate nor control. The effect of removing questions of power and agency from the study of globalization is to present the phenomena as natural, inevitable and benign. From a development perspective, this makes it very difficult to determine the causes of change and the appropriate sites for pro-poor reform (Newell, 2001).

At a policy level there is a tendency to depoliticize the globalization debate through appeals to benign management. For example, the DFID White Paper on globalization notes, 'Managed wisely, the new wealth being created by globalisation creates the opportunity to lift millions of the world's poorest people out of their poverty. Managed badly and it could lead to their further marginalisation ...' (DFID, 2000: 15). The structural power of relations of production is subsumed under a processual understanding of the term 'globalization'. Given the contested nature of the process, as well as the varied elements that make up globalization, the assumption that 'globalization' is 'creating wealth' seems rather vacuous. At the same time, we see evidence of what McMichael has called 'new managerialism' – a way of packaging political conflict as a management issue. In the White Paper, GATT/WTO, IMF and the World Bank, together with DFID, become the levers of change under globalization as they guide developing countries through privatization (DFID, 2000: 24), combating corruption (DFID, 2000: 25) and strengthening human rights (DFID, 2000: 27). The re-emphasis on responsible management can be seen as a rallying call around the merits of globalization on the part of the development community in the face of rising levels of discontent about the inequalities and democratic deficits that globalization produces, expressed, in part, by the anti-globalization movement.

The myths of consent and consensus

Encouraging an 'adapt or perish' view of the changes taking place in the global economy serves important ideological functions. The delegitimization of some policy options on the grounds that they are no longer tenable and the promotion of others has an impact on the direction of policy. The discourse of TINA (There is No Alternative) serves to absolve governments and other actors of blame for the consequences of their actions. Reckless investments and irresponsible speculation are attributed to unaccountable market actors over whom they allege they have no control. The myth of powerlessness associated with globalization also provides governments with a convenient alibi to make changes and impose social costs on society that would be difficult to justify by other means. Preventing wage increases, curtailing the powers of unions, restricting public expenditure and resisting calls for higher environmental standards have all been used in this way by industry lobby groups and neo-liberal political parties. Differentiating between the constraints that globalization actually imposes on governments, as opposed to those they choose to emphasize for strategic reasons, is, of course, a difficult task.

The myth of consent is another feature of the discourse of globalization. The myth that conceals the power relations behind it is that countries are freely selecting to open up and liberalize their economies because they have realized, post-Cold War, that the market delivers social welfare in the most efficient and even-handed manner. However, structural adjustment policies (SAPs), conditionalities, tied aid, exclusive decision making in key global economic institutions (such as the Organisation for Economic Co-operation and Development, OECD, and the International Monetary Fund, IMF) and the threat of retaliatory actions through organizations like the WTO have been some of the mechanisms by which the North has been able to use its leverage to promote globalization in the developing world. These pressures 'from above' have raised concerns that rather than globalization being a popular, demand-led process, governments are, if anything, becoming less responsive to the needs of their people. There are clearly areas of potential conflict between serving the needs of the poor and accommodating the demands of international capital when preferences for welfare provision and the provision of state support for key economic and social sectors are considered to be anti-competitive or trade restrictive.

The idea that there is a broad-based consensus in favour of global market integration is being challenged across the globe by a range of social movements. This suggests that the global business class that formulates and coordinates global economic policy through transnational business dialogues, global economic institutions and agenda-setting bodies like the Trilateral Commission (Gill, 1993) or the World Economic Forum does not speak for the majority of the world when it claims that what is good for them is good for the world's poor. While faith in the assumption that globalization would eventually deliver benefits to the poor remained, on the surface at least, unquestioned during the 1980s and early 1990s, by the late 1990s that faith was being shaken. Following in the wake of the Asian financial crisis, which devastated the economies of Southeast Asia, negotiations towards a 'Development Round' for the WTO and the attempt to enshrine investors' rights in a global accord by the name of the MAI (Multilateral Agreement on Investment), a disparate set of campaigns on issues ranging from child labour and the environmental impact of trade, to the behaviour of multinational corporations (MNCs) in developing countries and the rights of indigenous peoples have begun to focus on globalization. What appears to unite groups mobilizing around these issues is a sense in which the injustices they are confronting result from a similar set of processes that deny access and entitlements to the poorest in society.

Given the intensity of shocks and crises of various forms, which visibly hit the poor hardest, this disillusionment with globalization is unsurprising. By far the majority of the world's poor do not participate in globalization in terms of shaping the decisions that affect their lives, even though they are affected by them. Their lack of purchasing power and political clout necessarily means that this is the case. This is in spite of claims by protesters against globalization that they represent the voices of the marginalized. What is interesting, however, is the nature of the coalitions of civil society actors that are forming to protest against the different dimensions of globalization, forging linkages between social groups and articulating connections across different issues. While the manifestations of economic change differ according to the locale in which they become visible, the causes and processes that have brought them into being often have something in common. Global citizen action is, therefore, helping to identify the actors, interests and ideologies that drive the globalization process and benefit most from its gains, fixing our attention on the question of 'Who is globalization for?'.

The political reordering of the state?

In geopolitical terms it is sometimes argued that the term 'globalization' is misleading because it describes a trend which is largely confined to the relations between a small number of highly industrialized states and firms operating within the triad (East Asia, North America and Europe). The chapters in this book demonstrate, however, that it is a process with repercussions that extend far beyond the power centres of the global economy. They illustrate how international economic processes and social norms penetrate and impact, however indirectly, on the lives of most people, even if the architects of the current system and those who propagate versions of the 'Washington consensus' most vociferously are based in the OECD countries.

Increasingly, key decisions concerning global economic processes are being made at regional and international levels, generating concerns about representation and the emergence of democratic deficits when the demands of domestic electorates are subservient to decisions reached between unaccountable decision makers. The growth of regionalization has meant that an increasing number of areas of social and political life, with important development implications, are governed by what is best for the achievement of full market integration. This is especially so in regions where this process is most advanced, such as Europe. The imperatives of market access and creating 'level playing fields' have been the guiding principles for areas of policy that have nothing to do with trade, such as the environment (Grant *et al.*, 2000). The dynamic between state and market is clearly two-way, however. Institutions both react to and drive the process of globalization. We know from Polanyi (1980) that market activities are always socially embedded and inevitably shaped by the social and political pressures that create and maintain them. The World Bank and IMF have clearly played a significant part in creating the conditions for market expansion and globalized transactions by moulding the policies of states in a neo-liberal guise.

We have already reviewed some of the debates around the role of the state in a globalized economy in general terms. However, from a development perspective it is interesting to consider whether the developmental states that were considered to be central to the economic 'success' of many Asian economies are at an end. Interventionist regulation and the direction of markets by states is out of vogue in the policy circles that generate and sustain the enduring tenets of the Washington consensus, but neo-liberals struggle to explain the economic success achieved by East Asian countries that adopted a strong state model of development, which so squarely contradicts the anti-state emphasis of neo-liberalism (Hoogvelt, 1997). Despite efforts by World Bank economists to portray government interventions as merely 'aimed at creating macro-economic stability and a suitable environment for entrepreneurs to perform their functions by providing certain public goods', screening policies, financial instruments, and trade and industrial relations policies adopted by East Asian economies were blatantly market distorting (Hoogvelt, 1997: 203–4). Renewed interest in the importance of [good] governance also provides evidence of a step back, in some quarters, from the assault on the state associated with the height of neo-liberal Reaganomics. This interest is driven by a belated recognition that not only are strong states important for creating and sustaining market activity, but also that good governance is important both for creating an attractive investment climate and for targeting poverty (World Bank, 1997).

In this sense, it is perhaps more appropriate to talk about the reordering and reconfiguration of state power between government, capital and what is often referred to as the third sector (civil society). For some governments, this redivision of labour for undertaking key state responsibilities – decisions, for example, to privatize national industries and farm out the provision of state services to the private sector and non-governmental organizations (NGOs) – has been an active choice. For other, mostly developing, countries, this power shift has been to some extent thrust upon them as a condition attached to World Bank loans, as a component of structural adjustment policies or through tied aid from donors. Either way, this shift has implications for the poor, whose services are delivered by non-state agents keen to extract a profit or responsive to Northern governments, institutions and agendas. Accountability deficits quickly emerge in the transition from state-run to privately organized services for the poor that may undermine the goal of responsiveness they were meant to serve.

Another aspect of the governance of the global economy with important implications for development is the relationship between deregulation and reregulation. While some view the relationship as cyclical, whereby periods of deregulation (such as in the 1980s) are inevitably followed by periods of reregulation, such as the recent growth in forms of private and civil regulation (Newell, 2000; Clapp, 1999; Bendell, 2000), it is perhaps more likely that deregulation and reregulation co-exist. For example, in relation to business regulation, while there has been a failure to advance the regulation of MNCs at the international level, there has been a growth in industry codes of conduct and other voluntary agreements (Picciotto and Mayne, 1999; Braithwaite and Drahos, 2000). Similarly, while at the international level, legal *regulation of* global business actors is underdeveloped, *regulation for* business, in terms of regulatory arrangements that facilitate transactions and exchange, and that affirm the entry and exit options of multinational enterprises, has increased. Indeed, this is the basis of concerns that there is a mismatch between the rights that business actors have acquired through regional and global trade arrangements and the lack of corresponding responsibilities that they are expected to exercise (Newell, Chapter 11).

Clearly then, globalization is a contested process with outcomes that affect people well beyond the principal decision-making centres of the global economy. This inevitably means that the issue of whether the gains from globalization can be spread and the negative effects controlled, will be a question of political organization and institutional design, and the outcome of conflicts between competing social and economic forces over who sets the rules and for whom. Such rules are likely to be a product of tensions between the desire of some to see common rules, harmonized procedures and centralized procedures for rule making and the concern of others to preserve autonomy, diversity and difference in national economic and social strategies. These tensions are, in part, configured along North–South lines and are manifested in, for example, the Biosafety Protocol to regulate the trade in genetically modifed organisms (GMOs), which seeks to reconcile the interests of GMO exporters with the demands of many African nations, in particular, for the right to exclude imports on the basis of detrimental socioeconomic impacts they may have (Newell and MacKenzie, 2000).

The fora in which these matters are settled will clearly also make a difference. The mandates, ideologies and decision-making procedures of institutions will strongly affect their ability to respond to concerns about the development impacts of globalization. Representatives of the WTO have argued, for example, that considering the social and environmental impacts of trade is beyond the mandate of the organization, whose brief is restricted to facilitating the removal of barriers to trade. Similarly, concern has been expressed, by NGOs in particular, that the OECD is an inappropriate forum in which to negotiate a multilateral agreement on investment, given that it is biased towards Northern countries and is more concerned with investor rights than investor responsibilities. There are also broader questions about whether decisions of such significance to developing countries should be made in fora in which they are under-represented and insufficiently resourced to participate in effectively. Finger and Tamiotti raise these concerns in Chapter 5. For these reasons, international decision-making tends to privilege the powerful, who are better placed to shape the agenda because of a combination of structural power in the global economy and armies of lawyers and experts on hand to shape the deliberations in line with their priorities. Thinking creatively about multi-level approaches to decision making may allow for more equitable and efficient decision making. Strengthening local, national and regional decision-making arenas in the South may make institutions more responsive to development priorities and dilute the concentration of power that Northern countries and companies have over global, particularly economic, organizations. Questions of policy process, promoting inclusivity, transparency, coherence and equity are key to ensuring that globalization does not further impoverish the already poor.

Production and exchange under globalization

During the second half of the 20th century the value of world exports increased 60-fold[4] – a single, dramatic statistic that clearly illustrates the pace and scale of economic globalization and explains the emphasis given to international trade in globalization discourse. Little wonder that the WTO is regarded as the embodiment of globalization, even if these trends were in place before the body was created. Carr (Chapter 8) notes that during the same period, world output increased sixfold. The share of world gross domestic product (GDP) rose from about 6 per cent in 1950 to almost one-fifth in the late 1990s (Nayyer, 2000). In other words, the increase in the volume of international trade cannot be wholly attributed to increases in output. Per unit of output there is a higher volume of international trade, associated with the increased movement of goods across the world and changing patterns of production in the global economy.

Changing production patterns are reflected in the organization of production. Production systems have become more international in their nature –

with a growing proportion of raw materials, intermediate products and parts crossing national boundaries during the production process. Increasingly, international trade takes place during the production process rather than at the stage of end products. The share of intra-firm trading in world trade increased from one-fifth in the early 1970s to one-third in the early 1990s (Nayyer, 2000). At the same time, there is increasing vertical integration in the production system and concentration of production in fewer and larger companies. While the content of a product might be drawn from a greater number of countries, it is likely to have passed through fewer companies. In some cases, the production process is entirely under the control of one corporation (e.g. petroleum products). In many cases, production takes place within a number of contractually linked companies, but with the final buyer dictating quality and product specifications, and thus the technology used in production. For example, the detailed contracts set by Northern supermarket chains for goods supplied to them by Southern producers (see Barrientos, Chapter 9). This control can extend to marketing and distribution channels as mergers and acquisitions further concentrate ownership in the hands of larger companies. For instance, the influence of Coca-Cola, and other companies, on the sale of their products extends to the smallest of vendors (see Carr, Chapter 8).

While economic globalization entails changing patterns of production, it also produces changes in the nature of the goods and services being traded internationally. International trade in services is expanding rapidly. Under globalization, the processes of production have been shifting from manufacturing to service (information and knowledge-based) industries, from factory-based production to flexible labour patterns, with increasing amounts of subcontracting leading to outsourcing of production through home working (Peterson, 2000; Carr, Chapter 8). And increasingly, flexibilization of labour is based on these 'knowledge-based industries'.

Globalization in the organization of production leads to more complex systems, where the links between individuals, companies, institutions and national economies intensify. This complexity leads to more intense, less predictable and more rapid fluctuations. The internal systems within countries react unpredictably to external events. In Chapter 1, Dauvergne shows how financial shocks lead to immediate changes in production as people seek alternative livelihoods.

These complexities are made possible by new information and communications technologies (ICTs) and management techniques, which are themselves regarded as an integral aspect of globalization. The advantages of modern ICTs have not just been felt in the areas of e-commerce transfers and international capital transfers. They also enable the organization and management of information in more complex systems. In the global marketplace, information is becoming the key commodity. Since the information-driven globalization process is heavily dependent on new technological developments, it also ushers in an era of rapid and constantly changing technological processes and production methods. However, integrated supply chains facilitated by these media make Northern companies more vulnerable to adverse publicity regarding employment conditions or environmental impacts at the supplier end, because they also facilitate the ready international exchange of information between interest groups (Fabig and Boele, 1999).

The expansion of international trade in services and knowledge-based products has undoubtedly been enabled by modern information and transport technologies, reducing cross-border costs of such services. It has also been enabled by changes in the regulatory environment that permit the use of trade-related intellectual property rights (TRIPS). Ironically, another of the paradoxes of globalization has been that as international trade is liberalized and competition between countries is freer, the regulation or ownership of products, brands and knowledge is intensifying. Commercial regulatory control, it might be argued, has moved from the international level to the (transnational) corporate sphere, from product category to brand. As Barwa and Rai (Chapter 2) show, the TRIPS Agreement defines the tradeable knowledge product by identifying the boundaries of particular products and processes. This has allowed ideas, knowledge and information to be brought into the arena of international trade through regulatory protection of property rights (patents) in such intangibles. However, because 'patents privilege particular forms of knowledge ... stabilizing historically developed processes of production [they] entitle modern industrial companies to patent products and processes and deny nature's and people's creativity'. The global knowledge economy is resulting in the 'commodification of traditional, community or public knowledge, perhaps providing evidence of a 21st-century enclosure movement' (Miller, 2001)

How is the changing pattern of production affecting employment and labour markets? With the decline of Fordist patterns of production and dispersal of the labour force, there is also a decrease in the unionization of labour. The increased vulnerability of competitive states to the threat by MNCs of capital flight has resulted in attacks on the unionization of workers. Greater flexibility in the labour market within developing countries and industrialized countries has been brought about by deregulation in line with principles of economic liberalization. Chapter 1 describes the impact of short-term financial capital movements on employment in Asia – agricultural employment in Indonesia increased by 5.6 million following the Asian Crisis; while in Chapters 8 and 9, Carr and Barrientos show that the mobility of fixed capital affects socioeconomic groups differently. Part-time and temporary workers, often female, are the most vulnerable to fluctuations in production – brought about because of cost advantages elsewhere (within the firm) as much as by changes in demand. Deregulation and liberalization, however, have not extended to the international labour market to quite the same extent as for capital and goods transactions. Though globalization of the labour market results in temporary migration, controls remain in place in most industrialized countries. While there is disturbing evidence of the poor conditions of work in local labour markets supplying global centres, the effects of globalization on labour in local markets have not all been negative. Barrientos argues in Chapter 9 that women have gained opportunities for employment, income and enhanced status in some countries. New forms of employment, through subcontracting and outsourcing by large companies and multinationals to smaller local producers have enabled them to engage in the global economy.

Orthodox international trade theory is based on the concept that countries should concentrate on production that is based on available natural resources and existing capabilities, and trade for those products they cannot produce as efficiently. For instance, Carr (Chapter 8) characterizes Africa as an exporter of primary products, Asia as an exporter of labour-intensive manufactured products, and South America as an exporter of non-traditional agricultural products and of services. In the globalized economy, however, notions of comparative advantage have become centred not just on the final products that countries can produce, but increasingly on the advantages they might have within the production process.

The writers in this volume highlight that the competition on the basis of comparative advantage is now not so much between countries as between companies. Production within a company is moved from location to location to take advantage of relative differences in costs – of labour particularly. Thus comparative advantage can mean lower labour standards, lower environmental standards, weaker enforcement of the regulations that remain or merely 'regulatory chill'. Dogged pursuit of the logic of comparative advantage leads to the conclusion in the (in)famous World Bank memo that given that an amount of health-impairing pollution should be done in the country with the lowest cost, which will be the country with the lowest wages, '... the economic logic behind dumping a load of toxic waste in the lowest wage country is impeccable'.[5] At the same time, when it comes to exporting goods from developing to developed countries, there may be pressure to 'trade up' standards as gaining access to Northern markets means meeting tougher environmental standards (Vogel, 1997). Newell (Chapter 11) also shows that companies' social and ethical obligations, promoted by NGOs and consumers, are outstripping the legal restrictions on their investment practices. The interdependencies that flow from global integration create competing incentives. Dauvergne, for example, shows how short-term fluctuations in financial markets lead to changes in the sectors of investment – from export-oriented manufacturing to export-oriented agriculture and primary products, because these sectors are less dependent on foreign currency inputs and absorb the large pool of unemployed labour.

The structure of the book

As Mittelmann observes, 'the architecture of globalisation is too large to perceive as a whole, but if one moves to a finer scale, the structures become discernible' (Mittelman, 1998: 849). Case study approaches allow for a more micro-consideration of the sites at which globalization is manifested and the changes that are produced. The issues and actors discussed in the contributions to this volume highlight, therefore, a number of features of a trend that we often talk about in more macro terms. These themes are discussed in turn below.

The aim of the book is to focus on changes taking place in the institutions and actors central to development, brought about by shifts in the global economy. The chapters are clustered under three themes. We focus, in turn, on the consequences of globalization, the actors, institutions and movements that are operating in the new global political space, and on the strategies that are being developed to contest the impact of globalization on people's lives and ability to define development alternatives. Cutting across these themes we highlight three broad areas in particular – production and exchange in the context of small-scale enterprises, changing gender relations and feminist movements, and the environmental consequences of globalization and the movements that have emerged to challenge these. This reflects our concern with the consequences of globalization for the marginalized, as well as the politics of resistance to its negative outcomes.

A gendered analysis of economic and social regimes is, we believe, central to an assessment of the consequences of globalization, but equally important in understanding the processes that are constitutive of globalization. In thinking about gender, we address the inequalities that are at the heart of any enquiry into development and poverty, given that women are often marginalized in the formal economy, yet their labour is critical in undervalued but economically significant informal sectors and in household production. The chapters on intellectual property rights (Chapter 2), knowledge management (Chapter 6), women's work and organizations (Chapter 8), and codes of conduct (Chapter 9) all contribute to a gendered assessment of the processes and consequences of globalization.

Focusing on small and medium-sized enterprises (SMEs) is critical because micro- and small enterprises provide the means of employment and the livelihoods of most of the world's poor. Understanding how they are affected and might adapt to global economic change assumes enormous importance, therefore. Equally, a focus on the environment refers us to the natural resources that provide the 'inputs' for economic activity and the life-base on which we all depend for our very existence. Accelerated and more intensive exploitation of resources on a global scale, which globalization facilitates, can only further undermine the regenerative capacity of global ecosystems. At the same time, the prevalence of trade rules over social and environmental obligations makes effective collective action at the international level increasingly difficult to deliver. Together, these issues highlight one of the most important challenges for sustainable development in the 21st century: how to reconcile the need to eliminate poverty and reduce consumption in an equitable and just way within a system that has systematically failed to address either challenge.

Production and small-scale enterprises

The globalization of markets focuses attention on those whose livelihoods depend on traded goods and services, whether these are final or intermediate products. Expanded international trade and foreign investment, according to the protagonists for greater market liberalization, are supposed to result in employment and income gains for developing countries. Yet, we have seen how inward flows of foreign investment to developing countries flow into only a few countries. Export processing zones, one of the mechanisms used to attract foreign investment, account for only 2 per cent of wage employment in the least-developed countries (LDCs), where already 50 per cent or more are unemployed and whose exports account for less than 1 per cent of world exports.[6] In other words, export-oriented production does not account for the vast majority of workers in developing countries. The majority in developing countries will continue to earn their livelihood in small-scale production for local low-income markets.

Small-scale agricultural production is still central to the economies of most low-income countries, where the majority of the population remains rural. In India, for example, small-scale farmers produce 60 per cent of agricultural output and employ 90 per cent of the agricultural labour force (Acharya and Acharya, 1995). Worldwide, some 2.6 billion people, or 59 per cent of the workforce in developing countries, depend on agriculture for their livelihoods, mostly as smallholders or labourers (Oxfam, 2000). This is why the debate about how to protect the food security of the rural poor, in the context of global debates about the further liberalization of agricultural sectors, assumes such importance. Chapter 4 illustrates how questions of market access and domestic support bring together the competing demands of global agricultural exporters for the removal of barriers to trade and vocal domestic agricultural lobbies for subsidies and other forms of protection. The outcome of these deliberations will be closely watched by supporters and opponents of the WTO for evidence of sensitivity to the needs of the poor in the former case, and further proof that the WTO protects Northern markets while levering open Southern markets in the latter case.

It is not just in the agricultural sector that small-scale enterprises predominate, however. The 'informal sector' – 'unorganised, disorganised, clandestine, usually illegal, neglected by aid agencies, denigrated by economists, and harassed by officialdom' (Smillie, 2000) – comprises half the work-force in the rapidly expanding cities of developing countries. In terms of employment, the 'informal sector' accounts for between 8 and 41 per cent of total employment, 48 and 92 per cent of non-agricultural employment, and between 18 and 71 per cent of those employed in the 'informal sector' are women (Charmes, 1998). Such small-scale enterprises are the foundation for the private sector in developing countries, and form the base for private sector-led employment growth.

The challenge of globalization, therefore, is how the small-scale, marginal producer, working below the poverty line, will be able to take advantage of access to international markets and of market-driven open economies. In principle, SMEs could benefit from engagement in international trade as domestic suppliers to larger exporting enterprises, as exporters themselves of niche products, as importers of goods and as providers of support services to others engaged in international trade. Dawson shows in Chapter 3 that whether small-scale enterprises can profit from open economies depends on the nature of the enterprise, and concludes that 'while a relatively small number of enterprises has proved able to penetrate higher-value market niches, a much larger number has been unable to graduate out of the low-quality, low-value markets in which their clients are suffering from reduced purchasing power'.

Low-income operators of small-scale enterprises face significant barriers to engaging successfully in competitive markets. The constraints they face are the consequence of the interaction between the social and institutional environment and the current state of their production system. Or as Amartya Sen puts it, their 'ability to participate in the market economy is radically influenced by social arrangements for education, health care, micro credit, land reform, and other public policies' (Sen, 2000). There may be economic inefficiencies (relative to global markets) in their production process, or there may be local market failures in their access to relevant information or credit. While small-scale producers, in the context of international markets, may be shown not to be viable because they cannot adapt to liberalized market conditions, and exposure to competition shows that their livelihoods are economically obsolete, the social and cultural advantages of their being able to continue in production are unrecognized by the forces of the global market economy.

An OECD study has categorized SMEs into those that will be able to respond to economic reform and market liberalization, those that will not be able to survive the increased competition and those that will be unaffected (OECD, 1997). High-growth SMEs in sectors such as high technology and service may well benefit from greater access to global markets, though this still depends on the institutions and communities in which these firms operate. Even those fast-growing SMEs that the OECD thought would benefit from global markets will do so only as long as the process of globalization does not undermine their communities. However, as Barwa and Rai put it in Chapter 2, echoing Sen, 'participants come to specific markets with unequal capabilities and bargaining capacities and resources, which results in widely different market structures regulated by different state formations and characterized by more or less unequal power – class and gender are two bases for unequal power relations operating in the market'.

The ability of the state to make policies for SMEs that are justified in terms of the free market, for example the deregulation of SMEs, focuses our attention on the importance of understanding the institutional context in which SMEs exist (see Chapter 7). Those SMEs that are trying to adapt to more competitive markets, and being helped along their way by the removal of red tape, are potentially being placed in an even less beneficial position by the process of deregulation. Because they are not able to organize as well politically and provide the information that is required for policy makers, they are unable to influence which regulations are removed, and so which markets become truly global. In this sense, globalization provides an opportunity for big businesses in the domestic markets to reset the rules in their favour.

A second public policy question for SMEs in the context of globalization is the degree of support necessary to achieve developmental objectives. Dawson concludes in Chapter 3 that 'in a situation where domestic markets are often shrinking (particularly in non-export crop areas) and where access to higher-value domestic and export markets may well require more, not less, mediation by support agencies, the capacity of small enterprises to bridge the technological and information gaps themselves, without ongoing external support, must be open to question'. Some form of market regulation is required both to enable the continuation of the social benefits from production in small-scale enterprises by the vast majority of women and men in developing countries, and to enable them to enhance their livelihoods in a context of globalization. The SME policy dilemma under globalization, therefore, is how, within the rules set by international agreements and the liberalization agenda, national governments can protect and support such small-scale production.

Gender relations under globalization

Feminist scholars have made a strong intervention in the globalization debate. Cynthia Enloe's work, for example, showed that international debt does not just impact on women, it is based on the patriarchal power relations whereby women's work is invisible in the budgetary accounts of a country (Enloe, 1989). Without the assumption of women's work as 'non-productive' and of the care economy as a feminized sphere, the financial argument for structural adjustment policies could never have been made. Diane Elson's work too emphasizes the ways in which women's labour is being stretched beyond the bounds of the sustainable, as globalization in the form of debt regimes and structural adjustment results in diminishing safety nets and public goods (Elson, 1995). Bina Agarwal's work on the environment provides another important intervention, looking at the structural forces of capitalist development, which build on women's exclusion from access to land and land rights (Agarwal, 1997).

Women have been directly affected by these shifts. As traditional manufacturing industries have collapsed, women have become the main bread earners for the family. Work in Economic Processing Zones created in many states to attract foreign direct investment (FDI) is dominated by women. The relational power of women in the home has, however, not necessarily kept up with their new role. Traditionally women had to contend with the neglect of their interests by unions, and therefore it has not been a priority for them to look to existing unions to protect their rights. New forms of organization are therefore needed and are being developed to contest the disciplining regimes of globalized production chains.

In her article on globalization, V. Spike Peterson argues for anchoring the debate in analyses of the shifts in the processes of production. This, she argues, allows us to link the various elements of globalization and to rescue the political from the loud assertions of globalization as a 'natural' process (Peterson, 2002). Such a *political* understanding of globalization is important in itself, as well as for analysing the way gender relations are being refashioned. The various chapters in this book that address relations also take this view of globalization. The issues that these chapters raise are pertinent for our understanding of the shifts in production, and in ownership, as well as the new ways in which men and women are engaging with the global political economy.

In Chapter 8, Marilyn Carr makes the important point that, whatever the macroeconomic picture, changes in women's lives differ by sector and region. Within nations, Carr argues, 'men are the most likely to be able to take advantage of the benefits of trade and investment liberalization and are less likely than women to suffer from its negative impacts'. When countries diversify their production to offset dependency on a particularly crowded market, for cxample, Carr finds that more men 'are recruited into the new industries, which are more technologically sophisticated ...'. Men have greater opportunities to acquire the skills needed here, as a result of which we see women being concentrated in minimal skills industries.

Chapter 9 focuses on these minimal skills industries. The horticulture industry, dominated by women's labour, has, until very recently, not been well regulated and makes use of industrial products that are harmful to those working with them. While making the important point that women working in these industries do experience some sense of empowerment when earning wages for work, Barrientos focuses on the ways in which ethical trading has

become an important tool in challenging the globalized horticultural production regimes. The Ethical Trading Initiative (ETI) is based on the
International Labour Organisation (ILO) core conventions and 'formulated
a baseline code of conduct, which all member companies aimed to adopt as a
minimum standard, although this did not preclude them from also applying
an individual code'. ETI links various actors together – industry, governments
and markets, as well as individual consumers. Consumer consciousness has
become the target of much mobilization and education in recent years, and a
site of a great deal of NGO activity. The attempt is both to make the value
chains of products visible and therefore to account for labour that goes into
manufacturing of products, as well as to change the pattern of consumption
itself to reflect ethical concerns about conditions of work. Barrientos concludes that 'ethical trade does create new opportunities for flexible workers,
but there are clear constraints on its ability to address gendered employment
needs, and there are likely to be significant local variations in the extent to
which women workers are able to access potential gains from ethical trade.'

Barrientos notes that the changed employment patterns have not extended
to work within the household/family. Gender differences remain, and women
continue to bear the brunt of the workload – and the brunt of the changes.
While consumer and labour movements can highlight working conditions
within companies, they do not extend to the labour practices under globalization which impinge on the domestic sphere. 'Ethical trade on its own will
not lead to fundamental change for women, but in conjunction with other
aspects of social and political transformation under globalization, it .has the
potential to create new opportunities.'

If globalization has led to shifts in production with significant results for
existing gender relations, it has also fundamentally affected the regimes of
ownership. Perhaps one of the clearest examples of the attempts to regulate
ownership at a global level is the work of the WTO. Chapter 2 focuses on a
particular aspect of the work of the WTO – trade-related intellectual property
rights. Barwa and Rai argue that gender relations are both being disturbed and
confirmed by processes of globalization. They examine the process of patenting as intellectual ownership and show that boundaries of class, race and
gender are very difficult to cross. TRIPS, they argue, normalizes a reading of
knowledge and innovation that is excluding of women and those cultures
deemed not be modern and scientific: 'By discounting time and the historically
evolving nature of innovation, patenting institutionalises privilege ...'. The
debate about patenting of bio-organisms is examined to point out that under
the TRIPS regime, 'there has been a steady and substantial transfer of
resources from South to the North as the valuable products of informal innovation have been appropriated cost-free' (Cosbey, 2000: 8). They conclude, 'a
gendered analysis of the TRIPS Agreement reveals that the rules of the game
are predictably set by the powerful ... [and that] the successful promotion of

TRIPS can often reinforce the already unequal power relations between men and women ...'.

If the definitions of knowledge are changing the ways in which we think of ownership of ideas, these are also influencing the challenges we pose to the emerging regimes of regulation. In Chapter 6, Ines Smyth expresses the concern that an approach to knowledge that sees it as a commodity can have many negative consequences, even in the hands of NGOs that are seeking to challenge the global regulatory regime on these issues. Smyth examines the concept of knowledge management to point out that within its parameters, knowledge is indeed treated as a commodity, something that feminist writings have long challenged. NGOs are under pressure to account for their performance, as well as to compete with other NGOs for resources and market share. New skills are needed to do this – skills that can be traded in the knowledge market. However, Smyth argues, such a commodification of knowledge can undermine the principle of participation that most NGOs subscribe to, as well as ossify the creative impulse which has allowed the more successful NGOs to change with the times. Challenging knowledge management would, she concludes, lead to a shift 'from the shackles of systems and structures to granting knowledge its creative potential. This shift may also help NGOs achieve a kind of professionalism shaped according to their own models and principles, rather than those uncritically adopted from business ...'.

Thus all the chapters that deal with gender relations raise issues about globalization in terms of its consequences, the new actors mobilizing on the global stage, and the limits to responding to the terms of challenges embedded in the dominant regimes and discourses of power.

Sustainability and globalization

The relationship between globalization and natural resource use patterns is mediated by policies, institutions and processes from the local to the global level. These shape the contexts that govern people's access to the assets necessary for sustainable livelihoods. Although vulnerabilities to global change differ across regions, livelihood decisions in even the most remote areas of the world are increasingly affected by policies, institutions and processes that take place far away. Decisions about resource use are increasingly being taken by international institutions as well as national and subnational levels of government. For example, the recently negotiated Biosafety Protocol has important implications for the livelihood strategies of farmers, and intellectual property regimes create new patterns of ownership over resources that are locally held (see Chapter 2). However, international provisions governing global market activity, properly designed, can play a valuable role in safeguarding the poor from the negative socioeconomic impacts of globalization. They may compensate for the limits of state capacity by providing regulatory frameworks or other mechanisms for promoting the interests of the poor. This can help to address the current incongruence between the pace of global economic change and the ability of traditional mechanisms of international governance to ensure that the gains from such change are maximized and the losses minimized.

The economic developments most commonly associated with globalization mean a number of things for the environment.[7] For one, the ecological impacts of globalization are thought to be immense. Mittelman suggests 'unsustainable transformation of the environment under globalisation differs from environmental damage in previous epochs … large scale growth in world economic output since the 1970s has not only quickened the breakdown of the global resource base, but also has upset the planet's regenerative system' (Mittelman, 1998: 847). For many environmentalists then, the issue is how to regulate the process of trade liberalization in a way that minimizes environmental impacts. For others, however, the expansion of resource-intensive industrial activity which globalization requires means that there can be no reconciliation. Ecologist Edward Goldsmith argues for instance, 'The globalisation of economic development can only massively increase the impact of our economic activities on an environment that cannot sustain the present impact' (Goldsmith, 1997: 242). This is the impetus for the creation of alternative, locally oriented economic systems designed to insulate communities from the negative impacts of global restructuring and provide for local needs rather than global demands (Glover, 1999).

Whatever the benefits or losses associated with the emerging pattern of global economic development, it is clear that the internationalization of production, facilitated by technological change and reduced transport costs, has brought waste and pollution to new areas of the globe in a way that has spread the risks associated with environmental change. The export of toxic wastes to developing countries is an often-cited example, but Newell, in Chapter 11, also describes the way in which hazardous production processes have been relocated to poorer communities, North and South. Other concerns centre on the ecological impact of increasing levels of transport around the world, moving goods over longer distances,[8] as well as the sustainability of increased production and the expansion of consumer markets. Global market integration creates perverse incentives towards wasteful production patterns, whereby the prevailing economic rationale suggests that it makes sense to manufacture a product across multiple locations in order to maximize savings in production costs, whatever the ecological cost. What is 'rational' economically is not always so environmentally and socially. Export-led growth patterns boost income for some, but also increase vulnerability to fluctuating price structures and often require chemically intensive production methods known to be damaging to human health and to contribute to land degradation.

There is a fear that the imperatives of competing in the global market place force governments to prioritize economic objectives at the expense of environmental protection. Deregulation and liberalization are said to heighten pressures to lower environmental standards. The freedom of mobile transnational capital to locate where environmental regulations are weakest is one of the more vocal of a spectrum of concerns about the negative impacts of globalization. It was perhaps no surprise then that one of the grounds for stalling negotiations towards the MAI was that it would undermine standards of environmental protection by denying local and government authorities the right to uphold environmental protection as a legitimate basis for discriminating against would-be investors.

There is a sense in this understanding of globalization that enhanced economic integration creates an institutional crisis in which globalization removes the means of addressing the problems it creates. In other words, further intensification of current patterns of resource-intensive economic growth requires strong state intervention in order to check the worst excesses of this activity at the very time that the state is said to be in retreat (Strange, 1996). On the other hand, the increasing role that private investment is playing in implementing environmental measures is symptomatic of a broader shift towards environmental policy instruments that adopt a market-based approach and rely on the cooperation of private sector actors. Traditional command and control forms of regulation, in particular, are regarded as insensitive to the transformational capacities of the market and are being replaced by an emphasis on initiatives such as eco-taxation and the creation of markets in pollution permits.

The pace of economic change means that international environmental institutions are having to redefine their mandates to accommodate new challenges. At the same time, the Bretton Woods economic institutions have been attempting to cast their activities in a green light. There is a sense, however, in which negotiations on trade and financial matters have not been coordinated with efforts to address environmental problems. This has produced a number of conflicts over the trade-restrictive nature of environmental measures (most dramatically in cases over measures to protect dolphins and turtles). It has also given rise to calls for greater inter-institutional collaboration or the possible creation of a new institutional structure to reconcile some of the activities of trade and environment organizations and to redress the perceived imbalance between the WTO and existing environmental regimes. This has led former WTO director-general Renato Ruggerio and others to call for the creation of a World Environment Organization to act as a legal and institutional counterpart to the WTO.[9]

In Chapter 5, Finger and Tamiotti show how the WTO is responding to calls for regulations to protect the environment by endorsing the standards set by the International Organization for Standardization (ISO). They identify this move as part of a broader trend towards the privatisation of environmental regulation whereby non-government bodies set standards that are accredited by private agencies (Clapp, 1997). Their chapter explores the possibility of the WTO using these standards in preference to government non-tariff barriers, which are increasingly viewed as illegitimate. What this illustrates is the shifting contours of authority between the nation state and international regulatory authorities in relation to the environment; a complex tapestry of competing authority claims which serves to close off some policy measures and advance other institutional transformations.

At the heart of much popular concern about globalization is global finance. Perceived to be footloose and beyond the control of sovereign governments, the financial crises in Asia served only to heighten anxiety about the negative social and development implications of the mobility of short-term capital flows. One aspect, which has been neglected in the aftermath assessment of the socioeconomic costs of the crisis, is the environmental impact it has had in the countries of Southeast Asia. Chapter 1 explores these effects via an analysis of the changes in resource-intensive sectors that followed the events of 1997. Sensitivity to these concerns has been equally absent in the debate on the need for a new institutional architecture to regulate global financial markets. Dauvergne's analysis underscores the importance of assisting governments and communities in Southeast Asia to come to terms with the short- and longer-term implications of the crisis for the sustainable development of the region.

In thinking about the relationship between the global economy and the environment, we are inevitably drawn to the question of business practice. With annual turnovers that dwarf the GDPs of most developing countries, and the ability to make investments with enormous natural resource implications, as well as control of the technology and capital that is likely to be the vehicle for the implementation of many environmental policies, companies are central agents in the environmental debate. The need to respond to environmental concerns has brought companies into contact with NGOs in cooperative and conflictual settings (Newell, 2000). Such encounters have increasingly taken on global dimensions. Aided by ITC, local struggles have rapidly ignited global resistance and coalition building. Hence firms increasingly operate in a global environment where they are affected by the evolving norms and expectations about their social and environmental obligations, diffused through the activities of transnational NGOs. Chapter 10, about the attempt by the mining company Rio Tinto to involve local stakeholders in discussions about the impact of a proposed mining site in Madagascar and to fend off criticisms from environmentalists about the impacts of the project, highlights this process at work.

In a similar vein, Chapter 11 discusses strategies that NGOs and community groups have developed in order to hold corporations to account for their social and environmental responsibilities. Newell discusses the extent to which forms of 'civil regulation' (produced by the negotiation of codes of conduct or the creation of 'stewardship regimes') and attempts to hold transnational companies legally accountable for the impact of their investments overseas through 'Foreign Direct Liability' can act as a check on the growing power of transnational companies. He concludes that these strategies can each add something to an increasingly dense set of social expectations and legal standards that companies are expected to meet and observe. However, he questions their ability to counter the incentives that some firms have to benefit from lower social and environmental standards by exploiting the lack of protection available to the poor.

The very different ways in which developing countries interact with the global economy through local resource issues is a theme touched on both in Mulligan's discussion of Rio Tinto's work in Madagascar (Chapter 10), as well as Dauvergne's reading of the impact of the Asian financial crisis on environmental problems in Southeast Asia (Chapter 1). Chapter 10 shows that while local resource control is the issue for the community in Evatra, and not just a dimly perceived process of globalization, what is clear is that the global context of behavioural norms and political and economic pressures permeates the relationship between the community and the company in this locale. Similarly, Chapter 1 illustrates how the impacts of volatile capital flows are felt through shifting local resource use patterns as a result of economic dislocation. It is unsurprising, therefore, that resistances to globalization are often mediated through struggles over resource use and the allocation of property rights. The Joint Forum of Indian People Against Globalisation oppose what has been referred to as the 'recolonization' of India by transnational corporations (TNCs) and parallels have been drawn between seed patenting and the Salt Laws imposed by imperial Britain (Martinez-Alier, 1997). Hence decisions taken in the WTO about intellectual property rights are regarded by those whose resources are being patented as a form of bio-piracy (Shiva and Holla-Bhar, 1996).

What these chapters suggest is that there is a move to re-embed the market by creating incentives for positive investment practices and disincentives for irresponsible conduct. Informal mechanisms of accountability increasingly exist alongside formal legal obligations aimed at ensuring that companies are responsible not only to shareholders and consumers of their products, but to those affected by their operations. Public and private standard-setting bodies are also competing to define the future direction of the regulation of production and finance.

The changes in the global economy that these chapters describe simultaneously create opportunities and challenges for those concerned about the environment and give rise to an interesting series of debates about the dynamics of environmental politics in an era of globalization. What is becoming clear is that those concerned about the environment cannot afford to ignore the implications of the economic change that is taking place. If global economic integration proceeds without any attempt to reflect on its repercussions for global ecological security, it will undo in no time the environmental protection measures put in place over the past two decades. At the same time, it may also be true that the actors who are driving the globalization process forward cannot afford to ignore the ecological impact of their activities if they are to create new markets, reduce their production costs and maintain a degree of public legitimacy.

Part I. Globalization and its consequences

1 Globalization and environmental change: the case of Asia's 1997 financial crisis

PETER DAUVERGNE

Introduction[1]

OVER THE PAST three decades most of Asia experienced rapid economic growth. Many countries reduced poverty, improved education and saw substantial increases in life expectancy. As a result, the region has steadily emerged as a key pillar of the global economy. Yet these accomplishments involved severe environmental costs, which, according to the President of the Philippine Institute for Development Studies, left Asia 'the most polluted and environmentally degraded region in the world' (Intal and Medalla, 1998: 1). Asia's integration into the world economy also left the region highly vulnerable to currency speculators, market crashes and capital flight, especially in countries where political and financial reforms lagged behind economic growth. Few observers, however, foresaw how swiftly and forcefully the 1997 financial crisis would hit the region, and many were left sheepishly hiding their articles and books extolling Asia's economic miracle. Not surprisingly, few government or corporate leaders were prepared for the economic consequences of the crisis. Even fewer were prepared for the environmental ones.

The implications of the crisis demonstrate the difficulty of managing environmental resources in the context of economic globalization – where complexities are increasing as the links among actors, institutions, and economies intensify, as internal structures within countries react unpredictably to external events and as new technologies speed up the overall process of change.[2] Within this context of globalization, this chapter examines the environmental implications of the crisis for agriculture, fishing, conservation, air and water pollution, and forests in Southeast Asia and Melanesia, covering the period from the start of the crisis in mid-1997 until mid-1999, when it was largely over. It pays particular attention to the importance of changes to employment, income, global and regional trade, migration patterns, and global budgets and priorities. Overall, the analysis shows that the crisis exacerbated many existing environmental problems, as well as creating additional ones. This occurred as a result of both direct consequences and indirect implications of adjustments and policy reforms. It is important to emphasize here that the financial crisis alone is not responsible for all of these changes. Indeed, it is difficult, if not impossible, to isolate the implications of the crisis, especially given the simultaneous sweeping political reforms in countries like Indonesia. It is nevertheless clear that the crisis has significantly altered Asia's environmental conditions as well as the underlying forces driving environmental change in the region. The environmental changes set in motion by the crisis will continue well past the end of the crisis, and strong domestic and international measures to support environmental protection and conservation in the Asia-Pacific region are more urgent than ever before. Otherwise, a second crisis may well strike soon, this time ignited by an environmental collapse. To begin, the next section provides a sketch of the crisis.

Asia's financial crisis

The environments of the Asia-Pacific region were already highly vulnerable when Asian currencies began to crash in mid-1997, triggering financial crises throughout the region. Loggers had degraded much of the old-growth tropical forests, contributing to widespread deforestation (Dauvergne, 1998b). Forest fires had already burned huge areas, even before the 1997–98 fires in Indonesia burned nearly 10 million hectares, spreading a choking haze across Southeast Asia. Vehicle lead emissions in Asia were well above World Health Organization (WHO) standards. Lead in Manila, for example, had affected some children's IQ scores by 4 or more points (World Bank, 1999: 4; Cubol, 1998). Urban air and water pollution were at times overwhelming, especially in the megacities of Manila, Jakarta and Bangkok. Many of the poor in Southeast Asia and the South Pacific did not have access to clean drinking water or adequate sewage systems. Companies had disposed of substantial quantities of hazardous wastes improperly. Meanwhile, steady population increases were adding to these environmental problems. The population in Asian megacities was 126 million in 1995, with trends showing that this would more than triple by 2025, reaching 382 million (Asian Development Bank website).

Within a year, a large number of studies had been done on the causes of the financial crisis (see Krugman website; Roubini website; Griffith-Jones, 1998; Bello, 1998; Gates, 1998). These studies show that the specific causes of the economic downturns varied considerably across and within countries. While economic globalization set the stage and perhaps even magnified the crisis, an interlinked mix of specific regional and domestic factors sparked the crisis. These included excessive economic expansion backed in large part by private debt; inadequate regulation of, and weaknesses within, financial institutions; collusion, corruption, monopolies and inappropriate government–business relations; and external economic pressures and domestic political instability (World Bank, 1999: 2). The initial response to the crisis, both domestic and international, also seemed to exacerbate it.

The crisis started in Thailand and then spread to South Korea, Indonesia and finally the rest of Asia. Even countries like Vietnam, Laos and Cambodia – with non-convertible currencies, no stock exchanges, and largely rural and agrarian populations – were gradually dragged into the crisis as foreign investment, tourism and exports linked to Asia fell (Lamb, 1998).

Indonesia suffered the greatest economic turmoil. The economy shrank in 1998 by 13.7 per cent. In 1997 and 1998 the Indonesian rupiah depreciated, at times fluctuating wildly. In July 1997, it was around Rp2450 to the US dollar; by September 1998, it was around Rp11 000 to the US dollar. Prices for essential goods soared, while real wages fell by roughly 30 per cent (Feridhanusetyawan, 1999: 51). Many people in the sprawling slums of Jakarta faced food and nutrition shortages in 1998. Women appear to have been disproportionately affected by the hardships of the crisis (Baillie, 1998).

These changes will affect ordinary Indonesians well into the future. The United Nations Children's Fund (UNICEF) estimated in October 1998 that the crisis had pushed at least half of all Indonesian children under 2 into malnourishment, while 65 per cent of children under 3 had become anaemic. This has the potential, according to UNICEF, to threaten the intellectual ability of an entire generation, especially coupled with a rise in school drop-outs and a fall in health standards (Williams, 1998: 1).

The next section reviews some of the social implications of the crisis, paying particular attention to the impact on environmental management in Indonesia, where the crisis had the greatest impact.

Poverty, incomes, unemployment and migration: changing patterns

Poverty, lower incomes and unemployment are inescapably intertwined with environmental change. Many examples exist of poor people managing resources effectively, particularly when local institutions and social interaction create supportive conditions. Yet greater poverty and people's search for income – especially when this arises unexpectedly – frequently intensifies pressure on surrounding resources like land and water. Since the start of the crisis in Indonesia, for example, increasing numbers of local people have turned to illegal logging, mining and fishing. The Indonesian government estimates, for example, that 62 000 illegal miners are now operating in Indonesia, twice the number of legal miners. Many of these illegal miners are protected by local and regional politicians, bureaucrats and military officers. The Indonesian Minister of Mines and Energy estimated in mid-2000 that illegal miners were extracting 30 tonnes of gold, 4 million tonnes of coal, 3600 tonnes of tin and 2800 carats of diamonds every year (McBeth, 2000).

After mid-1997, unemployment increased while real wages fell in cities and towns throughout Asia. In Indonesia and Thailand, this apparently stemmed the flow of rural migrants to urban areas. It also pushed some people back to the countryside, although the exact numbers are uncertain. This had immediate impacts on rural environmental resources. For example, by January 1999 unemployed workers from Bangkok who had returned to their home villages were starting to occupy state forests to obtain land (Tangprasert and Ratchasima, 1999). The Indonesian government actively encouraged migration back to the countryside by, for example, making it relatively cheap for over three million urban workers to return home for the 1997–98 Ramadan holiday, while not providing support for the return journey. One indication of the apparent trend 'back to the countryside' is an Indonesian Central Bureau of Statistics survey that found agricultural employment in Indonesia increased by 5.6 million between February 1997 and February 1998.

This increase in agricultural employment in Indonesia alleviated some of the social and environmental pressures on cities and towns during the crisis. But it has simultaneously intensified pressure on rural agricultural land and water, especially since many of the migrants do not have a deep knowledge of sustainable agricultural practices. Marginal lands and forests are especially vulnerable as migrants and farmers stake out new areas.

Agricultural expansion

Sunderlin (1998: 2) points to five main reasons why expanding and supporting agriculture has been an attractive response to the economic and social effects of Asia's financial crisis. First, the agricultural sector is less dependent on foreign currency inputs, therefore the crisis affected this sector less. Second, adequate food supplies are essential for social and political stability, therefore governments had strong incentives to support this sector, especially when facing strong social pressures, as in Indonesia. Third, this sector is critical for absorbing unemployed urban workers who have migrated back to the countryside in search of work as well as rural youth who no longer leave in search of urban employment. In this way, agricultural employment was a crucial 'social safety valve' during the crisis. Fourth, increasing domestic agricultural output reduces the costs of expensive, yet essential, agricultural imports such as rice, soy and wheat. Finally, and in Sunderlin's view most importantly, the depreciation of the local currency allows countries like Indonesia to sell agricultural goods on the international market much cheaper in terms of US dollars – this is also the case for timber, mineral and fish exports. Moreover, the costs of agricultural production are primarily in the local currency (except for fertilizer and chemicals), while the profits are often in US dollars.

In October 1998, Indonesia's Forestry and Plantation Minister reiterated the government view that agribusiness was an important engine to help pull

Indonesia out of the economic downturn (*Antara*, 1998b). Expanding planta-tions will, however, generate great environmental pressures, especially the development of palm oil estates (examined later in the chapter). Moves to expand the production of cocoa, coffee, shrimp, rubber and pepper will add to these pressures.

Many Southeast Asian commodities fared well on world markets in the first year and a half of the crisis. For example, from mid-1997 to January 1998, the producer price of cocoa in Indonesia increased sixfold. From October 1998 to September 1999 Indonesia produced 336 000 tons of cocoa, a 6 per cent jump from the previous marketing year. The Indonesian Cocoa Association expects that Indonesia will be producing 500 000 tons of cocoa by 2005 (Sunderlin, 1999: 13). This expansion will have a particularly great impact on South Sulawesi, where most of Indonesia's cocoa is grown. Like cocoa, Indonesian coffee exports boomed in the first year of the crisis. By mid-1998 Indonesia had surpassed Vietnam as Asia's largest producer. While some coffee families prospered, this boom hampered government efforts to reclaim conservation forests as high coffee prices encouraged some families relocated from conservation forests to return and again grow coffee.

Fishing and conservation

Fishing policies in the Asia-Pacific region are often ineffective or distor-tionary. Low user fees undermine government revenues and encourage over-fishing. Monitoring and enforcement are weak, including in environ-mentally sensitive areas. This has led to 'substantial over-harvesting of aquatic resources' in the region (World Bank, 1999: 15).

As with agricultural exports, promoting fish exports is a logical response to the currency devaluations. Former Indonesian Agriculture Minister Soleh Solahudin saw great potential in fish exports. In October 1998, he declared that 'Indonesia has a good chance of becoming the world's biggest fishery commodity exporter' (*Antara*, 1998a). He pointed to one firm with profits in 1998 equal to its previous 12 years of operations. He estimated that revenue from exports of sea fishery commodities in 2003 would reach US$2.64 billion, while exports of coastal fishery commodities would hit US$7.36 billion. Shrimp breeding ponds in coastal areas were, in his view, especially important. To support these efforts, Soleh Solahudin announced in 1998 that the govern-ment was working on a scheme to provide fishers with low-interest credit, similar to the credit that some rice farmers now receive (*Antara*, 1998a).

The financial crisis also contributed to some changes in fishing practices, including illegal activities. At this point no one has systematically docu-mented these changes. Some anecdotal evidence exists, however. In Indonesia, despite severe damage to coral reefs, the use of dynamite to sweep fish from a specific area appeared to increase during the crisis. The use of cyanide to capture large fish for display tanks in places like Hong Kong and Singapore also appeared to become more common, even though this practice often kills the smaller fish in the area (*Wall Street Journal*, 1998).

The number of smaller, owner-operated fishing boats in Indonesia also appeared to rise. Higher diesel fuel prices seemed to encourage some fishers to stay closer to shore or move to new locations, to some extent altering their type of catch. More fishers also seemed to become involved in poaching. Some appeared to be selling from their boats at sea (such as to Japanese buyers), rather than going through regulated markets on land. Illegal fishing in Indonesia was so extensive by the end of the 1990s that, according to the Indonesian National Bureau of Statistics, the value of the annual illegal fish trade had reached US$4 billion, accounting for three-quarters of Indonesia's total fish trade (*Indonesian Observer*, 2000).

Urban to rural migration also appeared to put more pressure on local fish supplies. Rising prices in local currency terms for animals and eggs appeared to reinforce this trend by pushing up local consumption of fish products (although lower real incomes and unemployment simultaneously pushed down overall consumption). Further research is necessary to determine the potentially positive and negative implications of all of these changes for biodiversity and fish stocks.

Finally, the financial crisis increased the pressures on endangered animals and national parks. In Indonesia, local wildlife has become an increasingly important food source. Rare wildlife, some from the remotest areas of the country, is now available at local markets. Some wildlife, such as endangered macaques, has been sold to foreign fishers for food. Biologist Rob Lee laments: 'What's so sad is the rarest animals fetch little more than the most common wild-pig meat' (quoted in *Wall Street Journal*, 1998).

Air pollution

The air of many Southeast Asian cities is severely polluted. In the mid-1990s, the United Nations Environment Program (UNEP) ranked Bangkok as the second most polluted city in the world, after Mexico city. Jakarta was third (*Jakarta Post*, 1996).

Particulates and lead pose two of the greatest threats to human health in Asia. Motorcycles, diesel trucks and buses, industrial plants (especially small and medium ones) and kerosene are the main sources of particulate emissions. Leaded petrol is the main source of lead. Lower incomes and industrial output during the financial crisis appeared to reduce air and lead pollution as fewer vehicles and industries operated, although this still needs to be statistically verified.

For example, on the assumption that Indonesia would not recover to previous levels of industrial output quickly, the World Bank (1998: 105) predicted that by the year 2000 the crisis would lower particulate emissions in Indonesia by 17 per cent and lead by 20 per cent compared to previously projected levels. Any positive environmental impact on air pollution in Indonesia is unlikely to last long, however, as new investment – which often brings cleaner technologies – stagnates. Moreover, remaining industries now have less capital to invest in environmental technologies. In this context, firms are also more likely to sidestep environmental, health and safety standards to reduce costs. Finally, the immediate and longer-term effects of the crisis have undermined the ability and willingness of governments to enforce stricter standards on vehicles, a crucial step towards reducing urban air pollution. As a result of all of these changes, the World Bank (1998: 105) predicted that 'the medium-term impact of the crisis … will … increase the average emissions per unit of GDP by 5 to 10 per cent in 2005.'

At the same time, fewer government subsidies for fuel – such as the ones in Indonesia on diesel to support public transportation and kerosene to help poor households with cooking and lighting – could partially offset these more negative changes by raising prices, lowering consumption and fostering greater efficiency. Fully removing fuel subsidies may well be impractical, however, since it has potentially explosive political and social repercussions, as the riots in Indonesia following the fuel price hikes on 5 May 1998 demonstrated. The Indonesian government abandoned these measures within a week.

A similar scenario of greater air pollution in the long term appears likely in the Philippines and Thailand, although no conclusive data are yet available. One indication of the potential for a long-term increase in air pollution, however, was the decision by the Thai government in 1998 to delay introducing the 'Euro 2000 standards for diesel buses due to a backlog of unsold vehicles' (Asia Environmental Trading, 1998: 2).

Water pollution and sewage

Unlike particulates and lead, in some cases the financial crisis worsened water pollution in the short term. This has had an especially great impact on the lives of poor people. Even before the crisis, the World Bank (1998: 105) estimated that dirty water and inadequate sanitation was lowering the average life expectancy of people in the Asia-Pacific region by almost two years.

Irrigation systems in Southeast Asia are unreliable and urban water supplies are often filthy, in part because of poor sanitation facilities. The Asian Development Bank (1997: 30) estimated that 'Despite rapid and steady growth in income and wealth, at least one in three Asians still has no access to safe drinking water, and at least one in two has no access to sanitation services. Only in Africa is the situation worse.'

The amount of suspended solids in water sources provides a general measure of water pollution. Shakeb Afsah, senior policy advisor to US-Asia

Environmental Partnership, estimated that the financial crisis lowered monthly output from industrial plants in Indonesia by 18 per cent in the second half of 1997. Yet over this time the amount of organic waste per unit of industrial effluent jumped by over 15 per cent, apparently because more factories simply dumped untreated waste. As Afsah (1998: 1) notes, 'This finding contradicts the simple view that slower, lower or negative economic growth will reduce industrial pollution. On the contrary, pollution may increase because factories adjust their abatement effort in response to the lower regulatory inspection and enforcement, and higher pollution control costs.'

Afsah's work supports the argument that water pollution in some locations has increased since the crisis began, as firms have exploited weaker government efforts to monitor and enforce regulations. It further points to the strong possibility that illegal dumping of toxic wastes has also increased. Clapp (1998: 25) examines Afsah's study and concludes her analysis of hazardous waste in Indonesia and the Philippines: 'It is likely that similar results would hold for most hazardous waste generating industries.' This poses a serious health threat. Already, from 1975–88 toxic waste releases had increased in Thailand by 1200 per cent and in the Philippines by 800 per cent (Salim, 1998).

Aggregate figures do not of course reveal shifts in the specific location of water pollution. Even if the amount of water pollution increased overall, some communities will have benefited from the closure of an environmentally destructive firm, such as when the textile plant in Lagadar village in Indonesia, with a reputation for dumping waste into the nearby river, closed in mid-1998 (Yamin, 1998).

Tropical timber

Short-term implications of the collapse in demand

Japan and South Korea are the main tropical timber importers for Southeast Asia and Melanesia. Recessions and a slow-down in construction in Japan and South Korea drove down demand and prices for tropical timber at the end of 1997 and in 1998. In 1997, Japan's tropical log imports totalled 5.9 million cubic metres, 5 per cent lower than the previous year. In 1998, imports sank to 3.4 million cubic metres. South Korean tropical log imports fell to 1.18 million cubic metres in 1997, down slightly from 1.21 million from the previous year. South Korean tropical log imports dropped to 660 000 cubic metres in 1998 (ITTO, 2000: 70).

Largely because of the economic downturns in South Korea and Japan, total natural forest production in the Solomon Islands reached only 637 000 cubic metres in 1997 and about 650 000 cubic metres in 1998, far lower than a few years earlier when production exceeded 800 000 cubic metres. The

International Tropical Timber Organization (ITTO) (2000: 85) estimates that commercial log production in Indonesia fell from 31.5 million cubic metres in 1996, to 30.5 million cubic metres in 1997, and to 28.5 million cubic metres in 1998. Coupled with the loss of power of Solomon Islands Prime Minister Solomon Mamaloni in August 1997 and President Suharto in May 1998, the drop in demand for tropical timber helped to create greater opportunities in both countries to reform timber management. Former Solomon Islands Forestry Minister Hilda Kari even went as far as claiming in late October 1998 that the Asian financial crisis may have been a blessing, ending the 'looming environmental destruction' (Agence-France Presse, 1998).

These respites will not last long; meanwhile, serious problems remain. Total log production in the Solomon Islands in 1997 and 1998 was still well over the theoretically sustainable level of about 250 000 cubic metres. In Indonesia, illegal cutting may now exceed legal harvests (Tickell, 1999), pushing production far over sustainable levels (about 22 million cubic metres) and far over the conservative estimates of ITTO. Moreover, many companies simply stockpiled logs or left logs lying in the forest. By the end of 1997, log stockpiles in the Solomon Islands had reached 300 000 cubic metres, while as much as one million cubic metres of uncollected logs remained in the forests (Central Bank of Solomon Islands, 1998: 18). In Indonesia, almost 6 million cubic metres of uncollected logs lay in the forests in early 1998. Kari's comment that the crisis was a 'blessing' also seems overly simplistic, or at least highly optimistic, especially considering that the crisis left the government of the Solomon Islands – which relied on log exports for about half of total export earnings – on the verge of financial collapse as the total value of log exports in 1998 reached only $US36 million, a 47 per cent drop from 1997.

Nevertheless, important policy and administrative changes occurred to forest management at the end of the 1990s in both the Solomon Islands and Indonesia. The Solomon Islands government under Prime Minister Bartholomew Ulufa'alu (1997–2000) placed a moratorium on new licences. With support from the Australian Agency for International Development (AusAID), the Ministry of Forests, Environment and Conservation reviewed and consolidated forest legislation, including the Forest Resources and Timber Utilisation Act, the Environment and Conservation Bill, and the Wildlife Bill. The government passed new forestry legislation in mid-1999. The Forests Bill 1999 tackles some tough issues. It attempts to improve the process of determining customary forest rights and reaching agreements for timber sales. It proposes measures to ensure that harvest areas are suitable. It gives greater powers to the government to monitor log shipments. And it introduces a mandatory Code of Practice as well as performance bonds to require reforestation. A coup in June 2000 forced Prime Minister Ulufa'alu to resign, abruptly derailing forestry reforms in the Solomon Islands after government services and law and order rapidly deteriorated. The current crisis in the Solomon Islands is rooted in a dispute over land between traditional landowners from the island of Guadalcanal and settlers from the island of Malaita (many of whom settled on Guadalcanal after World War II). While the collapse of the economy following the Asian financial crisis did not 'cause' the coup, it did, however, certainly aggravate an already tense situation.

In Indonesia, the government, under pressure from the IMF to eliminate cartels and sever some of the collusive links among state and business officials, ended Apkindo's (the Indonesian Wood Panel Association) formal monopoly of the plywood industry, effective 30 March 1998. (Apkindo, under the control of President Suharto's crony Bob Hasan, dominated Indonesia's timber industry over the past decade.) The government has also announced plans for numerous reforms to forest policies, including limiting the size of concessions, transferring licences obtained through corruption or nepotism to cooperatives, forbidding new forest concessions, auctioning revoked concession licences and putting greater emphasis on community forestry. The government has announced plans to review the use of the Reforestation Fund, little of which has actually supported reforestation.

These changes, however, will not automatically translate into less pressure on Indonesia's forests. Many timber companies are moving into palm oil, rubber, and pulp and paper plantations, the expansion of which has already contributed to extensive environmental damage. Some reforms will have mixed environmental effects, such as removing restrictions on foreign direct investment in the palm oil industry and efforts to liberalize the timber trade. Some reforms may partly be illusionary, as informal rules and connections continue despite formal changes. Moreover, government commitment to implement reforms is inconsistent. By late 1998, the World Bank had become so frustrated with the lack of progress by the Indonesian government to reform forest management that it suspended payment of a US$400 million loan.

Long-term environmental effects on forests

The long-term impact of the crisis on effective forest management is even less optimistic. Several trends could increase economic and social pressures. The tropical timber industry in Southeast Asia and Melanesia was rebounding even before the crisis ended. In Indonesia, for example, demand for plywood began surging in April 1998 after a new Chinese government policy to reduce logging by 60 per cent. By mid-1998, Malaysia's decision to restrict timber exports further stimulated demand for Indonesian plywood from other Asian countries. Meanwhile, demand from the US, Europe and the Middle East remained reasonably strong. Firms began to re-hire mill workers. And, although total plywood exports for 1998 fell somewhat, the forest industry as a whole came close to meeting its export target of US$8.3 billion, partly on the strength of the pulp and paper industry (Sunderlin, 1998: 3; Akella, 1999: 79). Moreover, new migrants to rural areas, governments and firms have strong financial incentives to clear land and forests.

The economic and social effects of the crisis have also made it far more difficult for governments to monitor and enforce environmental policies as well as control illegal logging. The Indonesia-UK Tropical Forest Management Programme estimates that over 32 million cubic metres of timber was illegally cut in 1998 (Greenlees, 2000: 26). Some of the worst practices are in Kalimantan. Indonesia's Secretary-General of the Ministry of Forestry and Plantations admitted that every month as much as 100 000 cubic metres of illegal timber is smuggled from Tarakan, East Kalimantan, to the Malaysian state of Sabah (*Jakarta Post*, 2000b).

A pessimistic analysis of the long-term environmental effects of emerging trade patterns in Asia is consistent with previous studies of the links between currency devaluations and deforestation. For example, one study of Indonesia from 1981 to 1985 estimated that on average each 1 per cent fall in the exchange rate was tied to a 1.4 per cent jump in the deforestation rate (Capistrano and Kiker, 1995; summarized in World Bank, 1999: 12).

Finally, some of the greatest future pressures on the remaining forests of the Asia-Pacific region will come from the rapid expansion of plantations.

Plantations

The after-effects of the financial crisis have created strong incentives to develop more large-scale plantations, especially as capital starts to flow back into the region. Some of the most ambitious efforts are seen in Indonesia. Forest plantations covered around 3.8 million hectares of Indonesia in 1994. This area had more than doubled by the end of 1998 (Yoga, 1998). The future will see even more plantations. The government aims to make Indonesia one of the world's top pulp and paper producers. The government has a similar goal to overtake Malaysia as the largest producer of palm oil (used to make margarine, cooking oil and soap). This is an ambitious goal considering that Malaysia (especially Sarawak) is also aggressively expanding palm oil exports, a highly profitable enterprise for some firms in the early stages of the crisis. For example, Malaysia's largest palm oil company – Golden Hope Plantations – recorded a 30 per cent increase in net profits during the second half of 1997. Malaysia produced 10.5 million tons of crude palm oil in 1999 and expects to increase this to 14 million tons by the year 2010 (Reuters, 2000; *Jakarta Post*, 1999).

Indonesia is, however, already a formidable challenger to Malaysian palm oil exporters. Indonesia exported more than US$1 billion worth of palm oil and palm oil products in 1996. Over the past ten years, palm oil plantations grew from 600 000 hectares to over 2 million hectares. In September 1998, the transmigration minister even suggested shifting the massive transmigration project in central Kalimantan towards oil palm instead of food production (Down to Earth, 1998). By 2005, the Indonesian government hopes to increase the area for palm oil production to 5.5 million hectares (CIFOR News, 1998: 9).

The push in Indonesia to build a massive palm oil industry started well before the financial crisis (Potter and Lee, 1998). From 1967 to 1997, crude palm oil production grew on average 12 per cent per year (Casson, 1999). While the total area planted continued to grow during the crisis, the rate of expansion slowed slightly in 1998 and considerably in 1999. Production of crude palm oil also fell slightly in 1998 to around 5 million tons, the first decline since 1990.

A combination of factors explains this slow-down. Production costs were high while the global price of palm oil products dropped. Foreign investors remained wary of the political instability (*Jakarta Post*, 2000a). There were problems with distribution, marketing and credit. The 1997–98 fires and drought damaged production. And finally, the government's 40–60 per cent export tax on oil palm products – imposed from April 1998 to January 1999 to maintain domestic supplies of cooking oil – undercut incentives for exporters (Casson, 1999).

The after-effects of the crisis, however, have laid a foundation for further expansion. Reforms imposed by the IMF have eliminated constraints on foreign direct investment in palm oil plantations. Equally important, the depreciation of the rupiah has created a potential for even greater profits. With lower export taxes, lower domestic interest rates, more land available as a result of the 1997–98 fires and growing global demand for crude palm oil, the sector looks set to take off at an even faster rate, especially if Malaysia and Indonesia collaborate to control world crude palm oil prices (Sunderlin, 1999: 12). Indonesia is now ambitiously aiming to increase crude palm oil production to 15 million tons by 2010 (*Jakarta Post*, 1999).

The development of palm oil, rubber and industrial wood plantations can severely damage the surrounding environment. In Sabah, Malaysia, for example, the Kampung Sukau village security and development committee chair explained: 'The people in the plantations use tonnes of chemicals for the oil palm trees and they eventually flow into ditches and end up in the river. Our river is becoming severely polluted' (*Star* [The], 1998). So far, however, the greatest environmental impact of plantation companies has been their direct role in lighting the forest fires of 1997 and 1998 that swept Indonesia's outer islands. Klaus Topfer, executive director of the UNEP, remarked in April 1998 that Indonesia's 'forest fires may turn out to be one of the greatest ecological disasters of the millennium' (for details, see Dauvergne, 1998a).

Conclusion

Globalization is a complex process with diverse, multifaceted and uneven implications for environmental management. As part of this process, environmental ideas and the rhetoric of sustainable development have spread worldwide, reaching even the remotest parts of Asia-Pacific. All states in the Asia-Pacific region now have environmental agencies and environmental sections within government departments. States have signed numerous international environmental agreements. NGOs like Greenpeace and the World Wide Fund for Nature (WWF), as well as international lenders like the World Bank, now place even greater pressure on governments to address environmental problems. Even corporations have felt forced to develop strategies to cope with the globalization of environmental ideas and pressures (Fabig and Boele, 1999; Mulligan, Chapter 10). This globalization of environmentalism has been critical for the efforts to reform forest management now under way in many parts of the Asia-Pacific region.

Yet, at the same time, economic globalization has left states and firms in the Asia-Pacific more vulnerable to currency speculators, rapid capital flight and market crashes. This has profound environmental implications. Sudden economic downturns, such as the 1997 financial crisis, will fundamentally disrupt even the best environmental plans. Yet such a dramatic crash has the equally important effect of altering the underlying processes and incentives that drive environmental change. Recognizing these changes and then shifting development strategies to integrate these new conditions, as well as possibly take advantage of new opportunities for reform, are essential for better long-term sustainable management.

In the case of the Asian financial crisis, simple calculations cannot determine the costs and opportunities for environmental management. Instead, costs, benefits and opportunities have occurred simultaneously. Some economic costs of the crisis contributed to worse environmental conditions; but some changes had positive or neutral environmental effects. Moreover, different segments of the population absorbed economic, environmental and social costs to varying degrees. An environmental benefit for one group sometimes entailed severe economic, social or even environmental costs for another group. It is essential to recognize that as the lens and levels of analysis move, and as the underlying prioritization of concerns shifts, the conclusions regarding the net costs will naturally vary. Recognizing these complexities means accepting that both effects and interventions will have multiple interrelated repercussions. It further means that careful qualifications must accompany broad conclusions and generalizations.

It is important to stress here that, so far, relatively little research has been done on the environmental implications of the Asian financial crisis. This partly reflects the limited amount of reliable data available, although some patterns and trends have emerged. Detailed research is required on changes to water quality, industrial pollution, waste disposal, logging, fishing, mining and agriculture. There is also a need to examine systematically changes to environmental regulations and budgets, especially how the reallocation of resources within environmental agencies has affected conservation and enforcement. Further research is also necessary to understand the mixed environmental implications of changing trade and investment patterns.

Finally, there is a need to analyse further the link between globalization, economic crashes and environmental change. In particular, more research is needed on how rapid and intense change in a regional political economy alters short-term environmental conditions as well as the long-term underlying processes and incentives driving environmental change. Such research could potentially help firms, governments and donors respond more quickly and effectively when a financial crisis next strikes a developing region of the world.

2 The political economy of intellectual property rights: a gender perspective

SHARMISHTA BARWA and SHIRIN M. RAI

Introduction

THIS CHAPTER EXAMINES the trade-related intellectual property rights (TRIPS) to assess their gender implications as well as their impact on the present and future inequality amongst states. The arguments presented in this chapter reflect our concern to see TRIPS as socially embedded instruments of governance that regulate markets and are in turn interpreted by the functioning of markets. Women and men are differently placed on these patterned market grids and are affected differently by them. The embeddedness of TRIPS is reflected in the ways in which they define property rights. It is also reflected in what they do not address – the wider issues of social access to resources such as education, capital and law that are critically important to the processes of production of knowledges. Finally, we also examine the differential access that women of the South have to these processes as compared to those in the North. Thus this chapter unpacks the gender 'unevenness' of globalization even as the global barriers towards interconnectedness are being demolished. The closing section includes a few recommendations for meeting the challenges of the new global market place.

A gendered analysis of TRIPS needs to focus on access to and control over matters relating to intellectual property rights especially in the fields of science and technology. One of the least explored and least understood areas of gender and development is the issue of distribution relating to intellectual property and women's rights – why is it that women are always at the 'dying' end? It has been estimated that women own only 1 per cent of the world's property. Is it possible that TRIPS would be more accessible to women than the traditional property rights have been? In examining the new regimes of intellectual property that are becoming critically important under globalization, we find continued and wide discrepancies of ownership rights. Just as women experienced gendered regimes of advantage and disadvantage during the agricultural and industrial revolutions, and were less able to take advantage of the economic opportunities arising out of them, they seem to be equally disadvantaged in the context of the information–communication–technological revolution. This leads us to ask whether socially embedded markets, and more critically, regimes of ownership that are institutionalized through legal instruments and maintained through a 'web of surveillance' (Sell, 2001) as well as punitive sanctions can ever benefit women.

Women, of course, are not in themselves a unified category. In the context of TRIPS, divisions along a North–South axis are important, as are divisions along lines of ethnicity and class. The issue of location also poses questions for feminist politics. Is it our location that defines our politics, or is it our situated politics that allows different articulations of our located subjectivities?

The World Trade Organization and intellectual property rights

The World Trade Organization (WTO) was established on 1 January 1995 as part of the results of the Uruguay Round of the General Agreement on Tariffs and Trade (GATT). TRIPS were also agreed upon in this round of agreements. It sets out the obligations of member states to protect intellectual property rights within their borders.

What is the significance of TRIPS? First, TRIPS have for the first time brought the domain of ideas, knowledge and innovation into the arena of global trade. TRIPS are a set of agreements that regulate the granting of limited monopoly rights by the state to an innovator or inventor. 'They specify a time period during which others many not copy the innovator's idea, allowing him or her to commercialize it, and recoup any investment on research and development ... They trade off the welfare of the innovator, who deserves compensation for his or her efforts, against the welfare of society at large, which would benefit by unlimited access to the innovation' (Cosbey, 2000: 3). The emphasis here is clearly on trade-related and monetary 'compensation' on investment; it does not take into account the value of moral, ethical and non-monetary recognition of the innovator for an idea, an invention or an innovation. The problem of definition is thus twofold. On the one hand, it is about what counts as 'innovation' and on the other, it is about the recognized form of compensation. As we will see below, this particular reading of 'innovation' is particularly problematic for women as they bear far greater personal costs in terms of overcoming social prejudice to access the world of knowledge production.

Second, TRIPS define the nature of knowledge through identifying the boundaries of particular products and processes. There are three main types of intellectual property rights: patents, copyrights and trademarks. Copyrights cover literary and artistic works, as well as computer software, and trademarks are granted to names or labels denoting a particular quality, which distinguishes it from other products. 'All patents involve invention, but not all inventions are patented. An idea need be neither patented nor patentable to be an invention.' Patents cover 'any inventions, whether *products or processes* (our italics), in all fields of technology, provided that they are new, involve an inventive step and are *capable of industrial application*' (our italics) (Stanley,

2000: 1156–7). Two things stand out here. First, that both product and processes have now been brought within the remit of exclusive marketing rights. As a result, for example, farmers will not be able to keep seeds from their crops. As women form an increasing number of small and poor farmers, this provision is affecting them particularly. Second, patents privilege particular forms of knowledge – 'stabilizing' historically developed processes of production would entitle modern industrial companies to patent products and processes and deny nature's and people's creativity.

One of the most important issues that has emerged in the context of patentability is about the terms 'nature' and 'natural'. As Shiva points out, a patriarchal understanding of knowledge of nature has emphasized 'worked on' nature as natural: 'nature has been clearly stripped of her creative power; she has turned into a container for raw materials waiting to be transformed into inputs for commodity production' (Shiva, 2000: 4). Further, according to this view, 'to regenerate is not to create, it is merely to 'repeat' which is the same as passivity' (Shiva, 2000). The regenerating role of women and nature is then defined out of the sphere of innovation, excluding them from the regimes of patents and monopoly privilege. This is particularly evident in the case of the International Convention of the Union for the Protection of New Varieties of Plants, where 'micro-organisms' have been excluded from the categories of plants and animals and therefore brought under the patents regime. This has allowed for changes in the genetic makeup of existing varieties of seeds, for example, to result in a patent being granted for products of the neem tree and basmati rice among many other 'natural' products. This reading of innovation also goes against the recognition of the original reasoning for introducing patents, which was that innovation has high costs of development and low costs of reproduction. By discounting time and the historically evolving nature of innovation, patenting institutionalizes privilege – those who are left out of the loop (very often poor women are the majority of those excluded) fall progressively behind in the race for ring-fencing products for monopoly exploitation. As Cosbey points out, 'there has been a steady and substantial transfer of resources from South to North as the valuable products of informal innovation have been appropriated cost-free' (Cosbey 2000: 8).

Third, TRIPS signify a major innovation in the global regulatory regime. Unlike other agreements that define what members states may not do, TRIPS is prescriptive, in that it sets out what member states *must do*, thus encroaching upon the domain of national policy making in an unambiguous way. Further, by making TRIPS part of the 'cross-retaliatory' regime under WTO Agreements, the WTO has strengthened its regulatory power enormously. It now means that non-conformity in one area of regulation can lead to retaliation in terms of trade in areas covered by a different Agreement. TRIPS are therefore part of an extremely powerful group of regulatory mechanisms that all members of the WTO must put in place by 2005 at the latest. As we shall see below, countries of the South suffer disproportionately from such a prescriptive and encompassing regulatory regime.

Women and inventions

Almost two centuries ago, Voltaire declared, '[t]here have been very learned women as there have been women lawyers, but there have never been women inventors' (quoted in Stanley, 1998), and just five decades ago, Edmund Fuller wrote, 'For whatever reason, there are few women inventors, even in the realm of household arts ...' (Fuller, 1955).

To invent is to find, but it differs from discovery in terms of applications of discovery to practical use. Why are there so few women inventors? Some of the answers are obvious – invention usually requires money, materials and the opportunity to share ideas. A related subject is that of women's indigenous technical knowledge and innovation. Outside the world of formal science and technology, and far from the world of patents, is the everyday process of experimentation and adaptation, which has gone on for centuries in every part of the world (UNIFEM, 1999). Through language, problem diagnosis, and innovation and experimentation methodologies used by women who are custodians of such indigenous knowledge, it is also commonplace to hear that these developments are not non-scientific. They may be outside the scientific mainstream, but they are just as much the result of logical and internally consistent frameworks of understanding as other inventions. Until these 'alternative' forms of inventions are recognized as part of the 'real' science and technology that they are, there is a fear that women's extensive knowledge and contributions will not be given their appropriate value and worth. As a result, society will lose both ways – real gains to be accrued by society as a whole when modern science is combined with this indigenous knowledge, and loss of social equity which cannot be achieved unless women's intellectual property rights are properly protected.

Historically, few women have been financially independent, and most have been excluded from sources of education and intellectual stimulation (*New Scientist*, 1984). All these facts point to the usual feeling that women are 'trespassers' in the field of inventions – even though several path-breaking technological inventions have been made by women. Whitney's cotton gin (invented by Whitney's landlady), the Jacquard loom, the fire escape (Ann Connelly), filter paper (Melita Bentz), the sewing machine and several other such discoveries which made a profound impact on the quality of life prevailing at the time of each invention were all invented by women. However, the terms of the 'knowledge debate' highlight some of the difficulties, discriminations and prejudices women face while attempting to enter the domain of inventions.

Patents, property and the global market

Patents, as we have seen above, are forms of property. An old edition of *Encyclopaedia Americana* volunteers the information that 'Minors and women and even convicts may apply for patents under our law', hardly encouraging company. In 1910, women held only 0.8 per cent of the total patents at the US Patents Office. In 1954, a survey in the US found that although women received only 1.5 per cent of the total number of patents granted, the profits they received from them were, on average, higher than those of men. The range of women's inventions is now impressive: according to the United States Patent and Trade Mark Office (USPTO) Report, the most prolific woman inventor of US-origin patents from 1992 to 1996 was Jane Arcona, who was the named inventor in 82 patents. According to this Report, from 1977 to 1996, the corporate organizations named most frequently as owners of US-origin women-inventor patents were IBM (1272 patents), GEC (810 patents) and Eastman Kodak (738 patents). The US Navy topped the list of Federal Government organizations owning 264 US-origin woman-inventor patents. Patsy Sherman, commercial products development manager for the 3M company, contributed to 15 important patents including 'Scotchguard', the widely used stain repellent for fabrics. Yet this list comprises only the few women who have been able to brave and overcome the veiled unequal power relations operative in the marketplace, whether it is the global marketplace or the village market. Even these figures are skewed further when we consider that '95% of the world's patents are held in the North, and in information technology it is estimated that 90–95% of the world's research goes on in highly industrialised countries' (Cosbey, 2000: 11).

The inequalities persisting at different levels of the various marketplaces for women include access to, participation in, and having an equal stake and appropriate bargaining power in relation to the acquisition/invention of knowledge. Markets, it has been argued (Polanyi, 1980) are embedded in the dominant social relations. In discussing four dimensions of market power, White comments: 'the substance of market politics is characteristically about a number of issues: about the position of an agent or agents in relation to others within a market and their differential ability to extract resources through exchanges with other market participants; about the rules of the game and the nature of market institutions; and about the boundaries of the market' (White, 1993: 5). The participants in the market include the state, market organizations and formal associations such as trade unions, consumer groups, business associations, market networks, firms and individuals. The functioning of the market depends on the politics of state involvement, the politics of market structures and the politics of social embeddedness – of the state and the market (White, 1993: 6–10). In such a patterned market system, participants come to specific markets with unequal capabilities, bargaining capacities and resources, which results in widely different market structures, regulated by different state formations and characterized by more or less unequal power – class and gender are two bases for unequal power relations operating in the market. The neo-classical model does not query that individuals can pursue their economic self-interests in ways that have nothing to do with the 'best price'. Neither do they question the 'degree to which self-interest places economic goals ahead of friendship, family ties, spiritual considerations, or morality' (Block, 1990: 54). Finally, there is an assumption that instrumentality in decision making goes hand in hand with obeying rules and with maximizing interests, rather than a set of signals that can lead to conflictual economic and social behaviour in different groups of populations. The social embeddedness of markets is therefore not considered by neo-classical economists other than as a distortion. This embeddedness provides an explanation for the ways in which gendered regimes of patent-based property function. One can hardly be surprised that there are so few women inventors. What is more surprising is that inventions made by women exist at all and that they are not only patented but also commercially developed. As Cosbey points out, for example, 'large multinational plant breeders do not regard the South as a significant enough market to gear research toward varieties appropriate to the various regions ... It is to be expected that innovation done by Northern [funded] scientists will be in the interests of Northern producers' (Cosbey, 2000: 11). The result is that not only are women left out of the patents regimes almost entirely, but also the nature of research is typically skewed towards the needs of the North, trade and commerce, rather than towards the needs of the South and sustainability of life.

The Fourth World Conference on Women in Beijing in 1995 recognized that access to information prepares women to participate more fully in all stages of political and economic life. The Beijing Declaration and Platform for Action (1995) called on states and organizations to increase women's participation in and access to new technologies as a tool for strengthening women's economic capacity and democratic processes (www.undp.org/unifem/ec_tech.htm). The environment for debates on women's contribution to the technological advances of society and their protection in this regard has been building up for quite some time. This is evidenced by estimates that suggest that natural and physical capital account for less than half of the observed rate of growth, while more than half the growth arises from human sources (UNDP, 1990). This emphasis on human capital has been used to address the issue of gender-sensitive social and economic policies. The concern that human capital should not be allowed to decay during the adjustment period (Vivian, 1995) affirms that development should be equitable, gender-balanced, participatory and sustainable, and that it should also respect human diversity. This is the only paradigm that explicitly identifies gender equity as one of the main conceptual pillars for transforming the way the current world system operates.

As a result of the factors analysed above, the three riders of the apocalypse that could underpin the present position of women in the arena of intellectual property rights are as follows.

○ Intellectual property may be used contrary to the objectives and conditions of its protection – misuse determined by the rightful owner's status in society.
○ Market power resulting from intellectual property may be used to extend the protection beyond its purpose or the exclusive right may be used to enhance or extend or abuse monopoly power – depending on the bargaining capacity of the owner, based on economic, social and cultural factors.
○ Agreements on the use or the exploitation of intellectual property may be concluded in restraint of trade or limiting the transfer or dissemination of technology or other knowledge – a situation called restrictive contracts or concerted practice – again dependent on the intellectual and economic power of the owner (Acharya, 1996).

The underlying common thread in all three factors is the stake/bargaining capacity of the property owner in the property (in this case intellectual property). This is in turn embedded in several other factors that invest the owner with the power to negotiate adequately, or results in its opposite.

The interrelationship between these different issues extends to cover the protection of intellectual property rights at two distinct levels. First, as a multilateral development, affecting and being affected by multilateral trade liberalization and government trade policies, and second, as a microeconomic phenomenon driven by the strategies and behaviour of corporations where the changing dynamics of global competition and international competitiveness are the main concerns (Oman, 1994). Added to these factors are two issues identified by the United Nations Commission on the Status of Women, which further highlight the constraints faced by women with respect to intellectual property rights. These include inequality in women's access to and participation in the definition of economic structures and policies and the productive process itself, and insufficient institutional mechanisms to promote the advancement of women in this regard.

TRIPS – national and gender perspectives

Patent is property. The argument for patents is that inventors engage in the process of production of knowledge, which needs protection from piracy by others. The 'find' of an inventor is thus regarded as personal (or corporate, if the legal person is the group engaged in inventing) – something that is uniquely the property of the one who invents it. To qualify for patent right, the invention has to be novel, non-obvious and of practical use (Dasgupta, 1999). Thereafter, the right confers on the holder a time-bound monopoly of the given product to enable the inventor to recoup the cost of development of the product and also compensate for the risk undertaken. In addition, it is also expected that such rewarding of invention will encourage others to bring new inventions and thus help in the extension of scientific and technical knowledge that will benefit society as a whole. International protection of intellectual property rights has, therefore, been placed on the agenda of trade negotiations to safeguard the competitive position of some countries against intellectual piracy and the overly rapid diffusion of their comparative advantage.

Social knowledges, private patents: gendered and Southern challenges

As pointed out above, feminist understandings of knowledge and its creation have challenged the view that would allow intellectual production to be given the status of property. There are several reasons for this. First, such a view does not take into account the social history of production of knowledge. The stories we started this chapter with clearly indicate that the women's labour in the production of knowledge has been disregarded because the process of production has been linked with the public sphere, where women were not traditionally operative. Second, the definition of knowledge itself has historically excluded the knowledges accumulated and produced by marginalized groups; hegemonic ideas about knowledge have defined out 'other' knowledges as unscientific, superstition and even witchcraft. Such defining out means that historical knowledges are treated as the raw material for scientists to work on without due recognition. Finally, feminists have pointed out that knowledges are evolving, not static – that fixing a moment that is then frozen in the form of a patent does not allow us to recognize the building blocks of previous work in the area. The rules regime that is now setting the boundaries of this fixity is itself highly problematic, given that it seeks to stabilize the unequal relations of power – within society and between states.

Debates about the nature and processes of creation of knowledge have also made TRIPS an increasingly important issue between and among states. While global in its formulation, TRIPS and its enforcement through the WTO is resulting in sharpening differences among states of the North and the South. Most developing countries feel that the attempt by the TRIPS Agreement (Article 65) at a global standardization of patent laws is in conflict with the thrust on 'diversity' by the Convention on Biodiversity (CBD) signed at the Rio Earth Summit in 1992. They feel that intellectual property rights must not be in conflict with conservation and sustainable uses of biodiversity, an issue that been neglected by those who composed the TRIPS Agreement (Swanson,

1997). Questions are also being asked as to how far this patent regime would facilitate effective competition or dissemination of information. Some have even argued that it departs from the competitive ideals and further restricts the access of the poorer countries to technology (Stewart, 1993).

The two main objectives of an effective patent law are:

○ promotion of technological innovation by enabling the inventor to enjoy the fruits of his/her creative activities
○ transfer and dissemination of technology in order to curb piracy.

These views have been challenged on the grounds that they are Eurocentric views of culture and that determination of piracy, until such time as the universal patent regime is ushered in, would be judged by the principle of territoriality. Patent rights are not absolute and are to be judged in terms of their social utility, and, as such, costs and benefits may vary over space and time (Deardoff, 1993). Patent rights, while providing incentive to invent, simultaneously give rise to monopoly prices, which affect the consumer adversely. It has been found that about two-thirds of patented products are never produced but used to ward off rivals. While TRIPS is not very particular on the issue of compulsory licensing, several national patent laws (China, Argentina, Brazil) use it effectively to prevent the patent-holder from denying others access to the patented product, and make it possible for others to apply for permission for such use against a fee (Keyala, 1998).

The differential impact of the uniform patent legislation on less-developed countries is a major contentious issue between the two blocs of countries. Vaistos estimated that in 1972, 80-85 per cent of the patents were held by Northern interests (Vaistos, 1972). According to a recent document of the World Intellectual Property Organisation (WIPO), the citizens of developed countries hold 95 per cent of African patents, 85 per cent of Latin American patents and 70 per cent of Asian patents (GAIA and GRAIn, 1998). According to another source, the majority of biotechnology patents are in the name of companies originating in the West. In 1990, 36 per cent were in the name of US companies, 32 per cent in the name of European companies and another 23 per cent in the name of their Japanese counterparts – an aggregate of 91 per cent (Swanson, 1997). Given that an overwhelming proportion of patents originate in the developed world, patent protection is likely to lead to a transfer of income from the less-developed countries to the more-developed countries and thereby widen the income disparities between the two (Deardoff, 1993).

Biopiracy or value added? Patent dilemmas

The issue of biopiracy concerning patent rights on seed varieties has become the most controversial issue in the TRIPS Agreement. It stipulates that plant varieties are expected to be protected by patents, by a *sui generis* system or by a combination of the two (Dasgupta, 1999). As such, since the conclusion of the Marrakesh Agreement, there has been an explosion in the activities of large multinational firms to collect germplasms of different plant varieties located in the developing countries. After some cross-breeding with other varieties, they are producing new breeds of such plants and plant produce, which are being claimed to be unique and distinct and are being patented by the multinational firms in their own countries. Once patented, these plants become the private property of the patent-holder until the expiry of the patent right. Under exclusive marketing rights (EMR), the patent-holder of a product patented anywhere in the world would drive out indigenous competitors from the domestic market in any other country, as the patent is universally applicable. This places countries rich in biological wealth but economically poor in a very disadvantageous position. There are numerous instances of such patenting, which began with the commercialization of products made from the neem tree in India. It has since included other products such as the vegetable bitter gourd (karela), the spice tumeric (haldi) and the fruit jamun (a kind of black berry), as well as the African soapberry and the patent covering all genetically engineered cotton varieties. In all such cases, the crux of the issue is whether the knowledge relating to the development of such items is a social product subject to local common rights. Or should they be treated as commodities in which the profits generated from the development of the products involved in commercializing the products are treated as property rights belonging exclusively to the patenting party initially (Shiva and Holla-Bhar, 1996). There is an increasing feeling that the national laws that protect domestic innovations will have to be altered to conform to the patent laws of developed countries.

An important consequence of the concentration of patents with multinational companies in developed countries is the shift in focus for research and development from the public domain, universities and research institutions to private companies involved in maximization of profit. On the one hand, with public subsidy, once discovered, an invention can be disseminated without cost, and it can be shown that such 'common knowledge' products are efficient to finance publicly. On the other hand, private companies take the fruits of such basic research and make further investment in adaptive research for their commercial use. Although they cover only a small part of the total cost of research, they still claim patent (monopoly) rights to exclude others from accessing the knowledge. Other challenges to people's access and control of knowledge, technology and production processes include TRIPS preference for product patents, especially in the field of pharmaceuticals and drugs, which make it difficult and expensive for developing countries to gain access to new technologies. The 'classical pipeline protection' of Article 70.8 and 'exclusive marketing rights' (EMR) of Article 70.9 for countries in the transitional phase of switching from process to product patent miss the desired impact in view of the 'long' transitional period. In addition, the fact that once a product is patented in any one country it becomes automatically and universally applicable to all WTO member countries, denies the national governments the right to impose conditions that safeguard the interests of domestic industry. The patent-holder is thus endowed with two types of monopoly arising from patents and EMR. Given that patents are, in the majority, owned by developed countries, the benefit would accrue primarily to the multinational companies of the developed countries. Developing countries argue that the TRIPS Agreement further forecloses the avenue for them to acquire technology through the process of liberally using foreign technology or resorting to reverse engineering for their own technological and engineering progress (Hoggard, 1994).

Engendering the privatization debate

Privatizing knowledge production is gendered in different ways. First, this has historically been a process of exclusion of women (as well as some racial and ethnic groups). In Europe, research centres and hospitals became the domain of male scientists and researchers who denied the relevance of social knowledges to their work (Shiva, 1988). In India, lowest-caste people and women were excluded from education, and from even listening to the classical religious texts. Formalized education then has been a domain of denied opportunities for women. Further, in the global market systems dominated by hypermasculinized values that recognize only certain forms of knowledges, work and competition, even the male populations of Third World countries get 'feminized' through economic emasculation in the market place (Ling, 1997). This is evident in the case of the Warangal farmers of India, 500 of whom took their own lives in 1998–9, under pressure from a combination of local and global structural pressures (DAW, 1999: 10). Second, more recently, the post-colonial nation states have emphasized the need to develop indigenous strategies of modernizing their economies. This has led to two different strategies. Developing states have modelled their technological development on that of the West, at times by adapting existing technologies to their development needs. Patenting laws will result in the closing of this avenue of development. Without safeguarding the interests of the domestic industries, the product price of goods has a tendency to rise. This has different impacts on women and men, most startlingly in the sphere of health. As pharmaceuticals and drugs become more expensive, women's health is adversely affected. A recent study by doctors in the All-India Medical Institute in New Delhi suggests that far fewer operations are being performed on women and girls than on boys and men (*Times of India*, 25 April 2000). Second, there has been an emphasis on higher education rather than primary and secondary education. This has meant that girls have not been able to avail themselves of education – due to lack of resources at the lower rungs of the educational ladder and lack of expectation at the higher. Third, economic conditionalities imposed by structural adjustment policies on developing countries are leading to cuts in the public expenditure budgets of these states. These cuts are resulting in declining access to education and more health-related absences from school for girls and women. Average expenditure on education and health was about 3.4 per cent of GDP on education and 3.7 per cent on health for all developing countries, between 1988 and 1990, and only 2.8 and 2.4 per cent respectively for the poorest countries (DAW, 1999: 52). Indeed, even in countries that had very high levels of female education, such as Russia and China, liberalization and structural adjustment has led to a dramatic fall in female education. In China, for example, 70 per cent of illiterates are female. Finally, it has also been noticed that among multilateral aid organizations 'less and less importance is being attached to training poor women – indeed some agencies have abandoned it altogether in favour of micro-credit and savings schemes' (http://www.id21.org/static/4afl1.htm). Without training and with cuts in education, the levels of women's participation in creating formally recognized intellectual products will remain minimal.

Another important issue for the TRIPS regime is the unauthorized exploitation and appropriation of the full market value of the protected subject matter. Here, the inequality in market participation is important as both the protection of the inventor and subsequent commercial incentives are determined by the owner's position relating to market access and equal participation. As we have argued above, market access is socially determined, as is equal participation in the processes of production of intellectual property. However, we have also argued that a feminist and gendered perspective makes us sensitive to the social history of knowledge production and challenges the boundaries of privatised intellectual production. The market system, we would argue after Braudel (1985), can be understood only when it is placed within the context of an economic life and social life.

Can well-designed intellectual property regimes try to balance a recognition of the social history of knowledge creation and of individual or corporate inputs which enhance the products resulting from existing knowledge? Can regulatory boundaries be drawn within an intellectual property regime around incentives for the creation of knowledge and the social benefits derived from it? The evidence from our survey of the issues above does not lead to a sanguine conclusion. The terms on which intellectual property is being defined, and therefore regulated, does not seem to be sensitive to historically situated, informal networks of social knowledge. The need to privatize knowledge remains crucial to the regime of patents.

Put simply, intellectual property rights affect women and men as well as developing and developed countries in different ways. The key issues determining the differences are market access and competition policy (at both the national and international levels) (Sell, 1998). In the case of gender, in addition to these polarizations, women's property rights extend beyond the market to include structures of property that determine the endowments with which people enter markets and structures of reproduction that govern domestic divisions of property and labour. According to Palmer, social constraints that distort allocation of labour, and the rigid and socially sanctioned sexual division of labour that allocates the care of human beings to women's functions like a tax, further aggravate the gender blindness of allocative efficiency and have a bearing on women's participatory role in the market (Palmer, 1992). This is reflected in the TRIPS Agreement, where a new challenge is being posed to people's access, control and even knowledge of their livelihood resources.

Conclusions

Mrs Kaijoki's difficulties in making her patent a viable commercial product is a unique example of existing prejudice against women participating equally with men in the global market. The Winter Aquarium System, which she patented in 1989 in Finland, was launched for commercialization in 1994. But she is still struggling to be commercially successful. When interviewed by Ms Maila Hakala, ex-President of the Women Inventors' Network, she admitted that though there is no explicit discrimination on gender lines inherent in the legislation of TRIPS, there are no simultaneous safeguards against the 'brotherhood' network of men who are controlling her chances of equal participation. She feels bitter frustration at the long wait due to the unfair trade practices of agents and other colleagues, who are all men. To add insult to injury they frequently term her invention as an 'easy', yet they are waiting for her to give up.

   This experience proves that technological change and enhancing knowledge – the observable face of globalization – are primarily concentrated among male proponents from industrialized countries, operating on a winner-takes-all market concept, and that there is no in-built mechanism in the TRIPS Agreement to act as a safeguard in favour of the so called 'underclass'. This stereotyping is evident in spite of the fact that in 1990 estimated world sales of medicines derived from plants discovered by indigenous people and women amounted to US $43 billion; only a small fraction of this went to the people and groups who had preserved the traditional medicinal plants. Developing countries profit from the new technologies of the industrial world as much as they do from preserving and deploying the knowledge developed in the course of their own history – in most instances women have developed them. However, their weak positions cannot catapult them to a position similar to the Northern corporate groups, who are quick to patent the age-old knowledge developed by the community and for the community and to make the same community pay a price for the products that have always been in their custody. The technical interpretations of TRIPS in isolation would enhance the very inequality among nations and societies that it proposes to erase.

Institutional support mechanisms to encourage women to undertake the risks involved in innovative research and development are negligible. Facilities to run experimental trials and resources to encourage such ventures make the access points still narrower. And while in some countries initiatives have been taken, empathy with the unique role women have to perform in society is yet to be developed to make the conditions to facilitate them. Access to credit facilities or the lack of it has been a major deterrent to women's entry in this field. Formal financial institutions see a woman with an original creation to be tested in the market but without the conventional collateral as a double bad debt even before the loan has been approved. We need not venture further into the details of monetary restrictions facing women at every step thereafter.

Classification of many women's inventions and acknowledgement of women's creation or contribution to many inventions are important aspects of equal participation in the marketplace. Beginning with the inventions of fire and machines, both considered as male preserves, to herbal medicine, which became a significant technology the moment it was taken over by males, women have always been subjected to stereotypes – their inventions are 'domestic', mainly related to child, home and beauty care. Venturing out, they advanced into 'nurturing' kinds of invention for use outside the home and finally women entered into a variety of areas not associated with traditional stereotypes, such as biotechnology, including genetic engineering, etc. These assumptions, an integral part of any society's psyche, are a barrier difficult to surmount and when overcome pose a host of problems before the inventions can be patented and subsequently commercialized.

In a world of unequal partners, it is not, therefore, surprising that rules of the game (globalization) are asymmetrical, if not inequitable (Nayyar, 1997). The gains go to countries that have participated most actively in setting the rules (Page *et al.*, 1991). Developed countries of the West emphasize the close relationship between economic progress and protection and legislation on intellectual property rights, and feel this would further boost economic development in developing countries through an increase in employment and enhanced exports, and would act as an incentive for innovation and technological advance. On the other hand, developing countries focus on the double provision of patenting, which has led to several abuses, especially among developing countries (Ramachandra, 1977). According to the statistics of the Indian Patent Office, in 1998 the number of patents granted in India to foreign companies was 8229, while the figure for Indian companies stood at 1926. A UNCTAD report identifies the impact of the TRIPS Agreement on developing countries as 'ambiguous'; while reducing their access to technology developed in other countries it also imposes the cost of enforcement, which is particularly high in low-income countries (UNCTAD, 1996).

Our argument is that in any society, customary property rights are evolved to lessen transaction costs to individuals is valid generally – but this ignores the ideology of gender that places differential values on male versus female ownership and rights (including intellectual property) (Mukund, 1999). As such, the intellectual property rights legislation makes no provision for insulating the unique contribution made by women innovators, in the first place by acknowledging it as an innovation and thereafter protecting it from future unfair exploitation. Innovation for the universal formal sector signifies a proactive process where opportunities are created or sought and risks taken or supported. In the context of women, however, innovation extends within a broader band of activities, which sometimes may not be linked to the market or to changes in the machinery or equipment. It can bring about any change, however small, in the skills, techniques, processes, equipment types or organization of production that enables people better to cope with or take advantage of particular circumstances (Appleton, 1995). Women are not generally high-profile users of technical hardware but have important technical skills and knowledge and are engaged in complex production processes. They constantly innovate and adapt or contribute to the innovations and adaptations of others, but under the protective legislation of intellectual property rights their expertise goes unrecognized and is less valued. The apparent 'invisibility' of women's technical contribution is not rectified by this new legislation.

Reverting to the first of the three questions: whose rules govern the TRIPS Agreement, even if the rules are universally accepted, it will depend on the willingness of the powerful male-dominated lobby to promote them. Second, their successful promotion can often reinforce the already unequal power relation between men and women as the implementation of the TRIPS Agreement is dependent on domestic institutions which are often influenced by a close interplay of social and cultural factors. Finally, the third question pertaining to the mode of implementation – this is dependent on international institutions, which are usually not very effective, except when dealing with states dependent on them for financial assistance. This links back to the confirmation of the conflict between the powerful and the not powerful parties.

The four main issues that are most likely to have an impact on the future equal status of women, vis-à-vis the protection of intellectual property rights, are:

○ a capacity of states to bear the costs of adjustment to globalization
○ the need for institutional reform to manage globalization
○ the values which are to underpin the new global system
○ the complexity and ambiguity of the emerging transitional society.

For better and more effective protection of women's intellectual rights the following themes need to be explored and incorporated in any national or international legislation designed to achieve an optimum result:

○ Technological worlds of women and men differ according to social, economic, cultural and sexual relationships existing between them.
○ Women's knowledge of processes is rational and is based on a logical framework of understanding.
○ The space in which women live affects their patterns of production and use of technology, as do circumstances, such as national disaster, conflicts, environmental changes and market demands.
○ The innovations that women make are based on their perceptions of the priorities in all aspects of their lives and particularly on their understanding of the risks involved.
○ Women's knowledge and skills in food production, processing and marketing play a crucial role in household livelihoods and food security.
○ Technical information and skills are communicated to women and between women using different channels.
○ The national policy environment affects the ways in which women use, adapt and adopt technology (Appleton, 1995).

Based on these themes, a significant 'break point' in the implementation of the TRIPS Agreement would be an acknowledgement that the various disciplines of intellectual property rights covered in the Agreement will differ among countries (depending on their levels of economic and technological development and mode of implementation), as well as between women and men. 'We still live in a world where,' as Dr Rosalyn Sussman Yalow, winner of the 1977 Nobel Prize for Medicine for the discovery of radioimmunoassay (RIA) said, 'still a significant fraction of people ... believe that a woman belongs and wants to belong exclusively in the home ...'. To advance forward, women require competence, courage and determination to succeed. But this does not diminish the role of an enabling environment.

It is perhaps useful to end with another story of another woman inventor. Marie Curie did not patent her inventions. She insisted that she wanted no profit from them but to publish them to promote the study of radium and its applications. The so-called obvious technology of age-old communities is usually the real leap in knowledge as compared to all subsequent technology that is being patented with great enthusiasm. We do have choices. Instead of cherry-picking the best practices, which necessarily do not reflect the real position of women in the context of protection of their intellectual property rights, it will be useful and practical to challenge the TRIPS Agreement in order to press for the equal protection and participation of women inventors, entrepreneurs and others in their respective fields of technical advancement. Otherwise it may soon degenerate into a 'democratic masquerade'.

3 Stagnant backwater or dynamic engine of growth?: the small enterprise sector under globalization

JONATHAN DAWSON

Introduction

EARLY THEORIES ABOUT the place of the small enterprise sector in developing economies and societies were highly polarized. On the one hand, Marxist theorists dismissed the 'informal sector', as it was then known, as an irrelevance. It was seen as no more than a stagnant backwater whose primary functions were: (i) to develop new markets to a point where they were profitable for 'formal sector' exploitation; and (ii) to mop up the unemployed, thus acting as a brake on revolutionary pressures. Such was the dominance of the 'formal sector' in terms of privileged access to productive resources and markets that they believed the 'informal sector' to be incapable of meaningful development.

On the other hand, neo-liberal theorists were infatuated by the perceived dynamism of the 'informal sector' during a period when over-protected large state and private businesses were becoming increasingly moribund. Focusing on the individual enterprise and apparently oblivious to the possibility of structural constraints on growth, the neo-liberals argued that, given appropriate institutional support, 'informal sector' firms could become an important engine of economic growth.

Schmitz (1982) was among the first to attempt to relate these two schools of thought to each other. He concluded that while structural constraints unquestionably exist, there was some evidence of dynamism among small producers. The point, he said, was to move beyond ideological certainties to discover, in practice, what did and did not work. How could support agencies effectively enable small producers to become more dynamic and innovative?

This challenge has been taken up in all corners of the South. There is scarcely a country that cannot boast a raft of small producer support agencies funded and supported in their turn by the donor and international NGO communities. Twenty years on from Schmitz's proposal of the existence of a 'middle way', it is appropriate to examine in the context of globalization what impact these support agencies are having and to see whether, today, the sector more closely resembles a stagnant backwater or a source of dynamic growth. To quote from the title of a recent article by Kenneth King, pioneering researcher of the small enterprise sector in Africa, 'Growing up, but will the informal sector mature?' (King, 1997).

Definitions

In the current context, the term 'globalization' is used to refer to two related, recent and ongoing trends. First is the process of economic liberalization (generally under the name of structural adjustment), through which developing country economies have been tied more tightly into the global economy. Second, is the rapid development of communications technologies which have facilitated a significant increase in the speed and ease of trade and financial transfers.

'Small producers' is used here to refer to all those – artisans, craftsmen, smallholder farmers, etc. – producing on a small scale. 'Small-scale enterprises' is used to denote small, non-agricultural businesses. A common-sense definition of no more than 20 employees will be adopted to define 'small' in this context. (It should, however, be noted that in almost all comprehensive small enterprise surveys, well in excess of 90 per cent of firms are found to have fewer than ten employees.)

The impact of globalization on small producers: tracing the threads

Describing the impact of globalization on small producers is no simple matter. Globalization is a composite term used to encompass many different elements, each of which impacts differently on small producers of different types (the key variables being sector, size, export or domestic orientation, and levels of sophistication). The aim of this section is to attempt to disentangle some of the more important trends as they affect small producers. We shall look in turn at how small enterprises have been affected in terms of access to markets, technology, skilled labour and raw materials.

Markets

The opening up of many niches in international markets for small producers in recent years can be linked to globalization. There is today, for example, in the supermarkets of industrialized countries, a far greater volume and variety than ever before of speciality horticultural produce, a significant quantity of which is grown by smallholders in developing countries. There has also been a significant increase in exports of non-traditional forest products, including seeds, resins, essential oils, honey and so on. High-profile companies such as The Body Shop have played an active role in developing these niche markets.

The importance of fair trade and alternative trading organizations (ATOs) has increased significantly in recent years. Small producers in a variety of fields – traditional and non-traditional crops, handicrafts and other exotic ethnic goods – have gained a level of access to Northern markets through these channels that would have been barely conceivable a quarter of a century ago. In parallel, as ethical lobbies and consumer niches have developed in the North, so small producers able to meet the criteria set by specific quality seals of approval, such as those developed by the Soil Association and fair trade organizations, have enjoyed spectacular improvements in their market access. Moreover, these organizations generally pay a significantly higher price to producers than mainstream clients.

Domestically too, markets have opened up for small enterprises in the South. Devaluation, a key element of structural adjustment programmes, has pushed up the price of imported goods, creating numerous niches which, in certain cases and countries, relatively sophisticated and highly skilled small enterprises have succeeded in penetrating. These include high-quality clothing and shoes, furniture and a range of machinery, including food-processing equipment, hand tools and so on. In addition, small enterprises located in important cash crop-producing areas have often benefited from increased aggregate demand for their goods and services (see, for example, Dawson and Oyeyinka, 1993; Steel and Webster, 1991).

Finally, the shrinking of the state sector resulting from liberalization has created market space, some of which has been occupied by small enterprises. Where parastatal enterprises previously held a near monopoly in many domestic markets – including, for example, agricultural marketing, grain milling, and the provision of equipment, food and uniforms for public institutions such as schools and hospitals – today, small enterprises are often more active. In several cases, national or state governments have intervened to help small enterprises to exploit these emerging opportunities. In Ceara State, Brazil, for example, the state government has used its procurement policy to good effect as a way of stimulating strong growth in the small enterprise sector (Tendler and Amorin, 1996). There is also evidence of some increase in subcontracting linkages, with small enterprises supplying various goods and services to larger companies. Overall, however, especially in Africa, subcontracting has been a less important motor of small enterprise development than once had been hoped.

On the other side of the balance sheet, the trends inherent in globalization have also unquestionably led to the contraction of a number of small producer markets. As protective barriers have been dismantled, so imports have risen. This has been particularly damaging in countries where economic liberalization has been introduced suddenly and all at once. The countries of Southern Africa, which have shifted suddenly from command to open economies, have seen their manufacturing bases at all scales of activity decimated by the relative power of the South African and Zimbabwean economies. Imported second-hand clothing now represents a major threat to textiles and garment producers throughout Africa. Similarly, imports of cheap plastic and aluminium storage and cooking vessels have displaced many small-scale potters, basket makers and other artisans.

Indigenous capital goods industries have been hit by sharp increases in imports of many types of machinery and spare parts. Where the local market is relatively large and stable and where distribution costs are relatively low, imports have fared well. Conversely, small-scale, local production tends to remain profitable in those market areas where demand is sparse and irregular and where distribution costs are high. By way of example, small-scale producers of nuts and bolts in a number of African countries have entirely lost their market for small, standard items at the same time as they have come to dominate the market for relatively large, non-standard pieces.

Small producers are also being displaced from markets that they have traditionally dominated as a result of foreign direct investment. In Chapter 8 of this book, Carr describes how as shea butter has grown in importance as an export crop, so processing activities have progressively been taken over by large-scale plants, both domestically and overseas. An associated and potentially very serious problem for small-scale processors in the South (also described by Carr and by Barwa and Rai in Chapter 2), is the usurpation by Northern-based corporations of intellectual property rights of plants and crops that form the basis of many traditional small-scale economic activities. It is not yet clear what will be the practical impact of this development.

Finally, and to date perhaps most seriously of all, small enterprises have suffered from the drop in purchasing power that has generally resulted from structural adjustment programmes, particularly outside of the major export crop-producing areas. Inflation driven by devaluation has eaten into real consumer demand while wages have not kept pace. Newly introduced or increased school and hospital fees together with the abolition of subsidies on agricultural inputs have further exacerbated the problem.

In many areas, the effect on small producers of this factor alone has outweighed all of the opportunities and more favourable trends described above. That is, while a relatively small number of enterprises has proved able to penetrate higher-value market niches, a much larger number has been unable to graduate out of the low-quality, low-value markets in which their clients are suffering from reduced purchasing power.

A related problem here has been increased competition as the ranks of the 'informal sector' are swollen by new market entrants and retrenchees. The situation prevailing in many small enterprise markets could be likened to a cake being cut into ever-smaller slices.

Technology, parts and components and skilled labour

Small enterprises have benefited from a flow of modern production equipment and skilled labour from the contracting state sector. A number of

formally trained engineers and skilled workers have moved from retrench-
ment into self-employment in small workshops. In some cases, they have
succeeded in bringing their equipment with them or in purchasing appropriate tools at auctions following the sell-offs of state enterprises. For those able
to afford them, there has also been easier access to imported equipment,
spare parts and other components. The greater availability of imported glues,
dyes and resins, for example, has helped small-scale furniture makers and
tailors to move into higher value-added markets in several African countries.

While they may be more freely available, however, imported equipment,
parts and components are, by virtue of devaluation, significantly more expensive. Numerous studies of the small enterprise sector have found progressive
decapitalization as enterprises are unable to replace equipment that has
come to the end of its working life. A study in Nigeria, for example, found that
a quarter of sampled small enterprises had less equipment than ten years previously when the structural adjustment programme had been adopted
(Meagher and Yunusa, 1992).

Raw materials

Small-scale enterprises in several sectors appear to have suffered as a result
of increased exports of raw materials from the South. Carpenters and furniture makers in a number of countries, for example, have experienced
problems of both reduced availability and increased prices as a result of
exports of wood. Export of products based on uncultivated, non-traditional
forest products has in some cases led to over-exploitation. Open markets
have even resulted in the export of scrap metals from some African countries,
making production for local markets more expensive or impossible.

Analysis of the trends

In this section, we shall attempt to show some of the major lessons that can
be drawn from the above analysis. Four core lessons are identified.

1. *Those sectors in which globalization offers potentially the greatest direct
   benefits are, in the main, labour intensive and low-technology.* This is not to
   say that some relatively sophisticated small enterprises are not also deriving benefit from the trends inherent in globalization. As we have seen
   above, small enterprises that have been able to attract skilled labour and
   to purchase modern production equipment have enjoyed some success in
   penetrating domestic niche markets previously dominated by larger
   domestic competitors and imports. There is also evidence of the development in some parts of the South of subcontracting linkages between large
   companies and small-scale suppliers. These suppliers tend to be the more

sophisticated small enterprises that are able to adapt their working practices to the needs of the 'formal sector'. Nonetheless, domestic markets in
the South have generally remained depressed, and in most cases it is those
serving export markets that have derived most benefit from the opportunities emerging as a result of globalization. Export-oriented sectors in which
small producers are active include specialist horticulture, non-traditional
forest products, handicrafts and other exotic, ethnic goods. Enterprises in
these sectors are, in the main, small, rural and relatively backward technologically.

2. *The dichotomy between subsistence and growth enterprises that is often
   drawn is less useful as a tool in understanding the opportunities offered by
   globalization than the issue of market access.* Small enterprise theorists and
   practitioners have, for some years, laid much stress on the importance of
   distinguishing between 'growth' enterprises (relatively modern and sophisticated) and 'subsistence' enterprises (small, backward, informal). Where
   the former are believed to have significant potential for growth, the latter
   tend to be seen as stagnant and incapable of significant development.
   Consequently, assistance programmes aimed at promoting the development and expansion of the small-scale sector have tended to focus on
   'growth' enterprises. However, as we have seen above, it is in sectors in
   which small, informal, often rural-based producers (not all, for sure, but certainly among those active in sectors where export niches have emerged)
   that many of the opportunities associated with globalization are opening.

3. *The technology and information gap that divides small producers from
   large-scale business, both internationally and domestically, has widened
   dramatically.* During a period when there have been huge advances in communications and production technologies in the North (which have to
   some extent been extended to companies in the South), small-scale
   Southern enterprises have enjoyed at best only marginal gains. For small
   machine shops, for example – generally among the most sophisticated of
   small-scale enterprises – the prospect of successfully competing against (or
   cooperating in a subcontracting relationship with) larger domestic and
   international companies is more, not less, remote. For, while the machine
   shop may have acquired machine tools and formally trained labour as a
   consequence of liberalization, its larger competitors will generally have
   made a much larger qualitative technological leap, involving computer-
   aided design technologies. In a global economy in which access to
   information and modern technology are at a premium, small producers in
   the South find themselves further adrift of the competitive frontier than
   ever before.

4. *In the context of globalization, the capacity of small producers for meaningful innovation remains very weak.* For, if by innovation we mean the
   capacity of small producers to identify and successfully respond to new

market opportunities, independent of external support, the widening information and technological gaps are ever more unbridgeable. Information on international market trends is rarely available to small producers and knowledge of and access to export channels is almost non-existent. Moreover, only very rarely do small producers have the education, contacts and self-confidence to be able to seek out such information. Even when serving domestic markets, the capacity of small producers to undertake the necessary market research, identify new product niches, source and finance the necessary equipment, and move into profitable production is extremely limited.

Implications for small enterprise support

The first lesson to emerge from the above discussion is that the various trends inherent in globalization are throwing up fresh opportunities for small producers in the South. However, these trends are effecting a revolution in the shape and incentive structures of Southern economies: just as some new opportunities are presenting themselves, so others are closing. So, for example, while new market opportunities are opening for the producers of certain handicrafts and horticultural products, small-scale garment makers and potters are, in many cases, finding it impossible to compete with low-cost imports.

In this rapidly changing economic environment, it is more than ever essential that interventions aimed at promoting the development of small producers be based on a thorough understanding of the economic context. Subsector analysis (sometimes referred to as value-chain analysis) has emerged over the past decade as the principal tool for identifying the various economic actors and the scale at which they operate at each stage of the production, processing and marketing of goods in specific sectors. It is also used to identify points in this chain where small producers may have opportunities for increasing their participation and adding greater value. Too many small enterprise support projects continue to be built on the intuition of their designers or on outmoded ideas of the relative strengths and weaknesses of the small enterprise sector. In this period when economic incentive structures globally are undergoing rapid and radical transformation, subsector analysis is an indispensable tool in the process of project design.

A second challenge for small enterprise support agencies is in responding to the finding that, in many respects, it is in sectors in which relatively small and informal small enterprises are active that globalization offers many of the greatest opportunities. Here we return to the point made above about the diminishing usefulness of the distinction generally made between 'growth' and 'subsistence' enterprises. In the light of the findings discussed above, it is clearly time to think more in terms of growth *sectors* rather than growth *enterprises*.

The challenges facing support agencies seeking to support small producers in such sectors are substantial. Because the producers themselves are so far distant from market information and generally so ill-equipped to identify potential market opportunities, the roles of identifying and testing out such opportunities must be taken on by the support agencies themselves. In many cases, playing such roles successfully requires a substantial change in the culture of small-producer support agencies, which have generally had little exposure to markets and how they work.

There is, however, already much good practice in this field from which important lessons can be drawn. The role of ATOs and fair trade organizations has already been mentioned. In addition to providing information on niches in Northern markets, they are also often involved in the delivery of the skills necessary to enable small enterprises to exploit them and in the establishment of appropriate market distribution channels. Mechanisms now being used for the delivery of market information to Southern producers include the Internet.

There is, in addition, evidence among small-producer support agencies of a greater market awareness and of the employment of more staff with a private-sector background. A number of international NGOs, including the North American agencies EnterpriseWorks Worldwide and TechnoServe for example, now see the identification and development of market opportunities, both internationally and domestically, on behalf of their small enterprise clients as among their most important functions.

Similarly, Rural Enterprise Development Services (REDS), a wing of the Sri Lankan NGO Sarvodaya, identifies market opportunities and creates linkages between enterprises in the villages with which it works and exporters in a number of sectors, including handicrafts, fruit and vegetables. In a number of cases, the technical assistance and equipment involved are provided by the exporting companies. Having facilitated the linkage, REDS aims, where possible, to step back, leaving the relationship to develop sustainably without any further external input.

A key element in successful marketing strategies for small enterprises is that the support agency be able to identify and address the key bottlenecks in the production and marketing chain. In many cases, this requires the support agency to draw a clear distinction between target groups and beneficiaries. Often the most appropriate way of addressing a constraint faced by the target group of small enterprises is to tackle a bottleneck elsewhere in the chain. Assistance delivered by support agencies to relatively large marketing companies and to firms providing inputs and components has enjoyed considerable leverage in terms of its upstream and downstream impact on small enterprises (Dawson, 1997).

A further broad area of discussion in terms of the implications of the findings presented above for small enterprise support agencies relates to the most appropriate strategy for strengthening the capacity of small-scale manufacturers. One recent attempt at classification of technological support to small enterprises distinguished between *corporate* and *indigenous* approaches. The former approach mirrors that of a commercial organization: technologies are externally developed and distributed through strong market channels. The manufacturing enterprise receives from the support agency only the expertise required to manufacture the technology in question. The indigenous approach, on the other hand, emphasizes the importance of small enterprises themselves in the development of technology: the efforts of the support agencies focus on increasing their capacity for autonomous innovation (Committee of Donor Agencies for Small Enterprise Development, 1998).

The findings above present a challenge to the proponents of the indigenous approach. For, in a situation where domestic markets are often shrinking (particularly in non-export crop areas) and where access to higher-value domestic and export markets may well require more, not less, mediation by support agencies, the capacity of small enterprises to bridge the technological and information gaps *themselves, without ongoing external support*, must be open to question.

In short, for agencies seeking to enhance the capacity of small enterprises to innovate themselves, the questions that need to be addressed are:

○ first, given the large and growing information and technology gaps that are being driven by the process of globalization, what level of innovation are small-scale enterprises realistically likely to be capable of achieving?
○ second, in the light of this, in what cases and under what circumstances can an indigenous approach to technology development and dissemination be defended as cost-effective?

This latter point is important in terms of the capacity to attract continued donor funding. Agencies adopting a corporate approach are able, in many cases, to point to large-scale dissemination of specific technologies – including jiko stoves, treadle pumps and grinding mills – with very healthy cost-benefit ratios. This has always been more difficult for the proponents of the indigenous approach, since (i) most of the benefits are accrued downstream and after the life of the project concerned; and (ii) impact assessment is riddled with methodological problems, not least relating to issues of attribution.

Now, it is obviously important that small-scale manufacturers are not restricted to production of the handful of technologies that are easily amenable to large-scale dissemination through corporate approaches. Nonetheless, it is also true that the cost of interventions to enhance the general technological competence and self-confidence of small enterprises must be commensurate with the economic impact that they are likely to be able to achieve. In a depressed economic environment, this risks being modest.

Greater efforts need to be focused on the measurement of the impact of indigenous approaches to technology development and dissemination, to trace causal connections between technology-focused interventions and downstream benefits. This is required both to shed more light on what does and does not work and in which circumstances indigenous capacity-building can deliver value for money; and also, in such circumstances, to persuade donors, who are increasingly determined to achieve value for money, to continue funding.

Stagnant backwater or dynamic engine of growth?

So, what conclusions can be drawn as to whether the small enterprise sector today, in the era of globalization, represents more a stagnant backwater or a dynamic engine of growth? It is tempting to follow Schmitz's lead and conclude that the truth lies somewhere between the two poles. Nonetheless, it is unquestionably true that at present, grounds for pessimism are more apparent than those for optimism. While some niche markets have opened up for small enterprises, economic liberalization has seen a flood of imports and, in some countries, a resurgence of domestic 'formal sector' activity. In the face of these trends, small enterprises have in many cases been marginalized to those parts of the economy where demand is so weak and distribution costs so high as to render them unprofitable to their larger competitors. Moreover, growing information and technological gaps driven by globalization have left all but a handful of the most sophisticated small enterprises further adrift of the competitive frontier than ever. Serious doubts exist about their potential either for significantly greater integration into national and global economies or for undertaking meaningful innovation without the long-term assistance of support agencies.

This is not to say that small enterprises are no longer of economic significance: they continue to provide a livelihood for a huge number of households in the South. Nonetheless, in many respects the advances made by small producers as a result of globalization are characterized by high levels of dependence and vulnerability. Small producers are generally dependent on support organizations to identify and test out market opportunities and to continue to provide information and other forms of support. Their vulnerability derives both from the fickleness of trends in consumer taste in the markets of the North and from the potential or actual high levels of competition from other small producers in various parts of the world.

Globalization has accelerated the process of worldwide market integration. This has generated some opportunities for small producers in the South. However, it is perhaps more difficult than for some time to envisage the emergence of a dynamic, innovative small enterprise sector at the heart of any economy in the South.

4 Global trade and agriculture: a review of the WTO Agreement on Agriculture

BISWAJIT DHAR and SUDESHNA DEY[1]

Introduction

THE AGREEMENT ON AGRICULTURE (AoA) has remained in focus ever since the WTO took shape in 1995. The AoA seeks to provide the multilateral discipline to ensure comprehensive liberalization of agricultural trade, which was among the more important issues that the Uruguay Round negotiations took up for consideration. The inclusion of agriculture in the Uruguay Round marked a departure from previous rounds of negotiations in that for the first time GATT had decided to extend its authority over trade in temperate products, in the main, cereals. Tropical products, which include tea, coffee, spices, some oil seeds and vegetable oils (palm, coconut, etc.), have been governed by the GATT discipline, while temperate products had remained outside the purview of GATT.

The major issue that the Uruguay Round negotiations addressed was the removal of the plethora of distortions that had plagued global trade in agricultural commodities for several decades. In so doing, the negotiations brought into focus agricultural practices followed by the GATT Contracting Parties, and the outcome of the negotiations therefore brought up all aspects of the policy regime in the sector.

A comprehensive framework underlining multilateral discipline in the agricultural sector was finalized in the form of the AoA at the conclusion of the Uruguay Round negotiations at the end of 1993. The AoA seeks binding commitments from member countries in two areas. These include: (i) discipline in the subsidies regime; and (ii) enhanced market access through increased tariffication of all non-tariff barriers (NTBs). While emphasizing these objectives, the AoA also made reference to several non-trade concerns (NTCs) that would have to be taken on board while the Agreement was being implemented by the WTO member countries. These NTCs include food security and protection of the environment, among others.

In recent years, agriculture has received considerable attention in the WTO. Two factors have played a part in this process. The first stems from the nature of benefits that developing countries expected from the introduction of the WTO discipline through the AoA, the expectations of which have largely remained unmet. The second was the fact that agriculture was among the few areas that were to be reviewed in a comprehensive manner as a part of the built-in agenda of the WTO.

Several studies had indicated that the results of the Uruguay Round in the agricultural sector would bring significant welfare gains for a number of developing countries. In various scenarios worked out by the analysts, developing countries as a whole were expected to witness major welfare gains. Several of these studies indicated that countries like India and China would gain substantially as a result of the introduction of the discipline under AoA.[2]

The review of the AoA began in earnest in 1997, with the informal process of negotiations between the WTO members. The Analysis and Information Exchange (AIE) process threw up a large number of issues that were brought on to the agenda by the various members of the multilateral organization. These issues were mostly based on the experience that the WTO members had gained while implementing the commitments undertaken by them or by their major trading partners. The formal review of AoA began in March 2000 with the Committee on Agriculture setting a time frame for the process. In the period since then, WTO members have submitted their proposals which provide the backdrop to the negotiations.

This chapter attempts to highlight the present status of negotiations centred on the AoA. The ongoing negotiations are important in so far as they provide the basis for the trade-offs that different countries may agree to as the process of bargaining eventually takes shape. The chapter has three parts. In the first, the structure of AoA is briefly presented, looking at the main areas in which disciplines have been introduced. The second section discusses the positions taken by the major players as the ongoing negotiations on AoA have developed. This discussion is intended to provide a glimpse of the likely course of negotiations as the review of AoA gathers momentum. Finally, in the third section, a brief assessment of the proposals is presented.

Dimensions of agricultural policy introduced by the AoA

Agricultural policy making in the WTO member countries has been set within the contours of an elaborate structure that the AoA has put in place. As was alluded to above, there are two broad dimensions to this structure. In the first place, the Agreement has introduced several disciplines aimed at reducing the distortions prevailing in agricultural markets. And, second, AoA also indicates that some of the NTCs of WTO member countries, including those related to food security, would have to be taken on board. The following discussion provides the details.

Domestic support commitments

The subsidy discipline has been introduced by setting binding commitments on countries in terms of the support they can provide to their agricultural sector. According to AoA, the basis for calculation of subsidies is the Aggregate

Measurement of Support (AMS), which is to be calculated for each product receiving market price support, non-exempt direct payments or any other subsidy not exempt from the reduction commitment. All other non-product-specific support is to be put together into one non-product-specific AMS. The Agreement further provides that the AMS would have to include not only budgetary outlays, but also revenue forgone by the government and its agents. Additionally, the subsidy discipline stipulates that support provided to agriculture both at the national and subnational levels would have to be taken into account. This proviso is ostensibly aimed at including price support granted by federal governments in some countries.

At the same time, however, the AoA stipulates that several categories of subsidies would be exempt from AMS calculations. All these forms of agricultural support do not qualify for reduction commitments. In other words, WTO member countries would not have to decrease the spending on any of the programmes included in the exempt category of subsidies. These subsidies include domestic support policies that have, at most, a minimal impact on trade (so-called 'Green Box' policies included in Annex 2 of AoA) and the 'Blue Box' policies or production-limiting programmes appearing in Article 6.5 of the AoA.

In the exempt category of subsidies, i.e. the Green Box and the Blue Box taken together, two broad classes of support have been included. These are: (i) government programmes; and (ii) direct income support to producers. Included in the first category are government support for research programmes, pest and disease control, training services, extension and advisory services, inspection services, marketing and promotion services, and infrastructural services of various kinds. Among the programmes that have been included in the Green Box is a food aid programme for the poor, the details of which are discussed below. In a similar vein, payments to farmers under environmental programmes, or to producers in disadvantaged regions, would also qualify for exclusion, according to the provisions of the Agreement. However, the criteria for identifying such regions would have to be vetted by the WTO.

In the second category, two forms of income support would qualify for exemption: (i) payments under production-limiting programmes, including direct payments; and (ii) decoupled income support. Support for production-limiting programmes has been exempted from being treated under AMS to encourage countries to produce less and avoid creating conditions of glut in the market. This provision was included to address one of the main concerns that found expression in the negotiating mandate of the Uruguay Round, viz the instability in agricultural prices arising out of over-production. In addition to the Green Box policies, the other policy that would not be regarded as a part of the total AMS, but which forms a part of the support package that developed countries offer, is the direct payment to producers under production-limiting programmes.

Production-limiting support that can be exempted from being treated as subsidies can take the form of payments made on 85 per cent or less of the base level production, the base years being defined as between 1986 and 1988. Thus, production levels have to be fixed at 85 per cent or less than those in the base years in order to secure the exemptions that the Agreement provides for.

Also exempt from the calculation of the AMS are two other measures aimed at reducing the marketable surplus of agricultural products. Programmes for the retirement of producers, as well as resources employed in the past to produce marketable surplus, can be supported without being affected by the subsidy discipline.

The most important exclusion allowed is the decoupled income support. This is the principal form of support that US farmers enjoy. Further, the proposed CAP reform of the EU also entails adoption of a similar mechanism for providing support to European farmers.

The levels of AMS that countries have been allowed to maintain show significant variations. According to the rules that have been laid out, developed countries that provide low levels of subsidies to their agriculture would be allowed a 5 per cent ceiling on the quantum of subsidies they can provide. Developing countries have a higher ceiling of 10 per cent. This is in keeping with the special and differential treatment that these countries have enjoyed in the trading regime governed by the GATT.

The heavy subsidy-granting countries, on the other hand, have been treated differently. They are not subjected to any upper limits, but are expected only to bring down their subsidies by 20 per cent in six years. For developing countries, other than the LDCs, this reduction commitment has been put at a lower level of 13.3 per cent, or two-thirds of the amount by which developed countries are committed to decrease their support. An important aspect of the reduction commitments is that no schedule for bringing down the subsidies has been drawn up. In other words, countries have the freedom to undertake the reduction only towards the end of the six-year implementation period of the Agreement. The LDCs have been exempted from undertaking any reductions in the subsidies they provide.

Export subsidy discipline

The export subsidy discipline requires member countries to decrease the value of subsidies granted by 36 per cent compared to the 1986–90 level over the six-year implementation period of the AoA. The volume of subsidized exports would have to be decreased by 21 per cent over the same six-year period. Developing countries would have to reduce their subsidies by two-thirds of the levels stipulated for developed countries. As in the case of domestic support, LDCs would not have to undertake any commitment to reduce export subsidies.

Market access

Two mechanisms for committing countries to provide better market access opportunities have been identified. The first involves tariffication of NTBs and reduction of existing levels of tariff protection. The second is the establishment of minimum access opportunities for imports of primary agricultural products in case a country had imported less than 3 per cent of domestic consumption of such products between 1986 and 1988.

The proposed tariffication of NTBs and reduction of levels of tariffs already existing in countries is in keeping with the overall framework of the negotiations which aim at: (i) progressive reduction in the trade barriers; and (ii) increased transparency in the imposition of trade restrictions. It is further provided that NTBs, once tariffed, cannot be reintroduced.

The minimum access opportunities for imports of primary commodities would have to be established if countries avail themselves of the 'special treatment' clause. This clause, contained in Annex 5 of the AoA, provides that if the imports of primary agricultural products and their worked and/or prepared products were less than 3 per cent of domestic consumption, minimum access opportunities of specified orders would have to be provided.

The minimum access opportunities would become binding for developing countries, considering that they would no longer be able to apply NTBs for balance of payments reasons as freely as in the past. Article XVIII:B of the GATT, which allowed developing countries to impose such import restrictions, has been considerably watered down in the Uruguay Round Agreement. While under previous GATT provisions developing countries could generally take recourse to Article XVIII:B, the Understanding on the Balance-of-Payments Provisions included in the Final Act, indicates very specifically that WTO members would have to phase out their existing import restrictions measures within a definite time frame. Additionally, the Understanding provides that further imposition of import restrictive measures would be possible in the new trade regime only under exceptional circumstances.

Non-trade concerns in the AoA

It has already been indicated that although the AoA emphasizes the importance of trade in improving the agricultural sector in WTO member countries, it nonetheless highlights the need to give due recognition to the various NTCs in this sector. The preamble to the AoA provides some indication as to what can be treated as NTCs. It states that 'commitments under the reform programme should be made in an equitable way among all Members, having regard to non-trade concerns, including food security and the need to protect the environment, having regard to the agreement that special and differential treatment for developing countries is an integral element of the negotiations, and taking into account the possible negative effects of the implementation of the reform programme on least-developed and net food importing developing countries'. Food security and protection of the environment have thus been identified as the major NTCs that the AoA was mandated to address. The NTCs also find a mention in Article 20 of the AoA, wherein the need to continue the reform process that it has initiated has been emphasized.

These references to the NTCs notwithstanding, existing provisions in AoA do not provide clear guidelines with which to address these concerns. Among the dimensions that the preambular statement considers as NTCs, only the food security issue has found a mention in a very perfunctory manner. The only support for measures aimed at ensuring food security appears in the form of an exemption from the calculation of AMS, the expenditure which is made on public stockholding of food grains. Expenditure made for accumulation and holding of stocks of products would, however, be exempt from AMS only if these activities form an integral part of a food security programme identified by national legislation. This may include government aid to private storage of products as a part of such a programme.

The stockholding activities for food security have been subjected to several additional conditions. According to the AoA, countries will be allowed to make use of public stockholding of grains for food security purposes 'provided that the difference between the acquisition price and the external reference price (i.e. the ruling international price) is accounted for in the AMS'. This raises several crucial questions for countries like India, where the acquisition price for building food stocks had been lower than the international prices for a long time before the latter registered a steep decrease in the recent past.

There is another provision, included in the context of using public stockholding for food security purposes, that the beneficiaries will have to be targeted. Countries have been given the right to give food aid to the poor, but the poor will have to be identified on the basis of 'clearly-defined criteria related to nutritional objectives'. This proviso implies that the criteria adopted for identifying the poor must have the approval of the WTO and that the eventual decision as to who should receive food aid will be made de facto by the multilateral organization.

It is thus quite clear from the above that the AoA is considerably limited in its scope on issues pertaining to the NTCs. These narrowly defined measures, which are provided by the AoA to ensure food security, skirt the larger question as to whether or not trade can support realization of the objectives of food security, particularly in the developing countries. This reflects the view that trade can be the primary basis for ensuring food security in these countries. This perspective deflects attention away from domestic production systems and their capacities to ensure much-needed food security. This inadequate rendering of the NTCs in the AoA has resulted in an active discussion on these in the WTO Committee on Agriculture (CoA). Most countries have presented their views on the NTCs in the informal process of analysis and information exchange, which the CoA had initiated in 1997 for a better understanding of the issues, keeping in mind the mandated review of the AoA.

The review of the AoA was formally launched in 2000. Countries were expected to present their proposals leading up to the negotiations. In the following section the main issues that have been mentioned by some of the members in their proposals are presented. This discussion will help in understanding the future course of the AoA.

An analysis of the proposals on the review of the AoA

The mandate for a review of AoA is provided in Article 20. Besides providing for the time frame for the commencement of the AoA review, which is five years from the period when it was enforced, Article 20 contains three substantive points. First, it provides that members would take into account their experience of implementing the reduction commitment. Second, members will consider the effects of the reduction commitments on world trade in agriculture. And finally, members were expected to take note of 'non-trade concerns, special and differential treatment to developing country Members, and the objective to establish a fair and market oriented agricultural trading system'.

The informal process of negotiations among WTO members to review the extent to which each member had fulfilled its commitments with regard to the AoA began in 1997. This review was made primarily in three key areas of the agreement: domestic support, export subsidies and market access. With all the proposals having been submitted to the WTO CoA, it would be useful at this juncture to analyse the different country standpoints on some of the more contentious aspects of the AoA.

The proposals made by some of the more prominent members of the WTO for a review of AoA focus on all the dimensions introduced by the Agreement. Two sets of proposals are in evidence. In the first instance, countries have based their proposals on their respective experience of implementing AoA, which is in tune with the requirements of Article 20. Most of the countries in this group are the larger players in global agricultural markets. The second set of proposals are essentially those that reflect the concerns of WTO members arising from the basic structure of the AoA. This latter set of proposals has been made by several developing countries, among others.

The discussion below spells out the proposals of the WTO member countries, which, as mentioned above, were the more prominent participants in the review of the AoA. The issues covered in this chapter include those that are a part of the disciplines introduced by the WTO. These include *inter alia* market access, domestic support and export subsidies. In addition, the chapter discusses the views of the members on the issue of NTCs. Two features of the ongoing process need to be pointed out. The first is that the positions of the major actors in the agriculture negotiations seem to have moved very little since the Uruguay Round negotiations ended. The second and more significant point is that the number of active members of the WTO in the agriculture negotiations has increased significantly.

Market access

Two issues have engaged the countries on the question of market access. The first is the issue of tariffs and the second, tariff rate quotas (TRQs).

Tariffs

Countries making proposals for effecting changes in the tariff regime for agricultural commodities can be broadly divided into three categories. The first comprises of countries like the USA, Canada and the members belonging to the Cairns Group,[3] who have long pledged support for moving tariff reductions on to the fast track. The second set of countries includes Japan, Korea and members of the EU. The position of these countries in respect of tariff cuts has remained ambiguous. The third set of countries are those in the developing world, whose main interest has been to get the maximum market access for products in which they have export interest.

The USA has shown its continued commitment to pursue the goal of substantial reduction of market access barriers, including the pursuit of a zero-for-zero option in the agricultural sector. This has been spelt out in the form of two proposals that the country has made. The first is to reduce substantially or eliminate disparities in tariff levels among countries and to reduce substantially or eliminate tariff escalations. The second is to reduce substantially or eliminate all tariffs, including in-quota duties from the applied rates. Most importantly, however, the USA has remained silent on the issue of the inordinately high levels of tariffs, the so-called peak tariffs.

The agricultural exporters belonging to the Cairns Group have taken a more ambiguous position than the USA as regards market access. This manifests itself in three forms. One, the Cairns Group does not prescribe substantial reduction or elimination of tariffs on agricultural commodities by all countries. This prescription has been made only for products produced and exported by developing countries. The major ambiguity in this position is that it says that developing countries' products should have better market access, but remains silent on who the importing countries should be. In other words, it can be taken to imply that developing countries provide better market access to products produced in each other's territories and discriminate against the imports from developing countries. However, it is quite unlikely that this situation can emerge in practice.

The second level of ambiguity introduced by the Cairns Group members relates to the nature of tariff reductions. These countries have held that the market access opportunities for all agricultural and agri-food products should be on conditions no worse than those applying to other goods. This position is similar to a proposal that was made by the USA in the pre-Seattle consultations; that market access negotiations should be comprehensive in nature, including both agricultural and industrial products.

At another level, though, the Cairns Group appears more in favour of gradual elimination of market access barriers. Thus, unlike the position taken by the USA for a reduction of tariffs from the applied rates, the Cairns Group members are in favour of using the bound rates[4] as the basis for tariff cuts. Considering that most countries, developing and developed alike, had preferred to opt for substantially higher tariff bindings at the end of the Uruguay Round negotiations, the Cairns Group is in effect arguing for modest decreases in tariff levels. At the same time, however, the Cairns Group has supported the need to eliminate tariff peaks and tariff escalations.

Reduction of tariff peaks and elimination of tariff escalations has also been emphasized by Canada. In parts, the Canadian proposal goes further than that of the USA and the Cairns Group members. This is particularly manifest in the proposal to reduce the level of tariffs. Canada proposes reduction of tariffs which take into consideration the base rates of the Uruguay Round. Developing countries could find themselves in a bind if base duties are taken as a basis for tariff cuts. This was because the agricultural sector is most subject to quantitative restrictions and imports if any were canalized through the State Trading Enterprises (STEs). In such a situation, tariffs are generally non-existent. Canada's proposal for tariff cuts could therefore eliminate tariffs in a large number of commodities.

The European Community (EC)[5] has proposed a two-track approach to market access in agricultural commodities. The EC supports the proposals made by the USA, the Cairns Group and Canada for tariff reductions, even though the extent of tariff reduction sought is much lower. This is broadly in conformity with the somewhat protectionist stance of the EC in the area of agriculture. Accordingly, the EC has sought a reduction from the present bound rates and a minimum reduction per tariff line. The second track of the EC proposal pertains to the improved market access it intends to provide to the products originating from the LDCs by offering them zero tariffs. This proposal is a part of the position taken by the EC since the Seattle Ministerial Conference and its pledge to better integrate LDCs in the multilateral trading system.

Possibly the most conservative position on tariff reduction has come from Japan. According to Japan, 'appropriate tariff reductions should be decided in a manner that provides flexibility to individual products, thereby accommodating such factors as an individual country's current situation of production and consumption for each product, as well as the situation concerning international supply and demand, while at the same time recognising that a reform process is underway'. Japan has further argued that 'tariff levels of processed agricultural products should be determined, while giving sufficient consideration to the importance of the food industry, which has developed in unison with agriculture'. The fact that Japan is keen to keep its market for agricultural commodities protected is evidenced by the proposal it makes for reviewing the minimum access opportunities for agricultural products that the country had accepted at the end of the Uruguay Round as a part of the arrangement to enhance market access.

It is quite clear, therefore, that the Quad[6] has widely conflicting views on the issue of tariffs, with the result that there seems to be hardly any common ground between them. What makes the situation more complex is the strong position that the developing countries have taken articulating their interests.

India's proposals on the future of tariffs typify the position of developing countries. The proposals have argued that the tariff levels maintained by the developed countries were generally very high and that there is a need to reduce these tariffs. It has been suggested that two measures need to be adopted: (i) reducing the tariffs and tariff escalations by adopting an appropriate formula; and (ii) imposition of a cap on tariff bindings. As regards the developing countries, India has suggested that these countries should be allowed the flexibility to maintain appropriate levels of tariff bindings keeping in view their developmental needs and the high distortions prevalent in the international markets.

The members of the Association of South East Asian Countries (ASEAN) have argued for additional market access in tropical products in which these countries have significant trade interests. The next reform programme in agriculture, these countries suggest, must pursue the fullest liberalization in tropical products by applying further tariff reductions and eliminating tariff peaks and tariff escalations. As for the developing countries, the ASEAN members broadly adopt the approach that India had proposed, which is that these countries must be allowed the flexibility to accept differential commitments in the area of market access. An additional point that the ASEAN members have flagged in their proposals on tariffs is that the Generalized System of Preferences be elaborated and maintained as a part of the AoA.

There are thus three quite distinct and somewhat conflicting positions that emerge from the proposals made by some of the more prominent members of the WTO on the issue of tariffs. These differing perspectives are, however, not reflected in the second issue in area of market access, viz the issue of TRQs.

Tariff rate quotas

The issue of TRQs has two opposing points of view. While the USA, along with the Cairns Group and two developing countries, India and Nigeria, have indicated the need to expand tariff quotas, the EC, Japan and Norway have argued in favour of retaining the TRQs. However, some countries that have questioned the very utility of TRQs as a mechanism to enhance market access prospects in the regime introduced by AoA, have also indicated that should TRQs remain, they should be administered in a transparent manner.

The establishment of TRQs as a mechanism to ensure enhanced market access, has also been described as the 'tunnel through the tariff wall'. However, the implementation of TRQs has been one of the more contentious dimensions of the implementation of AoA because of two factors. One, the administration of the quotas has lacked transparency, and two, the quotas have not been filled to an adequate extent.

Quite akin to the issue of tariffs, the TRQs issue has seen a wide divergence of views among the WTO members. Three aspects of TRQs have been commented on by the WTO Members in their proposals. These are:

○ improving the volume of imports under TRQs either by improving the fill rates or by enlarging the quotas
○ making TRQ administration more transparent and non-discriminatory
○ the level of in-quota tariffs.

The positions of some of the key members as reflected in their respective proposals are recounted below.

The USA has highlighted that poor administration of TRQs and high in-quota duties have prevented exporters from filling TRQs. Very often exporters have been unable to meet market demands either because TRQs have restricted products or suppliers, or because imports have become more expensive. The USA has thus suggested that to improve the TRQ system members must agree to develop additional disciplines for TRQs that can ensure that TRQs do not hinder trade. The USA has also argued that WTO members must agree to reduce in-quota duties based on the historical performance of TRQ fill rates. It has opined that the lower the fill rates, the higher must be the cut. Hence members must cut tariffs keeping in mind the objective of reducing disparities across countries along with increasing TRQ quantities. They must also agree to an automatic trigger mechanism to reduce in-quota duties when the TRQ fill is low, along with substantial reduction of out-of-quota duties.

The USA has also emphasized the need for increasing transparency, non-restrictiveness and reallocation of TRQs. In its bid to make the system more transparent, it has proposed clarification and expansion of the Agreement on Import Licensing Procedures, guidance on transparency and GATT's Article X, 'guidance on timely and effective communication and information'. To promote non-restrictiveness, it has suggested that imports should not be limited to unprocessed bulk commodities, but should also include processed products.

The proposals made by the EC on TRQs point to the shortcomings that exist in their administration. The EC has insisted that these need to be resolved as they may affect the quota fill adversely. In other words, the TRQs system should not be embedded in the trade rules.

Canada has indicated that in-quota tariffs also pose significant access barriers, coupled with stringent quota administration procedures. Canada has suggested that members should be required to eliminate tariffs within quotas and expand the size of all tariff quotas to ensure that at least a common minimum end point is achieved. It has further suggested that if tariff quotas must remain, then they ought to remain as a provision on the import access opportunity and must not be based on the actual volume of imports.

The Cairns Group has made two suggestions in respect of TRQs. One, tariff quota volumes need to be substantially increased, and two, additional or strengthened rules and disciplines are needed to ensure that the tariff quota administration does not diminish the size and value of market access provided by the tariff quotas.

In keeping with its protectionist stance in the agricultural sector, Japan has proposed that the access opportunities that are required to improve market access should take into account the actual agricultural situation and the structural reform being undertaken in each country. The proposal emphasizes the need to take into consideration the stage of development of individual countries when the market opening for agricultural commodities is sought.

Several developing countries, including India, have proposed substantial expansion of TRQs for developed countries, leading to their eventual elimination. Developing countries, according to India, should be exempt from having any obligations to provide minimum market access. As regards TRQ administration, India has proposed that transparency in administration of TRQs needs to be enhanced by prescribing guidelines that would ensure:

○ complete uniformity across countries and products
○ adopting a common base period for calculating domestic consumption for minimum market access commitment by developed countries
○ mandatory filling up of TRQs by developed countries
○ strict application of the MFN (most favoured nation) principle in allocation of TRQs, with special preference being given to the developing countries having annual per capita income of less than US $1000.

Special safeguards

An engaging area of debate has been the question of whether developed countries should be given access to special safeguard (SSG) measures. Article

5 of the AoA, which contains the SSG provisions, allows countries to meet the increased threat from imports by imposing restrictions. There are three contrasting viewpoints on this issue in the proposals submitted by WTO members. Several countries from the developing world, including India, Pakistan, Haiti, the ASEAN members and those belonging to the CARICOM, have argued that these provisions must exist only for developing countries. According to these countries, developing countries, which currently do not enjoy the right to take recourse to SSG provisions, must be given this right. Others, like Japan, Korea and the members of the EC, emphasize that they must remain accessible to both the developed and developing countries, while the USA, Cairns Group members and Egypt have proposed elimination of the entire Article 5 (which provides for SSGs).

The SSGs are meant to be used only as a last resort in order to protect agriculture from unforeseeable fluctuations in the quantities imported, or in the price of imports. It is in the context of the latter that Switzerland suggests that the reference period should be the three most recent calendar years for which necessary statistical data are available. It also stresses the need to simplify the structure of additional tariffs to enhance transparency.

Japan, in fact, has suggested that a new safeguard mechanism must be introduced in situations of rapid increase of imports, especially for seasonal and perishable agricultural products.

The EC, which is also in favour of maintaining the SSGs like Switzerland and Japan, points out that the existence of the SSGs not only provides a limited degree of reassurance in case of a sudden fall in prices or surge in imports, but also prevents countries from taking recourse to the more trade disruptive safeguard measures permitted by the WTO.

Export subsidies

The issue of export subsidies has not been given the attention that it deserves during the ongoing negotiations. Nonetheless, the entrenched positions of the different countries are quite visible in the submissions that these countries have made before the CoA.

Argentina has explained the entire mechanism by which the developing countries have suffered, or are likely to suffer in future, as follows. Since 1997 there has been a fall in the demand for primary components of the export basket of many developing countries. Among other reasons, this was because some of the richest trading partners increased the use of subsidies during this period. This resulted in generating an even larger surplus, which was subsequently dumped on to the international market at subsidized prices. During the years 1997 and 1998, some countries used their accumulated export subsidies. For instance, the EU overshot its annual limits in terms of both budgetary outlays and volumes. The resulting downward pressure on prices of commodities in the international markets by virtue of unreasonable sub-sidization has not only affected the commodities involved directly but also substitute commodities.

According to Argentina, there are other extremely important issues that must be looked into during the negotiations. For example, the reform process must be continued and the experience in implementation of AoA must result in providing the expected benefits from the liberalization of the agricultural sector. Argentina proposed that, as a proof of their commitment, developed countries should make a down payment during the year 2001 by reducing their value and volume of subsidized exports from the existing level by 50 per cent. Argentina, as well as India, believes that a fair regime should ensure that no 'rolling over' of unused export subsidies takes place during the transitional period.

India, along with several other countries, has argued that export subsidiza-tion calculated by each country must include the export credit guarantees, price discounts and insurance programmes (in developed countries) that they provide. Poland, Norway and the EC have argued for inclusion of specific forms of food aid as well. In fact, the EC has declared that only after all forms of support to exports of agricultural and food products are treated on a com-mon footing will it negotiate to reduce its export subsidies.

The inclusion of the activities of the STEs has emerged as another con-tentious area in the negotiation process. While countries like Switzerland and the USA, which have a competitive private sector playing the lead role in exporting agricultural goods, advocate inclusion of STE activities, others, like India, remain silent over the issue. Apart from advocating for a progressive reduction of export subsidies to fulfil the budgetary and volume commit-ments, there is a proposal for the abolition of government funds and exclusive rights extended towards single-desk exporters.

While Japan has indicated that the unit value of the export subsidy ought to be bound and reduced progressively, Thailand, on behalf of the ASEAN group, has proposed an immediate elimination of all forms of export sub-sidies currently granted by the developed countries. For New Zealand, elimination of export subsidies is the key objective in the forthcoming nego-tiations on the review of AoA. In a further attempt to rid global markets of market-distorting policies, Japan has proposed that all policy measures cur-rently recognized as domestic support, but having effects of export subsidies, must be scrutinized and brought under the discipline on export subsidies.

Domestic support

The limits to the eventual elimination of all distortions from agricultural trade are quite clearly exposed in the proposals made by the WTO members on the issue of domestic support. This is the issue area of the AoA on which the developed and the developing countries hold the most contrasting views. Domestic support can be categorized either into market price support or budgetary support on the basis of the nature of payment, or into Green Box, Blue Box or 'Amber Box' on the basis of the use to which they are put and their mode of financing. The AoA recognizes that domestic support, whether in the form of market price support or budgetary support, could give rise to distortions in trade, a point that was elaborated in the previous section. But the AoA fails to recognize that Blue Box and Green Box subsidies that are exempt from reduction commitments can also give rise to distortions in trade. This is the common view of most developing countries that are natural low-cost producers of agricultural products.

Member countries belonging to ASEAN have pointed to the inequity in the domestic subsidy discipline introduced by the AoA, which allows the heavily subsidizing countries, most of whom are developed countries, to retain up to 80 per cent of their trade-distorting subsidies, while developing countries can subsidize their farmers no more than 10 per cent of their total value of agricultural production. In the view of these countries, it is imperative to remedy this distortion. These countries have proposed that in order to solve the existing disparities, developed countries must commit to a substantial down payment of aggregate and specific support from a determined base period, in absolute terms. In the subsequent phase, reduction commitments must be made at a disaggregated level, to ensure that all sectors are included in multilateral disciplines and to avoid distortions in the level of support between commodities. The reduction commitments must also include the Blue Box support measures in their view. It has been further suggested that the additional flexibility of applying *de minimis* levels of support must not be given to the developed countries. As regards the exempt category of subsidies, the so-called Green Box and Blue Box measures, the ASEAN members have proposed that these subsidies must meet the fundamental objectives of the WTO and that, above all, they are more responsive to countries' food security concerns.

On the issue of domestic support, India has pointed to the fact that some countries have complied with their reduction commitments on AMS by restructuring their domestic support policies and programmes. Some of them have even shifted the potentially 'trade-distorting' measures from Blue Box to Green Box. Some others have taken advantage of the inherent flexibilities in the AoA by including their Blue Box support during the initial period such that in subsequent periods they are not subject to reduction commitments. By virtue of this, they got the unintended benefit of achieving reduction in domestic support without reducing them authentically. India has suggested that developed countries should make a down payment of a 50 per cent reduction in domestic subsidies by the end of 2001 from those used in 2000, or reduce them by the amount above the *de minimis*, whichever is lower.

The Cairns Group has also advocated the adoption of a formula approach to deliver major reductions. The agricultural exporters have opined that all notifications must be made in a stable currency or a basket of currencies, such that inflation and exchange rate variations are accounted for. These countries have held that negative product-specific support should be allowed to be adjusted against positive non-product specific AMS.

According to the Cairns Group, the decoupled income support and other support included in Annex 2, and the production-limiting subsidies under Article 6.5 of AoA, are not as non-trade-distorting as they appear. This is because such payments entail insurance and wealth effects that increase the farmer's ability to take risk. They also increase land values, resulting in better maintenance of land. In addition, they subsidize the cost of production thereby enabling countries to capture a substantial share in export markets at the cost of more efficient producers.

The EC has taken a more predictable position on the issue of domestic support. Setting the terms of negotiations on domestic support, the EC had declared that it would negotiate to reduce support on condition that the Blue Box and Green Box measures would continue. But while it has insisted on the continuation of the Blue and Green Box measures, the EC has proposed that the rules concerning non-product-specific domestic support must be strengthened and the *de minimis* clause for developed countries must be reduced. The EC has further proposed that specific discipline must be applied to 'Amber Box' subsidies, i.e. the subsidies under AoA discipline that boost export performance by providing for the variation in market prices.

Although the USA has not specifically commented on the continuation or otherwise of the Blue Box and Green Box measures, it states that clear categorization of subsidies into exempt and non-exempt groups prior to strict implementation of the AoA is necessary. The USA, along with the Cairns group, nevertheless agrees that the formula should be different for developing and developed countries. It has further been proposed that the structure of the subsidies regime should be so adopted that it encourages a shift of production away from illicit narcotic crops. The USA has proposed an expansion of the Green Box measures to include those that promote sustainable, vibrant agricultural and rural communities. Towards this end, specific instruments have been proposed.

Net food-importing countries like Japan and Korea, however, appear be supporting their food suppliers. As regards the rules and disciplines on domestic support, Japan's view is that it is imperative to improve the requirements for decoupled income support stipulated in Annex 2 of the AoA so that it reflects the real situation of production, including that of the factors of production employed. Special attention must be given to staple crops, and at the same time tariff reduction should be based on final bound rates, so that it does not penalize member countries that have voluntarily reduced tariffs. To ensure consistency in the reform process, Japan advocates for the continuation of the Amber Box, the Blue Box and the Green Box. Korea has recommended a further exemption of compensatory support provided to promote multifunctionality of agriculture, along with more support for small-scale family farm households and for agricultural and rural development in developing countries.

Other developed members of the WTO, like Canada and Norway, who also play an important role in the international market for food and feed, have argued in favour of providing Green Box and Blue Box subsidies. Canada has been vocal about the provisions in the Green Box. It proposes a review of the criteria for identifying the so-called Green Box subsidies in the light of the experience and needs of the member countries. Canada has argued that if it can be ensured that programmes that have been included in the list of Green Box subsidies do not cause material distortions in production, then logically it would not cause material injury to producers in the importing countries. In view of the above, Canada proposes an overall limit on the outlays made on all types of support. Although Canada has a position strongly favouring the other developed countries, it supports the standpoint of developing countries by emphasizing the need for an overall limit or cap on all types of domestic support.

Non-trade concerns

NTCs have become an important issue in the ongoing review of the AoA mandated under Article 20 of AoA. As indicated earlier, two distinct kinds of NTCs have been brought to the negotiating table. The first is the issue of multifunctionality as proposed by the EU, and the second is the issue of food security. India first made the latter proposal during the informal process of consultations conducted by the CoA, which began in 1997. As will become clear from the discussion below, the two perspectives on NTCs are at a variance.

Multifunctionality

NTCs have come to the fore, with the EC emphasizing the multifunctional role of agriculture and India becoming emphatic on the need to ensure food security.

The EC has emphasized the role of agriculture as a provider of public goods. It calls for a number of possible actions to address this legitimate concern for the multifunctional character of agriculture to be examined through the development of multiple agreements, appropriate labelling of the rules and exempting compensation of additional costs to meet animal welfare standards from reduction commitments. The EC has committed itself to the continuation of the reform process enshrined in Article 20 of the AoA. It believes that in order to achieve sustained and continued economic growth in both developed and developing countries, strong public support is important, which can be acquired if the multifunctional role of agriculture is catered for through protection of the environment, sustenance of the vitality of rural communities and adequate attention to food safety and other consumer concerns, including animal welfare. Switzerland favours endorsement of rules that not only avoid harm to the environment, but also seek solutions favourable to the economy, social conditions and the environment.

Korea has emphasized the need for more specific provisions with adequate levels of government intervention to secure multifunctionality of agriculture, along with more practical and operational provisions for special and differential treatment to developing countries and more effective disciplines on export-related measures. The Korean government has appealed for each of the member countries to have the right to take measures necessary for the protection of human life and health. Thus appropriate measures should be taken within the WTO regarding consumers' concerns on food safety and quality and also on the potential risks of GMOs for human health and the environment. It should also encompass precautionary measures, as well as those surrounding consumers' increasing demand for informed choice. Indonesia, however, cautions that WTO rules should prevent non-legitimate claims of protectionist policies in the guise of multifunctionality.

Food security

Although the EC emphasizes the importance of the multifunctional role of agriculture, it also recognizes the role of agriculture in providing security in terms of the domestic food requirements of a nation. To help countries suffering from a food security crisis, the EC approves of aid either in the form of a full grant or measures that do not damage local food production and marketing capacities of the recipient countries. If food aid is provided in the form of credit, then the country's debt burden increases and hence the country is adversely affected in the long run. The EC believes that abuse of food aid should be prevented through the revision and strengthening of rules of food aid in Article 10 of the AoA and by promoting the development of genuine food aid donations instead of disposing of surpluses.

Seven countries of Latin America, which include prominent members of the Cairns Group like Brazil and Argentina, have presented an important perspective relating food security to trade. These countries have argued that trade promotion through export subsidies causes increasing food insecurity in developing countries. They have challenged the position held by some of the industrialized countries that subsidized exports of food grains are beneficial to the net food-importing developing countries (NFIDCs), since the beneficiaries have access to cheap imports. This argument, according to the countries presenting this viewpoint, is fallacious, as heavy dependence on imports of subsidized food can cause serious financial difficulties due to a more vulnerable balance-of-payments situation, regardless of the price of food. These countries have argued that effective solutions to the food security problem of NFIDCs can be achieved only if the domestic production capacities are strengthened in the import-dependent countries. For this to happen, paragraph 3(iii) of the 'Ministerial Decision on Measures Concerning the Possible Negative Effects of the Reform Programme on Least-Developed and the Net Food Importing Developing Countries' have to be put into effect. The paragraph in question instructs WTO member countries to facilitate technical and financial assistance to LDCs and NFIDCs so as to 'improve their agricultural productivity and infrastructure'.

India considers the issue of food security as being the key to future negotiations for the continuation of the reform process in agriculture initiated by the AoA. Food security, according to India, is directly related to livelihoods in developing countries. Agriculture employs over 70 per cent of the labour force in many low-income countries, besides being a significant contributor to their GDP. Agriculture is also an important source of revenue and foreign exchange in developing nations. Hence even small changes in agricultural employment opportunities or prices have significant socioeconomic effects on developing countries.

India has argued that, in view of the above, low-income developing countries need to meet their food requirements in a way that avoids constraints that developed countries have faced in the past regarding the procurement of food grains from the international markets. Since the world commodity market for food grains is significantly more volatile than its domestic counterpart, international prices, if transferred to domestic economies through imports, would seriously affect not only domestic prices but also the food income of the poor. The inadequate physical and institutional infrastructure for managing large quantities of imports and their distribution in rural areas makes import of food grains even more undesirable.

The ability of farmers to respond to market signals is also poor, since they often fail to shift their cropping pattern or allow for relocation. In the case of commodities like wheat, coarse grains, oil seeds, vegetable oils, sugar, dairy products, fruits and vegetables that are crucial for food security in developing countries, we find that high levels of export subsidies exist. In a situation where developed countries continue to perpetuate trade distortions through granting different forms of subsidies, developing countries should be allowed to resort to appropriate levels of tariff protection to protect their domestic markets. India has argued on this basis that any reduction of tariffs imposed by developing countries should be enforced only after substantial reduction of trade-distorting domestic subsidies and elimination of export subsidies. Besides, developing countries should also be allowed to revise the bound levels of all sensitive items. These views are in keeping with their overall perspective that food security concerns can be addressed in a meaningful manner only if the market access and domestic support disciplines are not adopted as the key policy objectives relating to the agricultural sector.

An assessment of the proposals

The proposals presented by the WTO members in the run up to the review of the AoA bring into sharp focus the structural imbalances that characterize the policy framework governing agriculture. The imbalances have become more stark in light of the ineffective implementation of their commitments by the major players in the market for agricultural commodities. The tardy implementation of AoA, particularly by the USA and the EC, have left most developing countries without the benefits, in terms of increase in exports, that they had expected from the liberalized trade regime at the end of the Uruguay Round negotiations. At the same time, the domestic production systems of some of these countries face the increasing threat of being rendered unviable.

The proposals made by different countries, particularly from the developing world, have made it quite apparent that a bilateral arrangement between the two dominant members of the WTO, which the AoA essentially represents, would come under increasing pressure as the negotiations on the review of the Agreement progresses. This has been eminently clear from the manner in which the proposals have targeted some of the key elements of the discipline introduced by the AoA. The subsidies discipline has come under increasing scrutiny, particularly since the AoA has made little impact on the ability of these WTO members to subsidize their agriculture. The impact of the unbridled spending on subsidies by the USA and the EC has been acutely felt in many countries where the viability of agricultural systems have come under threat.

It is in response to these prevailing conditions in the global market for agricultural commodities that developing countries have suggested a two-pronged approach. In the first instance, they have argued for a restructuring of the subsidies' discipline, in order that the prevailing deficiencies can be redressed. The second focus of the proposals has been to emphasize the importance of ensuring food security. The nub of the arguments presented in this context has been that domestic agriculture in the countries threatened by cheap imports needs to be strengthened so that food security can be ensured on a sustained basis.

Market access would remain a key consideration in the AoA given the fact that the Agreement is embedded in an organization whose basic focus is trade promotion. It is not unlikely, therefore, that the member countries of the organization would be led by the essential spirit of the organization and would present their arguments to enhance their market access prospects. And this has taken place despite the fact that a vast majority of the membership of WTO does not have significant interests in agricultural trade. The discussions on market access have been driven by more strategic thinking on the part of most WTO members. Many of the countries expect better prospects for themselves in the global market for agricultural commodities where trade barriers are expected to disappear.

From the point of view of developing countries, the issue of special and differential (S&D) treatment has remained largely unaddressed. The proposals made to the CoA in this regard have not been able to present a persuasive case for S&D and this could be a major impediment for the countries in the ensuing process.

Conclusions

The analysis of the proposals sent to the WTO by different member countries highlights key features of the negotiations leading up to the review of AoA. The first is that WTO members are keenly engaged in the review of an agreement that remains one of the key areas of the organization. The second feature of the negotiations is the highly polarized views that have been expressed by the more active members. What is quite apparent is that the positions of these countries have not moved from the ones they had held when the Uruguay Round ended. In other words, the process of consultations in the CoA does not appear to have paid many dividends in terms of moving countries towards adopting a consensual approach. The third, and possibly most important, feature of the process of consultations is the emergence of a third dimension to the negotiations presented by some of the developing countries like India. These countries have tried to focus on the problems they have encountered in an agreement from which they were expected to make major gains. The major impediment has been the lack of commitment shown by the larger trading countries to implement the AoA in an effective manner. While their gains have been non-existent, the developing countries have been under pressure to provide better market access by dropping all barriers. This imbalance in the outcome of AoA has been the focus of the developing countries' agenda. Whether this issue will be addressed in future negotiations remains a moot point.

Part II. New and old actors on the global stage

5 The emerging linkage between the WTO and the ISO: implications for developing countries[1]

MATTHIAS FINGER and LUDIVINE TAMIOTTI

Introduction

IN THIS CHAPTER, we try to uncover an emerging relationship between the World Trade Organization (WTO) and the International Organization for Standardization (ISO). We see this relationship as being particularly illustrative of changes that are occurring in the structures of global governance in the way environmental and other regulations may be introduced into a liberalized global economy. The relationship between the WTO and the ISO is of primary concern for developing countries, both in terms of competitiveness and in terms of access to global markets.

In the first section, we present the underlying dynamics of both deregulation and environmental protection, leading to the creation of new mechanisms of global governance. The second section shows how standards, and in this case environmental standards, might appear to be the most ideal form of contemporary global regulatory mechanism. In the third section, we discuss why the ISO and the standards it creates seem to be desirable for a range of global private and public actors. In section four, we explore the emerging linkage between the WTO, the promoter of global deregulation so far, and the ISO, the proposed solution to global regulatory problems. The fifth section highlights the lack of involvement of developing countries in the decision-making process of the ISO. This forms the basis of a discussion of the main concerns developing countries have when it comes to the implementation of ISO's 14000 series of standards. In the conclusion, the actor arrangements promoted by these new regulatory mechanisms are highlighted and critically analysed.

Liberalization and the environment: institutional restructuring

The present connection between the WTO and ISO 14000, a series of environmental standards, is, in our view, a result of a dual-process towards freer trade on the one hand and the privatization of global environmental protection on the other. Global trade has grown steadily over the past years, resulting from technological progress, low transport costs, deregulation and privatization of public enterprises in particular, and trade liberalization through successive multilateral negotiations in the framework of the General Agreement on Tariffs and Trade (GATT) and WTO agreements. Given that the threat posed by tariffs to fair trade has been reduced, promoters of free trade have identified new forms of trade barrier as a significant threat to liberalization. As a result, GATT (since the Tokyo Round) and now the WTO are increasingly targeting non-tariff trade barriers, such as technical or regulatory barriers to trade.

At the same time, environmental degradation has increased parallel to industrial development, and has further accelerated as a result of growing trade. Consequently, environmental regulations have been introduced since the 1970s, first at national and later increasingly at international level. However, as standard-setting moved to the international level, the need emerged to overcome fragmented national, regional and international authority structures, and to think of new and effective partnerships among all actors, including governments, business and NGOs. In other words, and parallel to a process of trade liberalization and deregulation, we observe the growing need to regulate, not only in environmental but also in labour matters. This is the crux of a growing tension between the trends of deregulation on the one hand and reregulation on the other.

The search for new forms of regulations, such as environmental standards for example, can be seen as an attempt to reconcile this *tension* between deregulation and reregulation. This approach has been brought about by two key trends: (i) the growing privatization of international (environmental) politics, characterized by the erosion of traditional nation state command and control policy mechanisms and the growing role of private and non-state actors; and (ii) the reorganization of international society. In this section, we shall address this latter point, while the former point will be addressed in the next section.

The past 50 years have been characterized by the expansion of international institutions and public actors with responsibility for carrying out international policies. Since World War II, the United Nations (UN) system with its various agencies, paralleled by the Bretton Woods Institutions of the World Bank and the International Monetary Fund (IMF), has evolved alongside the parallel process of trade deregulation brought about by the GATT, leading in 1995 to the creation of the WTO (e.g. Krueger, 1998). All three types of institutions developed together over the past 50 years, sometimes with overlapping missions and activities, a process that can probably best be understood in terms of institutional development. For example, the UN, with its multiple agencies, became increasingly fragmented and stretched ever further, which appeared particularly problematic when funds got scarce. On the other hand, the Bretton Woods Institutions, especially the

World Bank, increasingly involved themselves in the traditional UN terri-
tory of development by incorporating social development and sustainability
into its economic development agenda. The GATT, finally, developed a powerful liberalization agenda, and, in doing so, somewhat undermined the
agendas of both the UN and the Bretton Woods Institutions.

In the contemporary post-Cold War era of globalization, and the parallel
emergence of new global governance mechanisms, these international public
actors needed to reposition and redefine themselves. Such repositioning is
made necessary by new challenges resulting from globalization, public pressures, especially in the case of the World Bank (e.g. Cavanagh *et al.*, 1994),
lobbying by transnational corporations (TNCs) and because of serious financial pressures in the case of the UN (e.g. Alger, 1998; South Centre, 1997).
Today, we can observe an institutional realignment, whereby international
public institutions regroup around three key issues, all of which are crucial for
the management of international public affairs in the years to come. These
issues are security, sustainable development and trade regulation.

One can clearly see how the UN, under heavy financial pressure, is currently refocusing on issues of security (i.e. the safeguarding of international
boundaries, human rights protection and humanitarian intervention).
Increasingly, the traditional development work of the UN is being taken over
by the Bretton Woods Institutions, especially the better-resourced World
Bank. Indeed, the World Bank, the UN Development Programme (UNDP)
and the UN Environment Programme (UNEP), already linked through the
GEF (Global Environmental Facility), seem to be regrouping around the
issue of sustainable development, which might well lead to the creation of a
new 'Earth Bank'. Finally, there is the issue of trade and trade regulation.
Having actively promoted trade liberalization, the GATT and the WTO are
now increasingly under pressure from public opinion, developing countries
and TNCs demanding the reintroduction of some sort of trade regulation. In
order to meet this demand, however, the WTO will have to coordinate its
position with organizations such as ISO. The remainder of this chapter
focuses on this third dimension of institutional rearrangements – trade
reregulation.

The environment, as a cross-cutting issue, relates to all three dimensions.
Indeed, environmental degradation has become a security issue, hence the
by-now famous term 'environmental security' (e.g. Finger, 1991). Examples
are found in the potential conflicts arising from scarcity of natural resources
(such as water), or from transnational environmental damage (such as
nuclear disasters) (Timoshenko, 1992: 426). Second, since UNCED (the UN
Conference on Environment and Development), environmental protection
has also been reframed in terms of 'sustainable development'. Since then, UN
bodies such as the UNDP, but especially the World Bank, have been keen to
promote corresponding (sustainable) development projects. Third, the

environment also pertains to trade: indeed, while environmental protection was and still is considered an impediment to trade, it has also, as we shall show below, been mobilized as a justification for reregulating trade.

Deregulation and reregulation: from trade barriers to standards

In this section, we discuss a fundamental change from deregulation to reregulation. Parallel to this change, things that were previously labelled barriers to trade now become reframed as international standards, which are considered beneficial for trade. Moreover, as we shall see in the next section, we observe what can be called a process of the 'privatisation of international environmental governance' (Clapp, 1998). The result of both trends will be to make privately defined standards acceptable tools for global trade regulation.

Let us recall that the overall trend since the emergence of GATT is towards liberalization of global trade. Starting out with agricultural products, the Uruguay Round and the process of liberalization has gradually expanded to include more products as well as trade-in services. In this overall process of trade liberalization, the removal of technical barriers to trade (TBT) plays an important role. TBT measures are currently the main remaining barriers to free international trade. Although many of these barriers are not direct and open measures of protectionism, their effects may be characterized as trade barriers. Within the GATT of 1947, non-tariff measures were clearly forbidden in Article XI. Articles XX and XXI allowed states to use non-tariff measures only so as to protect health and the environment and their security interests.

During the Tokyo Round of Multilateral Trade Negotiations, the elimination of TBT measures was one of the major concerns for the negotiating parties. An agreement on technical barriers to trade was finally concluded in 1979, and entered into force in 1980. This agreement was part of subsidiary agreements dealing with the problem of non-tariff barriers to trade, and it was called the 'Standards Code'. But the Standards Code had two sides to it: on the one hand it was said that product standards, certification systems, test methods and labelling processes should be as 'unrestrictive' to trade as possible (Murray, 1997: 605). On the other hand, the Standards Code already encouraged the establishment of international standards and the use of these standards by contracting parties as a basis for national standards. By facilitating the harmonization of national standards, the Standards Code further promoted trade (Charnovitz, 1993: 274).

The main ideas of the Tokyo Standards Code were included in the Marrakesh Agreement of 1994, which established the present WTO. Indeed, part of the WTO Agreement is the Agreement on Technical Barriers to Trade, which seeks to ensure that regulations, standards, testing and certification procedures do not create unnecessary obstacles to trade. And, in order to harmonize these technical standards as broadly as possible, member states should actively participate in the elaboration of technical rules by relevant international organizations (Article 2.6 and Annex 3, paragraph G). Also, in its preamble, the TBT Agreement clearly recognizes the importance of international standards. The Agreement also encourages WTO members to employ international standards in existence, or whose 'completion is imminent' (Article 2.4). Moreover, the Agreement invites the signatory governments to ensure that the standardizing bodies in their countries accept and comply with a 'Code of Good Practice for the Preparation, Adoption and Application of Standards', embodied in the Annex 3 to the Agreement.

In short, free regional and global trade is making the need for reregulation increasingly obvious. This is both because TNCs want a transparent framework within which to operate, and because free trade leads to environmental and social impacts, which need to be addressed. While the 1947 GATT clearly was an agreement designed to promote deregulation, the present WTO seeks to prevent or to face some of the consequences of deregulation, especially in the social and environmental areas (e.g. Charnovitz, 1997: 112). An obvious illustration of the change that has occurred recently, and which now seems to push towards reregulation, can be found in the WTO Agreement on Technical Barriers to Trade, which encourages state members to use international standards instead of national ones. Consequently, the WTO is presently becoming a 'world competition agency', deregulating in some areas and regulating in others (Charnovitz, 1997: 112). However, the reregulating powers of the WTO are very limited, if not absent. Indeed, while it can make standards acceptable as part of an international trade regime, it cannot set the standards itself. The WTO must therefore look for other actors, preferably international private ones, who can do the job.

The privatization of environmental regulation

This section illustrates the process of privatization of environmental regulation, leading up to the definition of environmental standards as promoted by the ISO. Not surprisingly, these are precisely the types of standards that the WTO might be attracted to in regulating global trade.

When looking at the history of international environmental policy, it is apparent that the growth of environment protection measures is paralleled by the reduced involvement of states. This has occurred in several steps. Originally, international organizations and multilateral conventions used the traditional state machinery to implement environmental measures. In a second step, international organizations used NGOs for the direct implementation of environment commitments in certain countries, for example the way the World Bank uses local NGOs for project implementation. And now we are entering a third step, whereby states transfer the implementation and sometimes even the monitoring of this process directly to private economic actors from business and industry (e.g. Tamiotti and Finger, 2001).

As a result, voluntary initiatives by business and industry have been used over the past decade in order to improve environmental performance. Many kinds of such voluntary initiatives are available to companies and governments. Voluntary standards are gradually becoming requirements for access to international markets and there is much support for such standards. Economic actors (industry and business organizations) support them because they facilitate trade by reducing market fragmentation (Charnovitz, 1993: 271), but also because it increases their power along the supply chain. NGOs find them appealing because they offer a relatively direct way to influence environment protection, i.e. by pressuring companies that do not comply with the standards to which they have committed. For states, standards and corresponding certification is a way to transfer implementation and monitoring functions (and costs) directly on to the companies (Clapp, 1998: 298). Indeed, voluntary standards, which are enforced by indirect pressure (market-based incentives and disincentives), reduce the domestic costs of public legislation and enforcement by shifting enforcement costs to the producers of pollution rather than to the taxpayer (Pinckard, 1997: 439). Finally, certification bodies, such as Société Générale de Surveillance (SGS) or Veritas Ltd, are interested in standards because they can make profits from certifying private companies.

The UNCED was a great opportunity for large enterprises, particularly TNCs, to take steps, with an explicit reference to Agenda 21, to seek public endorsement for the fact that their activities conform and contribute to the goals of sustainable development. The majority of the industry associations' environmental codes and guidelines were actually issued in the months before and after the Rio Conference (UNCTAD, 1996a: 2). Indeed, UNCED provided the necessary impetus for action by referring to the need for international standards during various UNCED Preparatory Committees (Roht-Arriaza, 1995a: 501). In response, the ISO and the International Electrotechnical Commission (IEC) established an ad hoc Strategic Advisory Group on Environment (SAGE), which recommended in its October 1992 session the establishment of a formal technical committee (TC) on the development of environmental standards, to be known as the TC 207. It is in this context and in the aftermath of UNCED that a new type of environmental regulation, directly promoted by TNCs, has emerged. ISO 14000, a direct outcome of these efforts, is a new type of environmental regulation, which no longer focuses on the a posteriori control of emissions, but rather on operational techniques in the industry (Asher and Gupta, 1998: 315). ISO 14000 is thus the prototype of privatized environmental regulation (e.g. Krut and Gleckman, 1998).

Traditionally, ISO, a quasi-private body (and not an international organ-ization, as its name misleadingly states), sets technical standards. However, since the 1980s, with the ISO 9000 series (the ISO 9000 quality management system standards were first published in 1987), the ISO embarked on a new trend, evaluating the systems by which products are produced, rather than the products themselves. Owing to the success of ISO 9000 – the number of ISO 9000 certificates grew by nearly 40 per cent in 1997 – and in the context of the UNCED process mentioned above, ISO has finally focused its atten-tion on environmental issues with ISO 14000, a series of international and voluntary environmental management standards. To recall, the TC 207 was composed of six subcommittees which addressed the following aspects of environmental management: Environmental Management Systems (EMS), Environmental Auditing & Related Investigations (EA&RI), Environmental Labels and Declarations (EL), Environmental Performance Evaluation (EPE), Life Cycle Assessment (LCA), and Terms and Definitions (T&D). The ISO 14000 series of standards consists of several guideline standards and one compliance standard, the ISO 14001 Environmental Management Systems (EMS) (Fredericks and McCallum, 1995). The ISO 14001 specifies the basic requirements of an EMS that a company must meet in order to become ISO 14000-compliant. In order to obtain such a certification, a com-pany can either declare itself in compliance with the 14001 EMS standard, or it can have an independent third party confirm that the company's manage-ment is in conformity with the requirements of the ISO 14001 (Pinckard, 1997: 435).

It appears that for various reasons the ISO 14000 standards have become very successful, not least the fact that ISO is looked at by the WTO as a potential reregulator of global trade, as we demonstrate below.

The WTO/ISO relationship

So far, we have identified two parallel trends: on the one hand the trend towards reregulation as embodied by the WTO, and on the other the trend towards the privatization of environmental regulation, as embodied by the ISO 14000 standard. Both trends meet in an emerging WTO/ISO relationship by which a quasi-private body will increasingly become a legitimate actor for setting trade standards.

We have already mentioned the TBT Agreement, which recognizes the importance of international standard setting. Annex 3 of the TBT Agreement refers to a 'Code of Good Practice for the Preparation, Adoption, and Application of Standards'. On behalf of the WTO, the ISO (and the IEC) has been mandated to record the acceptance of this Code of Good Practice by national institutes (Favre, 1998: 2). Furthermore, the monitoring and enforce-ment of the TBT Agreement is a function assumed by the WTO Committee on Technical Barriers to Trade. In this context, the ISO and IEC are invited to attend the Committee as observers, and through that particular channel, regularly explain the developments occurring in international standardisation to the WTO members (Favre, 1998: 2). Further evidence of WTO/ISO cooperation is the ISO jointly organizing with the WTO a series of regional seminars, aimed at assessing the degree of market interest for developing international standards in order to facilitate trade. During the second such seminar in Buenos Aires in October 1998, the ISO vice-president highlighted the specific importance of international standards for the global integration of different national and regional markets. In parallel, the representative from the WTO explained that the WTO's objective was to ensure that standards do not create unnecessary barriers to trade, which is the reason why common standards are important. This not only perfectly illustrates the shift from trade barriers to standards, but also the emerging link between the WTO and the ISO.

The argument which says that international standards are good for free trade, while national standards are trade barriers, is now also made by the OECD's Committee on Standards and Conformity Assessment. In a survey this Committee conducted on standards and manufacturers from developed countries, it is shown that competition on the global market is restricted by a plethora of national standards, certification and testing requirements applying to consumer goods (Schwamm, 1997: 13). A global standard should reduce the risk of countries using environmental restrictions as a pretence for trade restrictions.

The lack of involvement of developing countries in TC 207

The standard-setting process of ISO/TC 207 raises several issues for international environmental law and policy, especially regarding its private nature. Indeed, some major stakeholders have not been fully represented, particularly during the early stages of the making of the ISO 14000 standards. Practically, decisions on the content of the ISO standards are formally taken by those who consistently attend every meeting (Roht-Arriaza, 1995a: 524; Roht-Arriaza, 1995b: 141). As a result, several basic concerns of developing countries have not been taken into account, such as the fundamental issue of transfer of technology. In other words, the ISO standards-setting process has diminished the role and voice of the developing countries in global environmental policy making (Clapp, 1998: 306). One interesting figure highlights the disparity: developing countries account for more than 75 per cent of the national standards bodies within ISO and yet they participate in less than 5 per cent of its technical work (Tobon, 1999). Reasons for this are manifold: first, the cost of travel to attend meetings is unaffordable for many less-developed countries. Because of the extensive number of meetings and working groups to attend during the annual session of the TC 207, the delegation of each country is usually composed of at least 15 representatives. Consequently, even if the less-developed countries manage to send one or two delegates, they will not be able to really influence the different working groups. The extreme technicality of the norm-making process within ISO 207 often prevents developing countries from being meaningfully involved in the decision-making process. In this context, UNCTAD has recommended that it may be appropriate for the ISO to review its internal processes to facilitate a wider representation and effective participation of developing countries and, if necessary, to mobilize financial assistance for them to participate in meetings (UNCTAD, 1997: 2).

The ISO has, on several occasions, manifested its concern about the lack of representation of developing countries. One could object that such a concern comes a little late: that once the ISO 14000 standards have been established by developed countries, mechanisms for participation serve only to legitimize these standards. Several events demonstrate the effort by the ISO and TC 207 to take developing countries' concerns into consideration. A first indication is the Memorandum of Understanding, signed in November 1998, between the ISO and UNCTAD. It pertains to a Programme of Cooperation, which seeks to promote a greater understanding of, and a more effective involvement in, international standardization activities by developing countries. The main reason here is the need to facilitate access to developing countries' products and services to world markets. The practical result of this memorandum is to allow for the participation of ISO and UNCTAD representatives in relevant meetings of each organization and to facilitate the exchange of information.

The ISO Policy Committee on Developing Country Matters (DEVCO) has also attempted to support developing countries' representation at TC 207 and to provide a forum for discussion of all aspects of standardization, as well as for the exchange of experiences between developed and developing countries. This programme was able to sponsor 22 representatives from developing countries in 1995 and 23 in 1996 (Clapp, 1998: 307). However, these funds remain very limited (Hutchinson, 1998). At its 1998 San Francisco meeting, the DEVCO has, moreover, noted the decline in financial support for DEVCO environmental activities and the consequent decrease in attendance by developing countries. Consequently, the ISO/TC 207 has adopted several resolutions calling for meetings to be held in developing countries, encouraging TC 207 members to contribute funding to the DEVCO programme and for allowing the greatest possible participation of member countries (ISO/TC 207 N278). However, in its last annual session in Seoul in June 1999, the TC 207 did not really achieve any progress in advancing the formal involvement of developing countries and NGOs in the standard-setting process. The only result has been the adoption of yet another resolution, which encourages ISO members to assist developing countries in actively participating in the work of the technical committee.

Concerns of the developing countries over the impacts of ISO 14000

The traditional approach of developing countries regarding the relationship between trade and environment has been one of deep apprehension. Such concerns surface regularly during the negotiation of new multilateral environmental agreements (Brennan, 1997). The argument is often that industrialized countries developed at a time when environmental standards and regulations were lacking, whereas these same countries are now seeking to impose stringent environmental requirements on developing countries. These environmental requirements, it is argued, prevent developing countries from competing in the world's economy. Moreover, in a context of globalization, developing countries have become much more sensitized to global market access issues (UNCTAD, 1996b). Indeed, developing countries increasingly perceive international environmental regulations and standards as disguised trade barriers imposed by developed countries. Such barriers, it is alleged, have been introduced to counter developing countries' competitive advantage over developed countries, in the form of lower wages (International Environment Reporter, 1999: 652).

It is in this context that the possible risks and negative impacts of the ISO 14000 standards on developing countries must be raised. Moreover, among the developing countries, there is a strong and growing feeling that the ISO 14001 is a market requirement (Krut and Gleckman, 1998: 76). UNCTAD has been particularly active in alerting developing countries to the importance of meetings of the ISO 14000 series. In October 1997, its Commission on Trade in Goods, Services and Commodities organized an Expert Meeting on 'Possible trade and investment impacts of environmental management standards, particularly the ISO 14000 series, on developing countries and opportunities and needs in this context'. One of the main issues raised by this Expert Meeting was the need for developing countries to be assisted in developing the necessary infrastructure to allow for credible, fair and rigorous certification (UNCTAD, 1997: 3). Indeed, UNCTAD's main concerns are not so much the standards themselves, but rather the process of certification. In this respect, UNCTAD seems to accept that such standards were not and continue not to be set in respect to developing countries' needs.

Rather, the costs, as well as the timing of the ISO 14000 certification process, are seen as being critical for developing country companies, and may represent real trade barriers. Indeed, the lack of certification structures in developing countries could severely restrict the ability of companies to adopt the standards. Moreover, even where there are certifying organizations, they often lack international recognition (Rotherham, 1998: 12). Depending on the different countries, the costs of seeking ISO 14001 certification vary widely. For large companies, the costs can range from $100 000 to $1 million per plant, and for small and medium-sized ones, one can expect costs ranging from \$10 000 to \$50 000 (Cohen, 1998: 650). Such costs, already huge for developing countries, should not be confused with capital and other costs relating to the management of environmental policies under the EMS. Consequently, the whole cost of the certification process is clearly not afford-able for most developing country enterprises. However, it remains affordable for TNCs operating in such developing countries, which are thus favoured by the whole certification process.

As a result of ISO 14001 certification becoming a necessary condition for doing business on the global market, some governments are reacting in such a way that may well lead to ISO standards losing some of their intended meaning. Some countries are progressively introducing pilot projects to help domestic firms be involved in the ISO 14001 certification process. For these governments, ISO third-party verification mechanisms emerge as a possible means for privatizing inspections of environmental regulations and saving money in the process. Moreover, several countries (such as South Korea) have already announced that they will offer relaxed inspection and licensing agreements to companies that obtain ISO 14001 certification (Rotherham, 1998: 12). There is evidence of a shift taking place when it comes to environ-mental regulation, from a traditional command-and-control regulatory framework to greater reliance on an environmental management-based approach (Speer, 1997: 227). If environmental monitoring systems and stand-ards are used as substitutes for environmental legislation, this clearly contributes to the erosion or at least softening of other existing environmen-tal regulations. Indeed, ISO auditors do not have any authority to make unannounced inspections. Moreover, the only thing auditors will verify is whether there is a commitment to compliance (and not actual compliance) with relevant environmental legislation and regulation. They will verify whether there is a process for identifying the relevant legal requirements, whether the process of setting objectives considers legal requirements – but not whether it meets them – and finally whether there is a procedure for eval-uating compliance, but again not assessing actual compliance. As stressed by Hauselmann, at best, certification will demonstrate that the organization does not have the excuse of ignorance when it is caught not complying with the legal requirements (Hauselmann, 1998).

Asian countries are particularly active when it comes to promoting ISO 14001. Japan, for example, is the leading country in terms of numbers of ISO 14001 certifications: as of 1 September 1999, there were 2400 certifica-tions registered; Germany, the second ranking country has only 1400 certifications.[1] Indeed, a number of Asian countries, notably Malaysia, Singapore, Thailand, Korea and China, now have government-funded ISO 14000 support systems, which offer technical and financial assistance to com-panies seeking certification (Gleizes, 1998: 460). China, for example, has recently launched an auditors' supervision board to monitor state-owned companies' compliance with the ISO 14000 series (International Environment Reporter, 1998: 17). The Chinese federal agency in charge of these questions was proposing that all state-owned industry would comply with the ISO 14001 by the turn of the century. Such government-supported certification programmes in turn illustrate a clear strategy on behalf of some developing countries to face the challenges of these new global regulatory mechanisms.

Conclusion: towards new actor arrangements

Being of private origin, ISO 14000 is still a voluntary standard. But this may only be a matter of time. Indeed, such private standards may affect the public sphere in many ways: global or regional trade agreements may explicitly recognize them, government regulations may refer to them for the definition of terms, and government procurement rules may adopt them (Roht-Arriaza, 1995a: 486). Furthermore, market pressure from consumers, financiers, insurers and competitors may become so strong that corresponding standards turn into prerequisites for companies wanting to do business in larger markets. As a result, ISO 14000 may become a de facto, non-tariff barrier to trade, keeping out small and medium-sized enterprises (SMEs), as well as companies from developing countries, especially the ones without government-sponsored certification programmes.[2] Moreover, there is a 'follow-the-leader' pattern, which means that more and more companies certify the standards, and in turn require certification from their suppliers and trading partners (Murray, 1997: 614). Consequently, TNCs can establish and enhance a monopoly position by promoting or even imposing international standards (Finger and Kilcoyne, 1997), which they can meet and their competitors cannot. In some developing countries, such TNCs might actually gain easy certification thanks to government support. On the other hand, ISO 14000 might also facilitate compliance with environmental laws by promoting uniform approaches to environmental management, as well as by harmonizing international environmental commitments and environmental impact assessments worldwide. In addition, the ISO 14000 standards call for continual environmental improvement: on the one hand, the certified company needs to comply with local regulations, while on the other, such compliance should result in the continued evolution and improvement of national environmental protection (Pinckard, 1997: 440). This is called the 'race to the top' perspective, i.e. a movement towards more and more protective environmental regulation. This, at least, is the theoretical argument for voluntary environmental standards, such as ISO 14000.

The emerging relationship between the WTO and the ISO in the field of environment protection is, in our view, a direct result of economic globalization and the subsequent transformation of the role of the nation state in international economic policy. Historically, governments have relied on public commitments such as treaties and domestic regulations to address global environmental issues. But economic globalization and trade have reorganized the relationships among the key global actors: as the UN increasingly focuses on security and the Bretton Woods Institutions on (sustainable) development, the trade arena is being rearranged among actors such as the WTO, the ISO, TNCs, states and domestic standardization agencies, working alongside private bodies, such as certification agencies and other business organizations. We predict that, as the need for reregulation grows, states will be only one among many other mostly private actors exercising authority. As we have shown with the example of environmental reregulation, it is likely that the WTO and the ISO, most likely together with certifying bodies and TNCs, will become the major actors in regulating international trade. States might then simply be used to enforce such reregulation domestically (Finger, 1998).

6 Slaying the serpent: knowledge management in development NGOs

INES SMYTH

And the serpent said unto the woman, Ye shall not surely die: for God doth know that in the day ye eat thereof, then your eyes shall be opened, and ye shall be as gods, knowing good and evil.

(Genesis: 3, 4-5)

Introduction

DEVELOPMENT NGOs ARE undeniably part of the social movements that, in complex networking and alliances, attempt to challenge economic globalization and propose alternatives to what they perceive as being environmental and socially harmful policies and practices. For some, this constitutes 'globalisation from below' (McGrew, 2000: 362).

In the past decade or less, development NGOs have become much more self-reflective about what they do and how. Learning and knowledge are among the themes that larger NGOs are most frequently debating. This is because, with globalization, both the opportunities and the need of doing so at greater speed and to a greater extent than ever before have grown greatly. Many are beginning to explore the meaning and practice of knowledge management.[1] The terminology is borrowed from the world of business management and much of the overall approach follows that adopted by the World Bank. Several development analysts have criticized and sought to develop further what the Bank says in relation to knowledge management.

Though supporting these criticisms, in this chapter I start from an unconditional agreement on the fundamental importance of information and knowledge in and for development, and on the need for all relevant organizations to engage explicitly with the challenges of creating, storing and disseminating both. However, I also wish to express some concerns at the route taken by NGOs in their current engagement with the notion of knowledge management. Primarily, I express concern that the approach sees knowledge narrowly as a commodity, as this can have many negative consequences. In particular, it may lead to the adoption of a sterile 'knowledge monoculture', and to create deep contradictions with NGOs' commitment to accountability, partnership and participation. In analysing these issues, I rely on insights that are derived broadly from a variety of feminist perspectives on knowledge and on development.[2]

In summary, the chapter expresses the worry that the current emphasis is too heavily on management, of both information and people, which could lead to the neglect of social relations embedded in knowledge. It may also fail to acknowledge and celebrate the unruly, infinitely creative and even dangerous nature of knowledge, and its potential for making men and women 'as gods', as indicated in the biblical quote at the beginning of the chapter. At an even broader level, the chapter questions the trends that are making development and other non-profit organizations adopt ways of working and principles increasingly closer to those of profit-oriented institutions. While professionalism is necessary to ensure that the activities of development organizations are effective and efficient, especially in a global context, some aspects of this may distort the fundamental characteristics that differentiate them from those for which profit is the reason for existence.

In the chapter, I focus on Oxfam[3] as a major NGO dealing with the issues outlined above. As a staff member, I have both an interest in the positions the organization takes on a range of issues and access to relevant material. In addition, I believe that given the size of the organization and the prestige and authority it commands, both nationally and internationally, its stance as well as its activities are likely to have profound repercussions among other Northern NGOs and among its Southern partners.

In the rest of the chapter, I will first reflect on the links between knowledge and globalization. I will then provide a brief account of what knowledge management is and how it is understood by development organizations such as Oxfam. Having summarized selected feminist contributions to the understanding of knowledge, I will examine the specific concerns mentioned previously, and their possible consequences. Finally, I will try to draw conclusions that I hope will encourage development organizations to adopt a more creative and critical notion of knowledge and how it can best be advanced in support of their objectives, especially that of promoting socially and environmentally just patterns of globalization.

Knowledge and globalization

There are intrinsic links between knowledge and globalization. To avoid unnecessary and lengthy debates, globalization can be simply defined as: '... the process in which economic financial, technical, and cultural transactions between different countries and communities throughout the world are increasingly interconnected, and embody common elements of experience, practice and understanding' (Pearson, 2000: 10). Pearson stresses that the process is greatly aided by the development of telecommunication and other technologies, which allow production and consumption to overcome distance and other similar boundaries. Such technologies, it will be shown below, are also what render knowledge management both desirable and possible.

Wilson (1999) follows a well-established tradition in noting that knowledge and technology are socially constructed and thus reflect existing power relations. This is true at the global level. Multimedia conglomerates with technological power (Made, 2000) control communication and information, as well as having political and economic leverage, often superior to those of states. At the opposite pole sit the people whose poverty and marginalization are almost universally accompanied by limited access to information and communication in all their forms.

Most developing countries are finding themselves in a similar position in relation to world trade. Poor countries are traditionally at a disadvantage because of their limited ability to invest in scientific and other research, hence the creation of a certain type of knowledge. International agreements and institutions are increasingly contributing to undermining the opportunities that such countries have to control knowledge and expertise, even then these are locally generated. In particular, the WTO's TRIPS Agreement forces member countries to adopt patent regimes that favour commercial interests and those of Northern countries, even when what is being patented is the fruit of local knowledge. The example used by Vandana Shiva in a recent public lecture is powerful:

> Patents and intellectual property rights are supposed to be granted for novel inventions. But patents are being claimed for rice varieties such as the basmati for which my valley – where I was born – is famous, or pesticides derived from the Neem which our mothers and grand-mothers have been using. Rice Tec, a US company as been granted Patent no. 5.663.484 for basmati rice lines and grains' (Shiva, 2000).

Knowledge management and knowledge as power

It is beyond the scope of this chapter to review the vast gamut of perspectives on knowledge and its meaning for development and growth. In order to assess the significance and the problems associated with the adoption of a knowledge management perspective on the part of development NGOs, it is nonetheless important to consider two sets of approaches: knowledge management itself, and the feminist insights on knowledge as power.

Knowledge as commodity

The literature on knowledge management is not only large, it is also to be found well beyond the boundaries of business management as an academic discipline. There is an abundance of newspapers and journals, both specialist and for a wider readership, that explains and extols its virtues. According to an article in the *Financial Times*, business and academic publications have recently recorded a 100 per cent increase in articles on knowledge management (Despres and Chuavel, 1999).

Definitions and explanations are extremely varied in clarity and detail. Some aim for brevity: 'Knowledge then can be considered as output(s) from a continuous feedback loop which refines information through the application of that information' (Bonaventura, 1997, cited in Webb, 1998: 1). Other definitions raise normative issues. 'Knowledge management is about structuring and managing an organization in order that people create and share knowledge and act on that knowledge in order to benefit the client an the organization' (Abell, 1998: 134).

Commonly, such definitions stress that although knowledge management relies greatly on the use of information technology (IT), knowledge itself is generated and held by people: 'If knowledge resides primarily in people and it is people who decide to create, use and share their ideas to attain business results, then Knowledge Management is as much about managing people as it is about managing information and IT' (Davenport and Marchand, 1999: 3).

While such definitions are necessary to set the scene for the discussion that follows, it is neither useful nor appropriate here to adopt one or the other. What is important is to stress that, in this context, knowledge is perceived as being at the core of, rather than additional and helpful to, economic growth. Other factors of production (such as land or labour) are not discarded as unimportant, they are simply relegated to a secondary position, since they are easier to obtain. Thus, knowledge becomes a commodity, in fact the most crucial asset for firms and the economy (Beijerse, 1999).

Insights from feminist theory and practice

A large body of feminist theory maintains that knowledge has been defined from a male perspective. Because of this, it is argued, socially validated knowledge has always excluded the perspective of women (Harding, 1991). In addition, feminist concerns with the causes and consequences of unequal gender relations have led to the frequent adoption, more or less critically, of ideas initially developed by Foucault. In this context, they have been engaged with debates that posit that knowledge and power are intrinsically linked, since the latter is manifested and organized through the former (Cameron *et al.*, 1992).

For some analysts, women's lack of power and authority is due to their social location in the private sphere. This 'silences' them (Youngs and Sreberny, 1999) and renders invalid the kind of knowledge they create and transmit in the domestic realm and beyond. This argument has also been applied to the situation of developing countries, and has led to the conclusion that Western knowledge and Western power are intrinsically linked: '... [there is] the impact of post-modern, post-colonial and feminist thought [which] have converged upon the truth claims of modernism and shown how the production of Western knowledge is inseparable form the exercise of Western power' (Crush, 1995: 3).

Feminists offer a variety of suggestions to overcome the problems and constraints imposed by this gender bias in knowledge. For example, Stanley and Wise (1990) propose to base critical inquiry and the creation of knowledge on an explicitly adopted and declared subjective standpoint, rather than on the kind of alleged objectivity that Western science, including the social sciences, considers indispensable. Part of this alternative is the necessity to recognize and celebrate individual practical experience, not normally accepted as valid knowledge.

Finally, feminists are among those who also stress the need to accept as valid forms of knowledge those that do not fit with or that even contradict the canons of Western objectivity and scientific rigor. At the same time, they warn that indigenous knowledge and other manifestations of these alternatives should not be idealized, since they are not immune from hierarchical power relations (Rai, 2002).

These insights derived from diverse feminist traditions are relevant here. They are useful to show that using feminist critiques of knowledge help stress, rather than deny, the importance that the creation and handling of information and knowledge have in all institutional contexts. As mentioned above, according to Youngs and Sreberny (1999) feminists have long recognized that knowledge is established within certain physical, symbolic and institutional boundaries that often exclude and silence women. They have attempted to break these boundaries at many levels, in theory and practice. Some of the relevant theoretical notions have been summarized above.

At the practical level, women's movements (and other social movements) in their diversity have adopted institutional forms that are largely non-hierarchical and rely on looser or more structured networking. The exchange of information across spatial and social distances has been both a purpose and a strategy of such networks. Advanced technologies for communication and information exchange are adding new dimensions and opportunities to these practices. They are also contributing to the effectiveness of some organizations in the global arena, where they are sharing the 'political stage' with governments, multinational agencies and firms (McGrew, 2000). During the meetings of the G8 in Japan in July 2000, the press referred to the anti-debt coalition Jubilee 2000 as: 'the biggest international movement since anti-apartheid'. It also described its global nature in the following terms: 'Thousands of activists across the world have collected signatures in tiny villages, sprawling shanty towns and the heart of middle England parishes' (*Guardian*, 21 July 2000).

Knowledge management and NGOs

As mentioned above, the interest in knowledge and its management is not the preserve of business. Development organizations are beginning to explore its insights and terminology for their own purposes. It is important to summarize the reasons that explain the attractiveness of knowledge management to development organizations, some of which also make it so interesting to profit-making organizations. One such reason is the breadth and speed of the social and economic changes usually referred to as globalization, or the 'process by which the people of the world are incorporated into a single world society' (Albrow, 1990: 9). In this context, the opportunities created by new communication technologies make it possible for more information to move faster and in ways that are more complex. The same opportunities make it imperative for organizations to have the capacity to access an ever-increasing body of this information and knowledge, and put them to use in shorter times than ever before.

For NGOs another reason explains the interest in knowledge management. This is the increasing pressure they experience to show that what they do 'makes a difference' in their struggle against poverty and inequality. Development organizations have become aware of the need, on one hand, to monitor and assess their successes and failures systematically and learn from them and, on the other, to do so in a way that helps them to compete with other organizations for the limited funds available (De Waal, 1997: 80).[4] Knowledge management seems to offer a framework to achieve both. A third reason lies in the transformation that the NGO sector as a whole has undergone in the past decade or so. It is widely acknowledged that NGOs, both in the North and South, continue to be alternative (to the state) providers of goods and services, while growing in their role of influencing development policies and trends. Knowledge management again helps deal with the challenges this poses:

> The moving beyond the development 'supply-side' to 'demand side' activities requires that NGOs develop new skills, partnerships and ways of working in order to help communities articulate their concerns and preferences, to manoeuver into negotiating positions with official bodies, and to mix technical operational skills with 'information age' communication, advocacy and networking skills (Clark, 1997: 45).

The opportunities of operating on a scale much beyond the local environment have been mentioned above.

The World Bank is leading the way, and its World Development Report 1998/99 declares knowledge to be 'central to development' (World Bank, 1999: 143). In Britain, the British Council is also reflecting on what knowledge management offers in practice and what kind of internal changes are required to ensure that its promises are fulfilled (Roman and Edwards, 1998). The Department for International Development (DFID) recently opened an online consultation on the topic of information, technology and knowledge for development, prior to the publication of its White Paper on international development in November 2000. Other development organizations are also exploring these themes, but through discussions and publications that remain internal to them, at least for the time being.

Oxfam and knowledge management

Oxfam's engagement with ideas of knowledge management has its antecedents in two traditions. One is in the leading role that the organization has played in promoting ideas and practices of participation, the other is its concern with internal systems for learning.

Participation

As in much of the development field, participation within Oxfam is perceived as an aspiration and a method of working. Both are rooted in the belief that poverty and injustice are not natural or inevitable. They are socially generated and are reflected in inequalities of access to material and non-material resources, which are mediated by relations of gender, age, ability and ethnicity. The organization also believes that one of the consequences of this situation is that perceptions of social realities, of needs and of rights are different, and depend on where people are located in this complex web of social relations, as well as on where they are geographically and historically situated. In so doing, the organization implicitly embraces a post-modernist view of both knowledge and power as being fragmented and diverse (Davies, 1994). Oxfam concludes that in order to both reflect its commitment to equity and to be effective, it must base its interventions on information and interpretations from this variety of sometimes contradictory sources, and must especially seek out the opinions of those who are usually less vocal. 'Oxfam believes that women and men have the right to participate in, and to shape, decisions affecting them: and that people are disempowered if this right is denied to them' (Eade and Williams, 1995: 15).

Participatory rural appraisal (PRA) and related methodologies (group discussions, maps and diagrams, rankings, etc.) are used extensively for this purpose, and are in themselves subjects of analysis, critiques and further refinement (Chambers, 1992; Holden, 1993). PRA has its roots in the data collection techniques known as rapid rural appraisal (RRA). It combines the original tools for data collection and analysis with a variety of sociological and methodological traditions that prioritize poor people's rights and ability to produce information about themselves and their problems, and to identify the solutions to those problems. Such methodologies and principles are also seen: 'to have the aim to strengthen the management capacity of community organisations and other development organisations' (Selener *et al.*, 1999: 1).

Oxfam stresses the difference between PRA as a process of learning and a set of tools (Neefjes, 1994), together with the belief that both are important to ensure participatory processes in the collection of information and the creation of knowledge.

Institutional learning

The second antecedent is in the belief shared by most development NGOs that the effectiveness and quality of what they do depend in large part on their ability to learn. For Oxfam, being a 'learning organization' has meant recognizing the variety of ways in which people in the organization learn, the barriers against such learning and the need to encourage the establishment of explicit systems to enhance the capacity for 'institutional learning' (Roche, 1995).[5]

Recent structural changes within Oxfam have required that considerations for learning remains central, for example through the setting up of regional management centres with a strong emphasis on learning, and of global groups working on organizational objectives.

Recently the focus has been shifting from a concern with learning to 'knowledge management'. In its understanding of the term, Oxfam puts the stress on the human element in knowledge management, as well as on the distinction between knowledge and information:

> What distinguishes knowledge from information is the value added through the experience, expertise and understanding of people. If knowledge is the product, learning is the process (Oxfam, 1998: 139).

In this shift, Oxfam has been, consciously or unconsciously, influenced by larger, international organizations such as the World Bank. The World Bank is playing an important role in promoting knowledge management. Some commentators have expressed concern at the fact that the World Bank is setting itself up as the Knowledge Bank, hence as the most authoritative source of knowledge (cited in Siochru, 1999). Others consider the Bank's focus on technical knowledge and knowledge of attributes as too narrow. Panos (1999) sees this approach as ignoring the political nature of knowledge and its links with power; the fundamental questions of access and control over it, and of which and whose knowledge is recognized as such, hence valued per se and in policy making. For example, the Report's attempt at endorsing the validity of 'indigenous knowledge' is limited to a scant and vague reference to instances where groups of Colombian and Rwandan women farmers were found 'to know more about how to breed improved bean varieties locally than did scientists from research institutes' (World Bank, 1999: 38).

Given these critiques, it is important for organizations like Oxfam to reflect seriously on the implications of their interest in knowledge management. Some of those are drawn out in a later section.

The commodification of knowledge

The key concern expressed in this chapter with regard to knowledge management is that the approach adopted by NGOs appears to 'commoditize' knowledge, and may lead to:

○ institutionally sanctioned and defined types and contents of knowledge, that ultimately lack creativity and have limited powers of regeneration, in addition to representing the selected views of those in power
○ possible contradictions with the commitment NGOs have to accountability, partnership and above all 'participation' as values and as practices in development.

As mentioned above, the emerging adoption of knowledge management discourse among development NGOs is borrowed from the language and priorities of the business sector. In that context, knowledge is clearly perceived as a commodity; in fact, it is said to be the most critical resource of modern firms and contemporary economies. As such, its effective management is necessary as it brings considerable competitive advantages. There is a similar slant in the approach taken by the World Bank. The Bank recognizes knowledge to be a public good, since to some extent it is 'non-excludable' (others cannot be prevented from using it once it is in the public domain) and 'non-rivalrous' (use by others does not alter benefits to oneself).[6] At the same time, the Report in which such issues are detailed, describes knowledge as 'capital', which developing countries can 'acquire from abroad' (World Bank, 1999: 27) (admittedly with some local adaptation). Knowledge can provide the most economically marginal countries with vast comparative advantages, in fact with the 'dynamic comparative advantage' through which they will be able to compete successfully in the global economy. In this light, knowledge becomes an economic asset and the panacea for all the economic and social disadvantages of poor countries and their people.

Some individuals within Oxfam appear to come close to this understanding of knowledge as an economic asset. To quote an internal document: 'We sell our experience in return for money for our work, is a not too cynical view of Oxfam's business ... information has to be converted into knowledge in order to be useful. Oxfam generates mountains of information, and tries to "sell" it ... How will we make sure that our shopping mall is where the knowledge hungry gathers? How will we make the knowledge on our Website a product people will buy? (Coventry, 1999, internal memo).

The quote may represent the standpoint of one individual in a large and complex institution. It also has the tone typical of spoken addresses, often characterized by being purposefully polemical. Nonetheless, it does reflect the type of ideas being discussed within the organization, though so far tentatively and informally.

Knowledge monoculture

The knowledge as commodity approach summarized above derives at least in part from the fact that knowledge management has its roots in business and management discourse. Feminist insights of the type mentioned earlier help identify other origins of the problem, as well as some of its consequences. According to Shiva (1988), the European men who came to be known as the fathers of modern science managed to displace all pre-existing modes of belief and instituted a new knowledge system which subjugated both nature and women. A key element of this was the deep-seated tendency to grant recognition and validity to innovation and knowledge only when those can generate profit. This position suggests that knowledge management may be unsuited to NGOs for a related reason. According to Shiva, one of the consequences of the masculinization of knowledge in farming systems is the way in which such systems have been controlled and modified in a direction that decreases diversity and complexity and creates monocultures.

In the context of business management, some commentators warn that the adoption of knowledge management and its reliance on IT discourages the validation and retention of multiple, complex viewpoints in favour of simplified, institutionalized versions of ideas and events (Malhotra, 1996). In the context of debates of agriculture and sustainability, Shiva (2000) states that: 'From the biodiversity perspective, biodiversity based productivity is higher than monoculture productivity'. Knowledge management may strip NGOs of diversity, in other words, of the possibility of holding a variety of diverse and even contradictory interpretations of reality, leading to a 'knowledge monoculture', and to decreasing creativity and powers of regeneration. The possibility for women and men to be 'as gods knowing good and evil', as suggested in Genesis, becomes very remote.

Accountability, partnership and participation

Borrowing notions of knowledge from the profit-oriented does raise other questions for NGOs. At a very immediate level, since by definition NGOs are also non-profit organizations, the pursuit of knowledge for profit appears to contradict one of the basic principles on which they are funded. Furthermore, the use of knowledge for gaining financial and other advantages in 'the market' can have other negative consequences. It could encourage practices that are counter to the much-prized virtues of transparency within and between organizations, networking for common purposes and accountability at all levels, all of which are said to characterize strong civil society and to ensure its sustainability.

It can also endanger another basic principle and way of working, that of partnership. Partnerships with communities and with private sector institutions, between NGOs and the state, and especially between Northern and Southern NGOs are being promoted by and for all actors in development and social policy. In particular, for Southern NGOs, partnerships are said to grant greater access to more information and influence, and for those from the North to aid sustainability and legitimacy (Jorgensen, 1996). A degree of skepticism exists towards partnerships based on pre-determined coordination and centralization (Pinder, 1999). But the consensus is that partnership should be promoted for the benefit of all.

An earlier section of this chapter reflected on the central place that participation has for a development organization such as Oxfam. It is perhaps the idea and practice of participation that are most at risk in the current interest that NGOs have for knowledge management. One of the definitions of knowledge management summarized earlier stresses that knowledge is different from information. At a very basic level this risk affects the possibility that all relevant actors in development may have to participate in the sharing of information.

In exploring the opportunities that knowledge management offers, NGOs should also consider a simple reality: that many of the countries, the organizations and the individuals they work with are severely disadvantaged in their ability to have access to and use information. As already mentioned, this disadvantage is fast becoming one of the most acute differentiating elements between Western industrialized and developing countries. There are many reasons for this. Access to the necessary technology, from the more conventional (books, paper and mail) to the more advanced (IT-based) has undoubtedly improved for many, but cannot be taken for granted. The political environment also plays a part in providing or preventing the conditions that ensure the optimal circulation and use of information. Within this environment, information itself is a 'political tool', which can both reflect existing hierarchies and help to create and reproduce them (Davies, 1994).

But is there really a contradiction between participation and knowledge management? Lack of participation of the most marginalized people and communities in development has led to a consensus of its importance. Rahanema believes that one of the many reasons why the concept of participation has become so popular among policy makers at all levels is that it is 'perceived as an instrument for greater effectiveness as well as a new source of investment' (Rahnema, 1992: 119). From this perspective of participation as an 'economically appealing proposition' (Rahnema, 1992: 118), the interest in knowledge management appears not as contradictory but as fitting the trend which sees NGOs getting closer and closer to the ways of thinking and working of other institutions, such as those that have a profit motive. As stated in the introduction to this chapter, these considerations should be located in the broader contexts of discussions on the pursuit of professionalism and the danger that it may render NGOs indistinguishable from profit-oriented organizations.

Feminist notions help to take these ideas on participation further. In an earlier part of the chapter, I summarized the links between knowledge and power which, according to feminist analysis, silence women and their knowledge, as it silences other voices outside those sanctioned by the Western scientific tradition referred to by Shiva. As already stated, the notion of participation as employed by NGOs reflects these differences in power, and the recognition and validation of alternative perspectives. In fact, the ability to build their interventions on 'indigenous knowledge' is often mentioned among the 'comparative advantages' of NGO practice, specifically in the fields of agricultural development and of natural resource management. While the universal validity of claims of comparative advantages and distinctive competencies of NGOs in relation to knowledge and information needs to be tested (Bebbington 1994), it is important to celebrate the efforts many NGOs make in developing practices which reflect this approach to forms of knowledge other than those emanating from a Western scientific tradition.

However, the questions posed by NGOs in the context of debates on knowledge management address much more the issue of 'how' knowledge and information can be developed and conserved, than that of 'whose' knowledge is validated by relevant processes and systems. Therefore, there is still a limited indication of how the current interest in knowledge management reflects the NGOs' sensitivity to the existence and the nature of indigenous knowledge systems, or of the unequal values attributed to different knowledge traditions. Furthermore, the emphasis on internal and institutional management, of both information and people, and the reliance on IT do not leave much room to consider the fact that most indigenous knowledge is passed on and stored in ways that are not easily 'managed'. Equally, such discussions have yet to broach the complex issues of the power hierarchies which, within any such tradition, give voice to some while rendering others voiceless, of the gendered nature of knowledge, and of the ways in which women are silenced, both within and outside organizations. Finally, the 'knowledge as asset' view reifies both knowledge and power, posing them as 'material things possessed by agents' (Long and Villareal, 1993: 157) rather than arenas where actors struggle to assert their own interpretations and their interests in the context of hierarchical social relations.

Some of these issues are being raised in organizations such as Oxfam. A recent document on knowledge management and its application to a specific project raised the following questions: 'How can the selection, analysis and organization of the knowledge content be determined? What are the implications for the intellectual property rights, i.e. who would have ownership of the knowledge one takes into the corporate knowledge base?' (Alvarez, 1999). These questions are to be welcomed and will certainly continue to generate important debates. However, so far they tend to be presented as additional practical and operational details, rather than critical challenges of some core notions of knowledge management, with substantial implication for future practices.

Conclusions

A better understanding of the ways in which people transform information into knowledge and use it towards the attainment of organizational goals is long overdue, as is the creation of systems that facilitate these processes. Advanced communication technologies, of which knowledge management makes extensive use, help voluntary organizations to overcome many problems of collaboration and networking they experience, by reducing time, costs and other limitations (Hallam and Walker, 1998), as well as providing other more conventional benefits.

NGOs that are participating in the debates on knowledge management and experimenting with related projects are to be complimented for daring to be innovative. Their work has the added advantage of helping to dispel the public image of the voluntary organization as a worthy but conventional and timid institution. Also to be applauded is the central role given to people in the position adopted by NGOs: 'Knowledge is expertise and vision of staff and others shared through any mean at the right time and just enough to transform reality' (Alvarez, 1998).

However, an uncritical approach to knowledge management may lead to many problems. A knowledge management discourse in development NGOs is relatively young, thus it can be hoped that some of the issues raised in this chapter will be taken into account, and a more mature and nuanced understanding will develop.

For this to occur, it is necessary that NGOs do not abandon, but rely fully on the basic principles and practices which distinguish them from other organizations and especially those that have profit as their goal: those of transparency, partnership and above all of genuine participation, in all its meanings. Ideally the reliance on such principles will lead to a shift of emphasis from knowledge management to knowledge creation, and from the shackles of systems and structures to granting knowledge its creative potential. This shift may also help NGOs achieve a kind of professionalism shaped according to their own models and principles, rather than those uncritically adopted from business, for-profit organizations. It should also enhance their ability to deal with global issues and to function in a much bigger arena than ever before, that of 'global politics' (McGrew, 2000: 357).

7 Globalization and small and medium-sized enterprises: the European experience

CHARLIE DANNREUTHER

Introduction

THE PROBLEM WITH these two terms – 'globalization' and 'SMEs' – is that they are frequently both widely used and poorly defined. Globalization can be understood to mean, among other things, the end of nation states, the expansion of information technology, the growth of financial markets and global corporations, and the rise of regional trading blocs (for a review see Dannreuther and Lekhi, 1999). SMEs can be defined in terms of employment size (e.g. fewer than 250 employees), turnover size and ownership structure (such as self-employed or private business), or they may enjoy a particular legal status regulated within national company law.[1] To write about either SMEs or globalization in an objective sense is, therefore, to make a number of assumptions about what we understand these phenomena to be and how we understand them to exist.

Recognizing this contestability of definition is not a new observation in discussions of the SME or the globalization debates. Much ink has been spent on defining both, and this chapter will not seek to resolve that particular debate. Rather this chapter begins by embracing the political nature of their definition to examine critically the association between SMEs and globalization in the European context. By embracing the fact that we cannot get a good understanding of either 'globalization' or 'SMEs' without understanding the context in which they are used, we can perhaps see how certain ways of understanding the world can become significant and have real influence. Our study will concentrate on the impact of the predominant liberal ideology in the interpretation and realization of these two terms. The study focuses on Western Europe and especially the UK, where the rise of the SME has been seen as significant, affected by the move to the right represented by liberal political parties and concerned with debates over the impact of globalization on their polities. These two political arenas – Europe and the UK – will help us to investigate how political ideologies help to construct relationships, justify arguments and propose solutions.

Globalization – the liberal view

The dominant view of globalization could have been written straight from the feather-quilled pens of Adam Smith and David Ricardo. They both believed that the private sphere (individuals and private enterprise) should be more important than the public (the state) because they both believed that the free market could ensure prosperity and harmony. For Smith, collusion in the market place, let alone intervention by governments, would undermine the purity of the market and impede the automatic distribution of resources through the market's mechanism of supply and demand. The liberal view of globalization sees the market as rightfully dominating exchanges between both private individual actors and societies.

These liberal views of the international political economy advance a number of assumptions about globalization and offer some policy prescriptions on this basis. The first of these relates to the importance of the individual, or the private sector, in the development of economic prosperity and in the distribution of resources. This takes place through the invisible mechanism of the free market – demand and supply – as opposed to the intervention by the state or public ownership. They point to global capital markets and new global forces of production as requiring economic governance above the national level (Omhae, 1990). The ideological basis for these arguments is not new. Liberalism was the guiding principle of the post-war international economic system (established under Bretton Woods) as a counterpoint to the protectionism of the earlier part of the century. Protectionism was seen, and still is in such important media as *The Economist* and *Financial Times*, as having a detrimental effect on world society either by promoting nationalism or at least limiting the benefits of free trade. That there was such prosperity and peace in the developed economies of Europe and the USA in the years that followed the World War II, was largely seen to have further legitimated these liberal ideas of free markets and increased trade. Indeed, once the main alternative of communism collapsed in 1990, the triumph of liberalism was seen as universal (Fukuyama, 1992).

The liberal view of globalization plays to the same ideology as those that supported the post-war liberal consensus. It supports the idea of the free market and favours the role of the private over the public. But supporters of the liberal view of globalization argue that a quantitative and qualitative shift has taken place. Quantitatively they identify changes in the volumes of trade and activity in the international economic system. Qualitatively globalization sees a marked change in the world economic landscape from that understood by terms such as internationalization and multinationalization. Unlike internationalization and multinationalization, globalization cannot be defined simply (Petrella, 1996). These former terms describe, respectively, the movement of goods across borders and the transfer of factors of production. In these terms, values are fixed and borders are still recognizable. But globalization describes more fundamental changes in the scope of action. These include the global, rather than national orientation of financial markets and corporations (Dicken, 1998), changing forms of regulation as supranational and regional governance replaces the national level (Omhae, 1990; Majone, 1996), and in the consumption of technology and goods (Petrella 1996). The impact of globalization is therefore seen as more fundamental than either internationalization or multinationalization. Not only do the goods and factors of production clearly cross borders, but the borders themselves are undermined; control is extended not only geographically, the very notion of hierarchy is problematized; people do not just become familiar with foreign cultures, their identities change; time and space do not just become less significant, they are redefined (e.g. Robertson, 1992: 8).

This liberal view is frequently ascribed to non-state actors such as business consultants and CEOs, as well as political leaders (Omhae, 1990; Fukuyama, 1992). Most of all, the international organizations that have governed the world economy for much of the post-war period, such as the UN, OECD and EU, also reflect this view. While the 'liberal globalizers' did not originate the term, they have clearly captured the public imagination and discourse through which globalization is discussed in much of Anglo-American political discourse. Globalization is a positive and, to a great extent, inevitable process, driven by economic and technological forces, that creates new forms of order (i.e. markets) to replace the old, outdated forms (i.e. nation states).

The state is therefore no longer capable of challenging global financial markets, credit-rating agencies and the other new gods of the global order. In this view of globalization the state can only react to the forces of globalization and preferably in quick time. Financial markets scrutinize economies and punish governments if they feel economic policies are inappropriate (as Francois Mitterand, President of France, discovered in 1982) or exchange rate values are wrong (as John Major, Prime Minister of the UK, discovered in 1992).

Globalization in action

But the argument supporting the political sovereignty of the private (in this case economic) actor over those of the state did not just arise in response to the new perceived threats of 'globalization'. Indeed, the French term 'mondialisation' initially emerged in the late 1960s. Globalization's heyday was as much due to the changing national political landscape of the 1980s that fostered the notion of a global economy as an antidote to nationalism, and sang the praises of free trade on both sides of the Atlantic and across European states. This liberal agenda that swept Europe was broadly known as the 'New Right', reflecting the more extreme free market orientation of traditional European conservative parties.

Cutting back on the role of the state also became an important concern for New Right parties fighting domestic level elections. For too long the 'nanny state' was seen to have controlled too many aspects of people's lives. This broad intervention was seen as a source of the social and economic decline of the period: guaranteeing full employment sapped entrepreneurial drive, high taxes punished innovators and risk takers, trade unions and burdensome industrial relations legislation impeded flexibility. These views led to the reorganization of the relationship between states and their societies in modern Europe that presented the extension of the market further and further into areas that had previously been the domain of the state alone.

The welfare state was also reformulated and in many cases significantly reduced. Once the embodiment of shared social responsibility in modern European capitalism, its main institutions – pensions, healthcare – were significantly restructured. Trade unions and corporatist industrial relations boards were also challenged as labour regulation was reduced (Ferner and Hyman, 1992). Meanwhile the management of state departments was reformed in line with private sector management practices (Hood, 1991). The policy trend across Europe from state interventionism to state-sanctioned regulation and from public to private management and practices was characterized as 'the rise of the regulatory state in Europe' (Majone, 1994). The common themes that justified all these reforms were classically liberal, emphasizing self-sufficiency, risk taking and entrepreneurialism.

SMEs and the liberal political project

So what did this have to do with small firms? How do political and administrative reforms at the national level combine with global financial markets to determine policies for SMEs? Politics is, above all, a practical matter and while the need for reforms demanded by (or justified in terms of) globalization were swingeing, the everyday problems facing politicians and policy makers – unemployment, competitiveness – needed solutions. In short, it would never be enough just to follow the behest of the financial markets or global capital. The state also had to act, and this is where the SME became such an important political device. SMEs provided politically acceptable solutions to political actors. It was not that SMEs were the best way to pursue employment or economic regeneration in under privileged areas – this was and remains heavily disputed.

SMEs were politically acceptable and sufficiently misunderstood to be presented as solutions to all manner of policy problems and political concerns. In addition, and because everyone understood the numerical importance of SMEs in the economy, they represented an important constituency. In many ways, policies to help SMEs became ready-made policy solutions for political problems. But if we are to understand why SMEs became the 'chosen ones' we also need to understand what the broader political and expert arguments were that led to the wide range of support for them. As we shall see, in many countries SMEs were core constituencies of the New Right and either already central to the economic constitution or becoming increasingly visible politically.

The notion of the SME, as managed by the committed and hard-working self-sufficient individual, has been employed as a powerful counterpoint to the centralized corporate economy throughout the European economy. Indeed the liberal political values associated with the individual entrepreneur were enshrined in the 'ordo-liberal' model of economic governance associated with West Germany's 'economic miracle' after the World War II. This form of economic governance promoted as much market freedom as possible with as much regulation as necessary, and was intended to act as a counterpoint to the centralizing tendencies of the German economy under national socialism. Furthermore, the German constitution allowed the political balance of power to be held by the liberal party, which, to some degree, represented this important sector. SMEs could and would promote freedom through the economy and so check the rise of fascism.[2]

The welfare state grew on the back of what is often called 'the golden age of capitalism', a period of full employment, sustained economic growth and stability (Marglin and Schor, 1990; Schonfield, 1965). During this period the small business sector was in many countries an anomaly to modern capitalist centralization and the policies that supported it. The Poujahd movement in 1950s France was, among other things, a social movement that grew as a protest against economic centralization. To a degree, small firms represented resistance to the economic centralization and modernization that characterized economic policy and planning of the period, and so were inevitably excluded. Yet as perceived benefits of centralized economic management and modern capitalism began to founder (especially during the economic crises of the 1970s), the respectable rebels of the middle classes took to the streets (Nugent, 1979). In the UK, the militant trade union activism of the 1970s was mimicked by the self-employed marches against VAT regulations (McHugh, 1986).

The rise in political awareness of SMEs took place very much in parallel with broader political reactions against this centralization of post-war economic policy and welfare state provision. Political support for SMEs therefore represented as much a change in the landscape of the instruments for managing the economy as for any inherent support for the entrepreneur. We can identify two reasons for this. First, the general tide of anti-welfare state and anti-trade unionism left the political arena open for reforming projects. SMEs or the small business sector in general was therefore a ripe constituency for the ideological crusade of the Thatcherite liberals in the 1970s. It is no coincidence, for example, that Theresa Gorman, one of Margaret Thatcher's most loyal supporters, established the Association for the Self Employed in the 1970s[3] (McHugh, 1986). Margaret Thatcher, the greengrocer's daughter, shared with the self-employed a dislike for the British establishment and made a public play of justifying her reforms of the state to them in later years.

Second, monetarist economic policy became increasingly popular across Europe replacing the Keynesian model that had previously dominated (Hall, 1993). Keynesian economic policies provided a role for the state to intervene against the economic cycle through nationalized industries, wage bargaining and large public sector projects. Monetarist economic policies mainly concentrated on keeping a stable currency by monitoring inflation and keeping it down. The two forms of policy looked at different statistics (employment versus inflation) and prioritized different instruments (government expenditure versus interest rates). So the rejection of Keynesian economic policies meant the removal of a whole apparatus of economic policy mechanisms, with few alternative measures. The difference in supporting SME policies was that these were all initiatives that would promote the liberal view of the market.

While the rhetoric of economic liberalism made New Right parties and SMEs natural allies, a new wave of findings in the academic community provided 'objective' and 'scientific' justifications for supporting the small business sector. A statistical trend emerged across industrialized economies that showed an increase in the stock of SMEs from as early as the late 1960s (Sengenberger *et al.*, 1990). This was seen to justify support for SMEs in two ways. First, neo-classical economic arguments saw SMEs as an important element of the economy through their filling of market niches. This 'dual economy' thesis provided an explanation for greater SME support. But in addition to implying increased economic significance, other academic studies lent greater weight to SMEs by concluding that small firms contributed to employment growth to a greater proportion than larger companies, many of which were shedding employment in response to the economic recession of the period. Perhaps the most significant of these studies was one conducted by Birch, which showed that from 1969 to 1976 small firms (fewer than 20 employees) accounted for 66 per cent of all new jobs in the US (Birch, 1979).[4]

While the change in ideology and greater credibility given to SMEs by academia should not be overstated – many states had already developed sophisticated SME policies (see below) – they created an important environmental change in the world of politics that contributed to new SME policies in the 1980s. Given these ideological claims, academic proofs and widespread political support, perhaps it is not surprising that SMEs have been picked up across the board as a kind of panacea for policy problems. Certainly the problem is not one of a lack of reasons to help SMEs.

What is wrong with the liberal view of globalization and SMEs?

In many ways, the liberal view of the SME and its relationship with globalization reflects the views held by SMEs. Entrepreneurs are frequently seen as individualists and the small business sector is traditionally the one that complains most about the burdens placed on it by government regulation. They also suffer most when the state intervenes, not only because they have fewer resources to ride the market distortions that arise from state intervention, but also because they lack the resources or ability to organize that are needed to influence government policy. But there are also problems in the assumptions of liberal (neo-classical) economics and liberal views of the globalization and the state that compromise our understanding of the small firm sector. Two examples illustrate this. The first is in the understanding of how more dynamic exporting SMEs, those identified by the OECD as potentially benefiting from globalization, work in relation to their environments. The second is in the ability of the state to make policies for SMEs that are justified in terms of the free market, notably the removal of red tape for SMEs. Both examples focus on the importance of understanding the institutional context in which SMEs exist.

High-growth SMEs in sectors such as the high-technology and service sectors may well, according to the liberal argument, benefit from greater access to global markets (Buckley, 1989; Fujita 1995a and b). The OECD, for example, sees globalization as affecting SMEs in two main ways:

○ fast-growing SMEs (5 per cent of total stock) benefiting from technological and communication change and representing 70 per cent of net new jobs from SMEs, will benefit from globalization and enjoy expansion and growth
○ others will see globalization as a threat or at least competitive challenge. There are three groups of these SMEs: those that will be able to respond and will in time benefit (approximately 25 per cent of manufacturing SMEs); those that will not survive because of increased competition (25–50 per cent of total SMEs at present); those that will not be affected (the rest, i.e. 25 per cent of the total). The last group will decrease while the first two will grow (OECD, 1997: 7).

Clearly the winners are those SMEs that have crossed the technological divide of the global age. The message for the others is 'adapt or die'. In short, there will be no space in a global age for SMEs that are unable to compete in a global market. Central to this assertion is the '… general agreement that globalisation is not reversible…' (OECD, 1997: 10). The assumption is that scale economies (which SMEs by definition do not enjoy) will swallow up all of the world's markets, from building the fastest motorbikes to selling the smallest snack in the most remote village.

Yet there are a number of problems with these assertions and observations. No matter how 'global' the local economy becomes, are we really going to lose all the local hairdressers and newsagents that fulfil our needs? Will we trust our individual looks to the scientific hair-cutting procedures of 'Unilever Global Hair Inc.', or will we look to someone we know and trust? When we go on holiday, will we feel happier cancelling the newspaper deliveries at a well-known local newsagent or an anonymous uniform in a global newsagent. Of course the local hairdresser could be awful and the newsagent a crook, but the importance of trust and shared history felt for the local, smaller business is lost in the liberal view of globalization and the small firm. In other words, values and culture are lost in the rational pursuit of efficiency.

This commitment to scale economies is a consequence of the orientation of traditional neo-classical economics analyses. SMEs and small businesses do not operate in the same way that large companies do, and alternative theoretical devices are required to understand the economics of the SME (Julien, 1993). For example, there is an important literature on the small firm that focuses on the institutional context in which it operates. Henrekson and Johansson argue that the variations in firm size distributions in Sweden are not explicable by the degree to which an economy is exposed to global competition (as one might deduce from the OECD report). Rather the relatively small number of SMEs in Sweden can be best explained '... as the outcome of the institutions and rules of the game pertinent to entrepreneurial activity in Sweden' (Henrekson and Johansson, 1999: 18). Among these they include tax policy, credit market policy, the national pension scheme and labour legislation (Henrekson and Johansson, 1999: 18–21).

In high-technology areas (where SMEs are seen to be the most resilient to the forces of globalization) the social context is paramount. The concept of 'flexible specialization', which famously explained the high growth of SMEs in Northern Italy in the mid-1980s, was premised on the notion that SMEs operated in a social environment that allowed them to spread risk and cooperate in a more flexible fashion than the rigid procedures of the traditional hierarchical firm (Piore and Sabel, 1986; Diwan, 1989).[5] This focus on trying to understand how small firms are embedded within their societies also has important implications for the way in which we understand SMEs to work.[6] For example, Autio argues that the emphasis on atomistic (that is individual entrepreneurs) as opposed to systemic approaches (which focus on the environment in which SMEs develop) has meant that '. . . the general conception of new, technology-based firms may be mistakenly biased towards high growth or at least the aspiration of it' (Autio, 1997: 197). Indeed, even those high-technology-based SMEs that do want to expand at a great rate will be greatly affected in their technological development by their national (de la Mothe and Pacquet, 1994) as well as regional (Keeble *et al.*, 1998) contexts. Furthermore, their decision on where to invest abroad is very likely to be influenced by the cultural proximity of the host country (Fujita, 1995a and b).

Institutional analysis can also help us understand how SMEs are excluded from important political decisions – even when they are made in the name of small firms. This is clear in our second criticism of the liberal view of SMEs and globalization. The Deregulation Initiative was presented under Margaret Thatcher and focused on the removal of red tape. This would promote international competitiveness and increase global investment. She thought that national market regulations would be unnecessary under the European Community's Single Market Programme of the late 1980s. In other words, the policy was to replace national regulation with regional regulations, just as the liberal globalization guru Kenichi Omhae would have advocated (Omhae, 1990).

But the policy was also strongly identified with small firms, that had consistently called for relief from regulatory burdens since 1979 when the Conservative government came to power, and represented an important political constituency for Thatcher at the time (see above). In the first report to deal with deregulation, Norman Tebbitt, then Secretary of State for Trade and Industry, made the link with small firms abundantly clear:

> This report is about burdens on business – the burdens imposed by central and local government regulations which bear hardest on small firms. (DTI, 1985: 3)

The report went on to place some considerable weight on small firms suggesting that departments strengthen their arrangements for consultation with small business organizations and obtain a greater understanding of their working environments (DTI, 1985: 14). It also argued for a structured analysis of legislative proposals, a small empowered central government body and that regular reviews of existing regulation should take place. These were respectively realized in the Compliance Cost Assessment (CCA), Enterprise and Deregulation Unit (EDU), and a number of White Papers and reports that reproduced concerns over existing legislation and targeted new ones (Froud and Ogus, 1996). Relaunches of the initiative built on the existing principles, especially by formalizing the CCA procedure and increasing its scope to all legislative proposals,[7] while later proposals established a Small Business Litmus Test (SBLT) to facilitate the involvement of small firms.

Despite these procedures and reforms the small firm representatives felt systematically excluded. Individual small firms lacked the ability to provide the information for CCAs and the time and resources to attend the Task Forces – one group had to lobby the government for compensation for small firms attending the Task Forces. One representative from a small business organization suggested that he would not let a CCA near one of his members, and others pointed out that the SBLT was pointless as it would not be filled in by a representative sample. Another representative said that 99 per cent of his organization's members would not be affected by most legislative proposals, and those that did participate in the SBLT were more likely to be politically motivated, more eloquent or less busy (author's interviews). While the SBLT correctly identified the need to target specific firms, it provided little help in achieving this goal.

Even the groups themselves, which were better positioned to respond in comparison to individual small firms, seemed unable to fulfil the demands the Deregulation Initiative placed on society. One group's executive officer saw the volume and breadth of issues involved in CCAs as imposing an impossible burden on his time. Other groups addressed this problem by organizing surveys on specific issues on a limited range of issues (author's interviews). But these consultations were exceptional to a few groups only, and related to specific policy proposals, which were in turn selected by the executives of the groups. While this form of information may have been useful to the CCA process, it was not carried out in uniform response to the CCAs, nor was it carried out by all the representative groups. Small businesses were only contacted directly in a random and arbitrary fashion and only contacted indirectly at the discretion of the interest groups' executives. In both cases, the information that derived from the small business population was qualitatively inferior to that provided by larger businesses in respect of the demands of the deregulation initiative.

This brings us to our second criticism of the liberal view of globalization and SMEs: liberalization policies made in the name of SMEs and globalization may not help SMEs, despite the rhetoric. While SMEs were clearly important in legitimating the Deregulation Initiative, they were important only because of the liberal agenda that was being advocated.

Conclusion: globaloney

The assumption that high-technology SMEs will benefit from globalization depends on the institutions and communities in which these firms operate. Even those fast-growing SMEs, which the OECD thought would benefit from global markets, will do so only as long as the process of globalization does not undermine their communities. And those SMEs that are trying to adapt, and being helped along their way by the removal of red tape, are in fact being placed in an even less beneficial position by the process of deregulation. Because they are not able to organize as well politically and provide the information that is required for policy makers, they are unable to influence which regulations are removed, and so which markets become global. In this sense globalization provides a perfect opportunity for big businesses in the domestic markets to reset the rules in their favour.

But it does not have to be like this. Many commentators now reject the very core observations of the liberal view of globalization. They do not see globalization as 'irreversible', nor do they accept the extent to which it is either different to what was happening one hundred years ago or having the huge effect that its reputation implies (e.g. Hirst and Thompson, 1996; Boyer and Drache, 1996; Berger and Dore, 1998). There is huge diversity in the way that SMEs have been supported by different national regimes across Europe.[8] There are also significant variations both within countries and in regions that cross between countries. What is clear is that when we consider helping SMEs we need to consider the context in which they exist and how that can best be adapted for those who work there, rather than beginning all our policy discussions from an ideologically informed perspective of 'global-ization – the unstoppable'.

Perhaps when we discuss globalization and SMEs we need to ask 'which globalization' and 'which SMEs' it is we are talking about. Then we can start to talk about what we really understand globalization to mean and the extent to which we find it acceptable for those SMEs that we wish to support. Too easily in Europe, globalization has been used as a:

> . . . rhetorical device to discipline expectations of what is feasible in terms of social expenditure and welfare entitlements. (Watson, 1999: 127)

Part III. Contesting globalization

8 Challenging globalization: the response of women workers and entrepreneurs to trade and investment policies

MARILYN CARR

What is globalization?

GLOBALIZATION IS MANY things to many people. In its broadest sense, it is all types of economic and cultural transfers between nations – including cultural domination of the media and widespread use of the World Wide Web. In its narrower sense, it encompasses the economic exchange of goods and services internationally, and international financial flows. Internationally traded services are an expanding category which include those such as travel and tourism, which are traditional, as well as those such as telecommunications, accounting and business consultancy, which are very new and growing rapidly (Schoettle and Grant, 1998).

Possibly because of the high profile acquired by the WTO, there has been a tendency for the globalization debate to concentrate on trade policy and its impact on flows of goods and services. This is indeed important as the volume of world exports increased 16 times between 1950 and 1996 – as opposed to six times for world output – mainly as a result of trade liberalization (DAW, 1999). And, as we shall see, this has had an enormous impact on the patterns of employment for women and men in developing and developed countries. But financial flows are just as, if not more, important. Such flows are huge and growing – and are now bigger than official flows (aid) in all regions except sub-Saharan Africa. There are several types of international financial flows, the most important of which are:

○ Foreign direct investment (FDI): an investment transaction in a country's domestic production capacity by foreigners, with a management component. FDI expanded by 30 per cent between 1983 and 1989, during which time exports expanded by only 10 per cent. FDI now accounts for 40 per cent of total external finance to developing countries (Shoettle and Grant, 1998). It is talked about a lot, mainly because it has created so many jobs in Export Processing Zones (EPZs) in developing countries – particularly for Asian women. However, total employment in EPZs in developing countries is only 27 million which, at only 2 per cent of total wage employment in these countries, is a mere drop in the ocean (FIAS, 1998). Also, as we shall see in the following section, FDI is causing loss of livelihoods in some regions, as well as exploiting the natural resource base and leading to exports of crops rather than increased domestic food security.

○ Private portfolio investment: an investment transaction by foreign investors in domestic productive capacity, without any management component, usually through purchase of equity on the local stock market. This is more volatile than FDI and is basically what caused the Asian financial crisis. In 1997, there was a net outflow of private funds of $US20 billion from East and Southeast Asia (with massive impact on women in particular) versus net inflows of $US70 billion in 1995 and $US80 billion in 1996 (Joekes, 1999). Unemployment increased from 5.3 million people in 1996 to 18 million in 1998 – and the majority of those displaced were women. Those living in poverty increased from 30 million to 50 million over the same time period, with women and girls suffering the most (Singh and Zimmit, 1999).

Before looking at the specific impact of trade and investment liberalization on women and men, there are three major points to make about economic globalization:

○ Distribution of gains between countries has been very uneven, with the North benefiting much more than the South. Northern countries have been able to protect their own industries in the past in a way that the countries of the South are not able to do, given the emphasis on liberalization of trade and investment. Northern countries are in a much stronger economic and bargaining position than those in the South. It is estimated that 70 per cent of the gains expected to arise from the Uruguay Round will be accrued by the North, leaving only 30 per cent for the countries in the South. Even then, the bulk of these gains go to a very few Southern countries. The same is true of FDI – ten developing countries get about 75 per cent of all FDI in developing countries. African countries in total get only about 1 per cent (DAW, 1999; ODI, 1997)

○ Distribution of gains within countries is also very uneven – both in the North and the South. In particular, the share of wages has been declining relative to that of profits – partly because of incentives given to investors and partly because labour is increasingly exploited, driving wages lower and lower (Rodrik, 1997). The share of women versus men is less clear cut and, as we shall see in the next section, the situation varies considerably between different regions of the world and over time. However, such evidence as does exist suggests that men are the more likely to be able to take advantage of the benefits of trade and investment liberalization and are less likely than women to suffer from its negative impacts

○ Also with countries, the increased openness of trade brings increased instability. So, although we may need openness for the sake of economic gains, it is important to recognize that the poor become even more vulnerable under volatile conditions (as evidenced in the Asian crisis), and there is a role for the state and civil society institutions/associations to ensure social protection for these vulnerable sectors. Unfortunately, governments are now less able to respond because revenues are decreasing as tariffs and taxes are reduced as part of the globalization process. One estimate is that as much as one-third of total tax revenue may have been lost in many countries as a result of trade liberalization (DAW, 1999). Thus, at the same time as the poorest segments of the population are becoming more vulnerable, the tax base is being eroded. In addition, employers are less concerned with providing benefits/security to their employees because capital is more mobile than ever before and less dependent on the goodwill of the labour force (Rodrik 1997). It is estimated that less than 5 per cent of GDP goes on social protection in most developing countries, and that a large and increasing proportion of workers have no form of benefits from their employers (WIEGO, 1999a).

Gender impact of trade and investment policies

The gender aspects of trade and investment liberalization have received increasing attention over the past four or five years, but there is still a lot more research and action required. One major finding so far is that it is not possible to generalize. When the United Nations Development Fund for Women (UNIFEM) first commissioned work on Women and the New Trade Agenda in 1992,[1] women from the regions advised that this could not be dealt with at a global level because the differences between regions are so great. As a consequence, research has now been carried out in most regions, and regional policy dialogues – based on the findings of this research – have taken place over the years in Delhi, Brazil, Bangkok, Harare and Mexico.[2] As the following examples illustrate, these have shown how complex the situation is.

Asia

In the Asia region there has been export-led growth, through which large numbers of jobs were created in labour-intensive activities and particularly in garments for export – where women account for over 80 per cent of the workforce in most cases. This has led some researchers to refer to industrialization as being female-led as well as export-led (Joekes, 1995).

One of the most spectacular cases of female-led industrialization is that of Bangladesh. In 1978, there were four garment factories in the country. By 1995, there were 2400 factories employing 1.2 million workers, of whom 90 per cent were women under the age of 25 years, and garments were employing 70 per cent of women in wage employment. (Bhattachararya, 1999). The question that is asked is whether this is good or bad for women. Wages are very low and working conditions are not good. However, unskilled women in export-oriented factories are paid almost the same (90 per cent) as unskilled men, as opposed to only 57 per cent outside these factories. Also, women say that this work is much better than the alternatives (Joekes, 1999; Kabeer, 1995). This leads us to exercise some caution when discriminating against clothes produced by vulnerable groups in developing countries. For example, a US bill on child labour under the age of 15 in garments in Bangladesh made thousands of girls redundant, but they still had to earn a living, so they ended up with working conditions that were worse than before (Fontana *et al.*, 1998).

While trade policies have an impact on women, gender also has a bearing on trade policies. A good example of what can happen comes from Pakistan. Pakistan is similar to Bangladesh in that it has very low literacy rates, especially among women, who have few options for productive employment. The government has had a policy of export expansion, and exports are heavily focused on cotton and cotton textiles, which is a heavily male-dominated industry (88 per cent of workers are men). There was a very sluggish response to the export drive because (for a variety of sociocultural reasons) women could not be mobilized to expand the labour supply as happened in Bangladesh (Fontana *et al.*, 1998).

Sri Lanka has a much higher literacy rate than Bangladesh and Pakistan, but there are still thousands of young women going into garment production in EPZs. Garments are now a bigger export item than tea, and the women to men employment ratio has gone up from 1:4 in 1963 to 4:5 in 1985. However, the fact that women still receive low wages and have very poor working conditions prompts us to ask whether gender equality really has increased. In addition, 500 000 women from Sri Lanka are now working in the Middle East. This makes a big difference for the country as their remittances bring in more foreign exchange than do tea exports, but it is not necessarily benefiting women themselves. They work under appalling conditions and get to keep little or none of the money for their own use (Fontana *et al.*, 1998).

The Philippines provides a good example of how – even though women may be the first to get jobs in periods of export expansion – they are also the first to lose them when something goes wrong, as in the Asia crisis. By early 1998, over 200 garment factories had closed in the Philippines with immediate loss of income for factory- and home-based workers. Women have to seek alternatives such as horticulture, but this is difficult because of their restricted access to credit, training, improved technologies and markets. So they resort to vending, which does not require much input, but also results in tiny profits (Carr, 1998).

What is likely to happen in Asia in the future? In particular, will the level of labour participation among women remain high? There are two issues involved here.

○ What approach is being taken to increased competition among developing countries for markets for labour-intensive products such as ready-made garments, shoes and electronics? There appear to be two strategies. The first is to diversify into different types of products for export, which have higher profits and less-crowded markets. In countries where this is happening, the proportion of women employed in EPZs is falling as more men are recruited into the new industries, which are more technologically sophisticated and which demand higher skill levels (which men are given greater opportunities to acquire). In Malaysia, for example, the proportion of women workers in EPZs fell from 75 per cent in 1980 to 54 per cent in 1990. The second strategy is to try to maintain or increase market share in existing export industries by undercutting competitors – usually by cutting labour costs. This is what is often called the race to the bottom and is neither good for the women workers nor for the countries concerned. It is a common phenomenon, however, and we are now seeing a real downturn in the prices for garments and shoes in world markets precisely because corporations are able to bid down labour costs in developing countries. Neither of these strategies seems to work in favour of women (Joekes, 1999).

○ What will happen after the Multilateral Fibre Arrangement (MFA) is phased out in 2005? This arrangement has so controlled trade in textiles and garments over the past decades that there will be some quite dramatic shifts occurring – many of them in Asia, where textiles and garments are a major export industry. It will be very important to start examining the likely outcome of the end of the MFA as soon as possible so as to plan for likely changes well in advance. For example, in Bangladesh, the garment export industry is based on imported fibre from India and other countries. In 2005, India may be more interested in exporting directly, so unless Bangladesh builds up its textile production capacity before then, millions of women's livelihoods will be at risk (Bhattachararya, 1999).

Africa

In Africa, exports are still linked to primary commodities, the prices for which are in slow decline in world markets. Also, many traditional women's industries are in jeopardy because of cheap imports from Asia and FDI from Europe.

Agriculture is the major source of exports in Africa, and many governments promote export of cash crops – often with serious consequences for domestic food security. For example, in Ghana, the government has supported an export drive based on cocoa, which is a crop totally controlled by men. However, women are generally expected to provide unpaid family labour, which leaves them with less time to devote to production of food for family consumption and for sale (Fontana *et al.*, 1998). Women's own crops are not seen as important and are not supported or protected from imports (although they could be according to WTO regulations). Thus, in Ghana, and in several other countries in West Africa, imported cheap rice is bringing the price down for produce of domestic (women) farmers, with all that this implies for incomes and domestic food security.

There is a similar situation in Kenya, where the government has been promoting the export of tea. Here land has been diverted from food crops (controlled by women) to tea – and only men are allowed to be licensed as tea producers by the State Marketing Board. Women have to put in long hours in harvesting tea, but have no control over the income resulting from sales. Research has revealed that although tea-producing households have higher income than those which do not produce tea, they have higher levels of malnutrition because women have little or no control over income in the former (Ongile, 1999). It is findings such as this that have led governments such as that of Namibia to reverse previous policies which supported export crops, and to increase support to subsistence farmers, and especially to female-headed households (Stark and de Vylder, 1998).

Another interesting trend in the agricultural sector in Africa is that of the promotion of non-traditional agricultural exports (NTAEs) – primarily fruits and vegetables and cut flowers aimed at the European markets. These do offer some hope of increased incomes for women, who represent about 90 per cent of the workforce in this fast-growing sector (DAW, 1999). In many ways, this is a replay of the garment export industry in Asia, with large corporations dominating the commodity chain, and with women working on large-scale 'factory' farms for very low wages and in very bad working conditions. In fact, the conditions are worse than in the case of garments, because of the high use of pesticides and resulting physical and mental health risks. However, women do get wages straight into their hands and have more control over income than when they work for their husbands on smallholder export crops (DAW, 1999; USAID, 1999). On the negative side, however, is the effect that this type of 'factory' farming is having on soil fertility and on the availability of food locally.

A similar phenomenon has been happening with African countries that have been promoting fish exports. A particularly striking case is that of the three countries surrounding Lake Victoria. Here, government has encouraged foreign investment in modern fish-processing factories around the lake. There are now 50 of these, which employ very few workers and which export fish to Europe and Japan. This has resulted in thousands of women losing their jobs in smoking and sale of fish in local markets. It also means that little or no fish is available to eat locally, with disastrous effects in terms of rising rates of malnutrition among children (IUCN, 1999).

Another example of how FDI may affect women's livelihoods in Africa comes from Burkina Faso and other countries in West Africa where shea nuts grow wild. Shea is a commodity that has been collected, processed and used by women in West Africa for centuries as a cooking oil, a body lotion and for medicinal purposes. Now there is a growing and profitable market for shea butter in Europe, North America and Japan for use in cosmetics. However, the women who collect the nuts get very little of the high price that the final product brings in the North. They usually sell the unprocessed nuts directly to middlemen for export, as a higher quality of processed product is demanded in Northern markets than African women can provide with their existing level of technology. Thus, one study estimates that shea butter in Northern markets sells for 84 times more than the price paid to African women for the raw material (Provost, 1995). The price of shea is likely to go even higher if the EU follows through on its proposed policy to allow shea butter to be used as a substitute for cocoa butter in chocolate manufacture (Bekure *et al.*, 1997). However, the fear is that FDI will be attracted to the area to establish processing facilities and that local women will benefit very little or not at all from the booming market for the commodity they have nurtured for years.

An associated problem relates to that of intellectual property rights. Under the TRIPS Agreement of the WTO, it is now possible to patent life forms if they have been altered in some way for new and innovative uses. Shea butter runs the risk of becoming patented by Northern researchers or companies in much the same way as have many other products such as neem and turmeric (from India) and brazzein (also from West Africa). Neem, which has been used by women farmers as a pesticide and fungicide for generations now has more than 35 patents on it in the US and Europe, mainly for its pesticidal properties. Local communities receive no share in the profits accruing, and are already victims of reduced access to this traditional resource due to increased market prices. Turmeric has been used in India as a magic cure-all from time immemorial. In 1995, two American scientists were granted a US patent on the use of turmeric for healing wounds, claiming it to be novel. The Indian government challenged the patent and managed to win the legal battle, otherwise this patent would have prevented Indian companies from marketing turmeric for wound-healing in the US, and could have made it illegal for Indian companies to use Indian turmeric for this purpose even in India! Finally, brazzein is a substance found in a West African berry, which is

500 times sweeter than sugar. American researchers have obtained a patent in the US and in Europe for a protein isolated from the berry and plan to market it worldwide claiming that it is their invention. They have no plans to assist the West African people to share in the estimated US$100 billion a year market (Kaihuzi, 1999).

The other major sources of livelihoods for women in Africa are traditional industries such as food processing and handicrafts, and vending and hawking – all of which have been affected by trade liberalization. In the case of traditional industries, there are many accounts of women basket makers and cooking oil processors being displaced by cheap imports from Asia. While it would be wrong to argue for protection of inefficient production, there are, nevertheless, hundreds of thousands of livelihoods being jeopardized or destroyed in this way, with little or no support available to enable women to upgrade their industries or to diversify into other areas. In the case of vending or hawking, recent research in countries such as South Africa shows that foreign traders are now entering from elsewhere in the region, bringing with them new and different types of products. Faced with competition, many women vendors end up working for these (predominantly male) newcomers with resulting cuts in income and independence. And even vendors are becoming tied into multinational corporation chains with companies such as Unilever selling their soap through them and with Coca-Cola renting out kiosks (Skinner, 1999; Kapila, 1999).

Latin America and the Caribbean

In this region, 'modern' services are a fast-growing export sector. The region also has a large well-educated female labour force. In fact, it is the only region where – in several countries – women's enrolments in schools outnumber those for men. In Jamaica and other Caribbean islands, there are now many relatively prestigious and well-paid jobs for women in 'digiports', which focus, for example, on data entry for US airline companies. Women often represent 100 per cent of the workforce in these zones, but despite their relatively high education levels, they still are paid only 57 per cent of men's wages (Fontana *et al.*, 1998).

In several other countries in Southern and Central America, it is traditional services – vending and domestic service – that account for the bulk of women's employment. In Mexico, for example, 70 per cent of women's employment is in these types of service. However, 80 per cent of all exports are manufactured goods – a large proportion of which are in sectors such as ready-made garments in which women comprise well over 50 per cent of the labour force working mostly in EPZs (Cardero *et al.*, 2000). However, as in Asia, the proportion of women in EPZs (especially near the US border) is declining with increased liberalization. For example, the share of women in the export sector as a whole fell from 45 per cent in 1991 to 35 per cent in 1993 (Ghiara, 1999), and of those still working in the export sector, increasing numbers are located in EPZs furthest away from the US border where wages are much lower (Cardero *et al.*, 2000).

As in Africa, many Latin American countries have a growing trade in NTAEs. For example, in Chile, fruit exports expanded by 258 per cent from 340 000 tons in 1982 to 1.2 million tons in 1994. This expansion has resulted in many peasant farmers being displaced from their land – some of whom now make up the 300 000 temporary labour force that works on the new NTAE farms and plantations. The majority of these temporary workers are women (as opposed to only 5 per cent of permanent workers), and although there has been some raising of status for women as a result of earning wages, the temporary and uncertain nature of work, as well as the low pay and inadequate working conditions, tend to limit this effect. As in other parts of the world, distribution of returns in this industry are very uneven. For example, in the case of seedless grapes in 1993/94, producers accounted for only 11 per cent of costs (of which only a proportion went to workers), while exporters, importers and Northern retailers accounted for 89 per cent of total costs (Barrientos *et al.*, 1999)

Analysis of examples

There have been various attempts to put these trends into frameworks and theories. Some of these include:

○ the integration thesis, which suggests that economic development first decreases and then opens up paid employment for women and that trade liberalization speeds this up
○ the exploitation thesis, which asserts that economic development and export-led growth are made possible only through exploitation of women, and that while the country may benefit as a result of increased export earnings, the women who do the work do not get their fair share of these benefits
○ the marginalization thesis, which states that the development process works against incorporating women into the labour market on equal terms with men, since they are seen as surplus labour to be forced into paid labour when needed at low wages, and then let go again when they are not needed (Joekes, 1999).

As we have seen above, these different theses are the subject of much debate. In particular, continued increases in female employment in EPZs now seem far from certain with the trend towards more technology-intensive export goods. There is also some evidence that women in EPZs feel less exploited and marginalized than they did in alternative economic activities.

A more action-oriented framework – which enables us to a gain a broader picture of the impact of globalization on women's work and to identify appropriate interventions – is that of value chain analysis. This looks at the distribution of gains from trade in a different way. It considers international distribution of value added in the production and sale of goods that are sold in global markets. It also looks at the distribution of power (Gereffi and Korzeniewicz, 1994). Much of the work done on value chains has been on labour-intensive manufactured goods such as ready-made garments and shoes. This covers companies such as Gap, Levi Strauss and Nike, which control the commodity chain as buyers but do not own production plants. Production is outsourced to producers in Asia and Latin America, with millions of factory workers and home-based workers involved at this stage of the production chain. These millions of workers (most of whom are women) are paid very low wages and end up accounting for no more than 10 per cent of the total cost of the finished goods. The other 90 per cent is accounted for by the advertising, distribution and retailing end of the chain.[3]

There is more limited work being done on NTAE value chains, including one study on the horticultural producers and workers in Africa who are linked to five major supermarket chains in the UK (Dolan et al., 1999); and those in Central and South America who are linked to supermarket and fast-food chains in Canada and the USA (Barndt, 1999; Barrientos *et al.*, 1999). As was seen in the previous section, these chains are also buyer-driven, with the vast proportion of gains being siphoned off by Northern importers and retailers.

In addition, there is now some work in progress looking at value chains for non-timber forest products (NTFPs). These products, which have been nurtured and used by communities in the South for centuries, are now finding expanding and profitable markets in the North as interest increases in the use of natural products in cosmetics, foodstuffs and pharmaceuticals. Over 150 NTFPs, including gum, essential oils and medicinal plants, are now traded internationally on a significant scale, usually without the communities where the raw materials originate deriving much benefit from the profits arising (FAO, 1995). As in the garment, shoe and NTAE chains, the gatherers of NTFPs have very little power and are not in a strong position to bargain with those further up the chain for increased returns for their labour or their traditional knowledge. The complexity of these chains is illustrated in Figure 1, which outlines the various links in the shea butter value chain – from local women who collect shea nuts in Burkina Faso to the international cosmetics and confectionery companies in North America and Europe. Plotting these chains helps us to determine more precisely who is doing and getting what, and is a useful first step in determining where and how to intervene in order to help bring about a more equal distribution of gains and power.

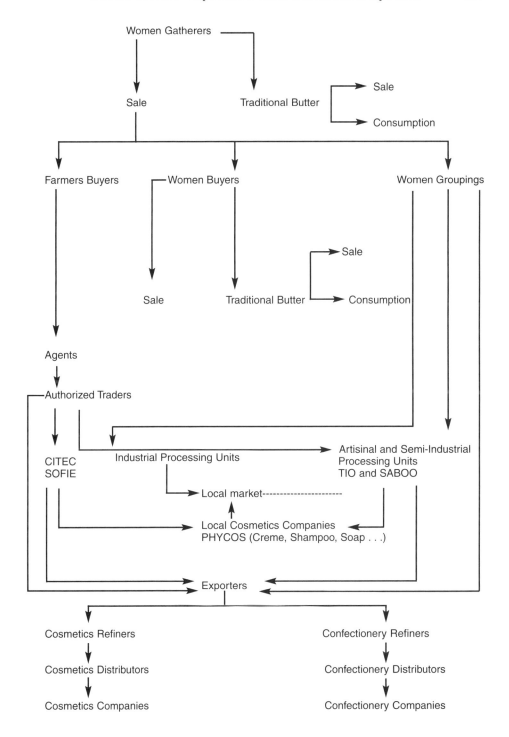

Figure 1   *Value Chain of Shea Butter in Burkina Faso*

Research so far indicates that likely points of intervention would include:

1. organizing those who are weakest in the chain so that they can bargain for better prices
2. assisting rural communities where raw materials are found to do some processing and get some value added by increasing access to improved technology
3. helping primary producers to cut out some of the middlemen in the chain by increasing their access to information on prices and markets (through, for example, use of community telecentres), and introducing new ideas such as marketing directly through the Internet. (WIEGO, 1999b).

Women's responses to trade and investment policies

Responses to trade and investment policies will be different for different categories of women workers and entrepreneurs. These include:

○ own-account workers (e.g. vendors/fish smokers/beer brewers) and home-based workers in subcontracting chains (e.g. garment workers)
○ small-scale women entrepreneurs (with fewer than five employees)
○ domestic workers/casual workers/plantation workers
○ small farmers.

There has been a tendency in the literature to concentrate on the enterprise and the entrepreneur, rather than the self-employed worker or the worker in subcontracting chains. While the former are, of course, important, they are considerably fewer in number and better able to argue for their economic rights than are the latter. As a consequence, this section concentrates on the responses of own-account workers and home-based workers.

There are millions of women street vendors and millions more who work at home brewing beer, baking and doing other kinds of food-processing operations. In addition, as we have seen, there is a large and increasing number of women who work from their homes involved in garment making and other labour-intensive activities and who are linked through subcontracting chains to large formal sector companies. Estimates are that – in this last category alone – there are 40 million women in China and 30 million in India. In six sub-Saharan countries where attempts have been made to enumerate home-based workers, it was found that over 50 per cent of all enterprises were home-based; while in Egypt, over 50 per cent of women's and over 10 per cent of men's enterprises are home-based.[4] These are the people who tend to be at the bottom of the value chains that were mentioned in the last section.

Of interest is the fact that home-based work is equally common in developed countries as in developing countries. There are an estimated one million women home-based workers in the UK, and in Australia the number of home-based workers in the clothing industry doubled every year between the mid-1980s and mid-1990s, with total numbers rising from 30 000 to 330 000 within a decade. This means that for every factory worker in the garment industry in Australia, there are an estimated 15 homeworkers (Carr *et al.*, 2000).

Organizing of own-account and home-based workers is a first step in assisting them up the rungs of value chains and assisting them to empower themselves both economically and politically. Quite a lot of this organizing has already been done around the world at the local and national levels, and increasingly at the regional and international levels.

One of the most impressive examples of local-level organizing is that of the Self-Employed Women's Association (SEWA) of India, which is the oldest trade union of women who work in the informal sector. Since 1972, when it was founded, SEWA has organized women engaged in home-based work, street vending and casual work, and has provided a range of services (financial, health, child care and training) to it members. Today, it has a membership of over 250 000 women. Other successful examples of organizing include: the Union of Embroiderers in Madeira, Portugal; the Self-Employment Women's Union in Durban, South Africa; UNITE in Canada; and the Textile, Clothing and Footwear Union (TCFUA) in Australia.

Several of these associations have won major victories for their members. For example, in Australia, TCFUA, working with other organizations such as consumer, church, community and student groups, organized a consumer campaign with broad-based public support and media coverage to encourage retailers to sign up to a code of good practice regarding their employment of homeworkers. The trade union and its allies in the campaign won an industry-wide agreement – which is legally binding – covering the terms and conditions of homeworker employment (TCFUA, 1995, 1996). In India, SEWA was a moving force in pushing through an ILO Convention on Homework, which potentially will benefit not only its own members, but also women in the informal sector worldwide.

Recognizing the need for a globalization of the labour force within the context of increasing globalization of economies and markets, the various unions, grassroots organizations and NGOs working with women informal sector workers – in both the North and the South – have recently begun to establish linkages across national boundaries and across continents. In the mid-1990s, at two separate meeting in Europe, these organizations came together to form two international alliances of women in the informal sector: one of home-based workers called HomeNet; and the other of street vendors called StreetNet.

It was at the first HomeNet meeting in 1994 that the founding members (under the leadership of SEWA) planned a global campaign for an international convention that would recognize and promote home-based workers.

The culmination of that campaign was the June 1996 vote at the annual general conference of the ILO in favour of an international convention on homework. HomeNet now has active members in over 25 countries, with a newsletter that reaches a very wide audience in 130 countries. Its main activities are to assist with national-level organizing, to seek implementation of the ILO Convention on HomeWork, to assist its members to form linkages on a worldwide basis and to link members with emerging markets.[5]

At the first StreetNet meeting in 1995, the founding members (again with SEWA very much in evidence) drafted an International Declaration that sets forth a plan to create national policies to promote and protect the rights of street vendors. A longer-term objective of StreetNet is to build the case and mobilize support for an ILO Convention on the rights of street vendors.[6]

While HomeNet and StreetNet are helping women to organize locally, nationally and regionally – and increasingly at the international level – they still have several needs.

○ The need for information on what global economic reforms are going on and how they affect their members: the global economic policy process is very complicated. Impacts are unclear, and it is not clear as to where, how and when to intervene to make a difference. Further research – especially into value chains – would help to see what is happening, and further research on the process of trade policy making would help to see how to intervene and when. UNIFEM, CIDA, WEDO and others have started producing primers, which aim at increasing women's understanding of key trade issues and the trade policy process.[7]

○ The need for links to the policy process: information is only half of the battle. There is also a need to be able to interface with decision makers. An example of this is how UNIFEM assisted HomeNet/SEWA to reach the ears of key policy makers by convening a policy dialogue between them and the Asian labour ministers prior to the 1996 ILO conference at which the ILO Convention on Homework was discussed. This prior sensitization went a long way towards helping HomeNet/SEWA to ensure that the vote went in their direction.

○ The need for access to emerging markets: own-account workers in particular need a way to link more effectively with emerging global markets and a way to bypass the intermediaries in the value chain who rake off so much of their profits. There is a role here for research into international markets and assistance to women producers to gain access to modern ICTs.

○ And finally, the need for assistance in organizing globally. StreetNet has not yet started international organizing, and although HomeNet has made some international linkages, there is still much to learn in terms of organizing at this level.

To respond to the needs of the international alliances of workers and producers, a new international coalition, Women in Informal Employment: Globalizing and Organizing (WIEGO), was formed in 1997. This brings representatives of the workers alliances together with the researchers, statisticians and international development organizations who can help to respond to their needs for statistics and research, as well as links to policy makers and global institutions and markets. Its name reflects two of its major concerns: that women informal workers are an integral part of the globalizing economy; and that women workers need to be organizing at local and international levels in order to respond effectively to the new opportunities – as well as the negative impacts – associated with global trade and investment.

WIEGO has a Secretariat at Harvard University and five major global programmes, which respond to the priority needs of the alliances:

○ urban policies, particularly as they relate to street vendors
○ global markets (i.e. trade and investment policies), particularly as they relate to home-based workers
○ social protection for workers in the informal economy
○ statistics on the size and contribution of the informal economy;
○ the organization of informal sector workers as well as their representation in relevant policy-making bodies at all levels.

Each programme is coordinated by a part-time programme director in liaison with an active expert working group.

Specific activities of WIEGO to date include:

○ action research studies of street vendors in South Africa, Kenya and India, including policy dialogues with municipal authorities
○ development of regional frameworks for measuring the impact of globalization on women workers in the informal sector
○ design of research studies to analyse global value chains for garments, food processing and NTFPs from a gender perspective
○ development and implementation of a pilot scheme in India to link grassroots women producers with global markets
○ design of pilot studies aimed at promoting social protection for women workers in the informal sector
○ analysis, compilation and dissemination of existing data on the informal sector from a gender perspective
○ testing of improved concepts, classifications and methods of data collection, and promotion of their use in official labour force and establishment surveys.[8]

WIEGO, HomeNet and StreetNet are relatively young organizations, which have been created as a response by an already disadvantaged section of society to the forces of globalization. Their establishment and the rapid expansion in their membership suggest that women homeworkers and own-account workers recognize the need to organize and take collective action. While tools such as value chain analysis help them understand better the effects of changing production patterns under globalization, their capability to respond to the large and powerful actors in the global economy is through coming together and participating in the policy processes at both national and international level.

9 'Flexible' female employment and ethical trade in the global economy

STEPHANIE BARRIENTOS

Introduction

GLOBALIZATION AND ECONOMIC liberalization have led to significant changes in the patterns and conditions of female and male employment, especially in export production in developing countries. Important features of this have been the relative increase in female employment, the expansion of 'flexible' work and, associated with it, a deterioration in the conditions of employment. Many have talked of the feminization of labour, through the loss of traditional male jobs and also the 'downward spiral' in labour standards as aspects of a globalized economy. But globalization is a complex and contradictory process, yielding both positive and negative effects. Recently, ethical trade has gained momentum as a means of improving employment conditions in the export production of some global consumer goods. Ethical trade is a paradox of globalization, which could potentially help to reverse the downward spiral in labour conditions. But given the feminization of the labour force, an important aspect will be the extent to which it can address the employment needs of both female and male workers.

From a gender perspective, globalization has had particularly significant effects. Women have tended to be more concentrated than men in marginalized 'flexible' forms of employment, where labour standards are poor. The gender division of labour within the household has usually not adapted to the changing employment position of women, and they continue to carry the majority of community, domestic and childcare responsibilities in addition to their paid work. Globalization has clearly impacted on to the lives of both men and women, but for the latter it has often meant an increase in the overall burden of work they carry. Despite this, the increased opportunity for paid employment outside the home has also had empowering consequences. Many women have been drawn into paid employment for the first time, increasing their independence and potential bargaining power within the household. Going out to work can also increase the chance for social interaction and potential for collective organization. While at one level, women workers are often marginalized, both in their forms of employment and ability to participate in traditional (male) labour organization, at another level new opportunities are being opened up for them.

Ethical trade could provide new means of addressing the problems of workers in global export industries and create a space for the voices of more marginalized workers to be heard. The term 'ethical trade' normally relates to codes of conduct being adopted by some large northern companies to ensure that producers along their supply chains in developing countries adhere to core labour standards. There is an issue as to whether ethical trade should cover environmental and broader aspects of corporate social responsibility, but to date it has focused on employment conditions alone (Blowfield, 1999). Many individual companies are adopting codes of conduct independently, but in the UK and USA there are also initiatives for company collaboration with NGOs and trade unions to develop a joint approach. The main sectors where ethical trade is gaining a hold involve the retail of clothing, footwear, food and other domestic goods. Given that a significant proportion of women are employed in these sectors, these codes could have important gender implications. But much female employment is 'flexible', casual or temporary work, and there are important questions as to whether codes of conduct initiated in the North can genuinely address the employment needs of these more marginalized workers in the South.

This chapter considers the gender dimension of ethical trade and its implications for flexible female labour. It draws on research carried out on gender and horticulture in South Africa and Chile to provide examples of the issues raised in the application of ethical trade. It examines how ethical trade has arisen in the context of globalization, and whether codes of conduct could address the practical and strategic gender interests of more marginalized workers in export industries. It also considers whether ethical trade could help to open up new spaces for collective organization among workers, which embrace the needs of women, and which could be effective in the context of globalization. It concludes that ethical trade does create new opportunities for flexible workers, but there are clear constraints on its ability to address gendered employment needs, and there are likely to be significant local variations in the extent to which women workers are able to access potential gains from ethical trade.

Female employment and globalization

The effect of globalization on employment has been marked, especially for female workers. The most important effect has been the increase in 'flexible' labour. This term usually relates to work that is temporary, part-time, on short-term contracts, homework or self-employment (Hakim, 1987). In all these cases, the worker does not have a permanent contract or enjoy the security or benefits of permanent employment. Women in particular have been drawn into this type of work, both within domestic and informal sector production, but especially within the growing export sectors associated with globalization. As a consequence, female participation in the labour force in many developed and developing countries has increased significantly during the past two decades (Standing, 1999).

A number of factors have been central to changes in the patterns of employment associated with economic liberalization often imposed on to developing countries through structural adjustment programmes. A central element has been the deregulation of labour markets. Many governments have abolished regulations covering the rights of labour and terms and conditions of employment, where they existed, or the lack of enforcement of legislation has rendered it meaningless. Another factor has been the employment effect of trade liberalization and the focus on promoting export production. The lifting of trade barriers has led to a fall in previously protected domestic production and its associated employment (often with a high male concentration). In its place domestic informal sector production has expanded – a sector where there has always been a high female participation, insecure work with little observation of labour regulation.

At the same time, the expansion of export production based on the 'comparative advantage' of developing countries has helped to generate new forms of employment. This has happened in industry, through subcontracting and outsourcing by large companies and multinationals to smaller local producers in the production of a range of goods, including textiles, clothing and electronics. It has also happened in agriculture, with the expansion of cash crops, and especially NTAEs, which we shall examine later. In much of this export production, given the increased level of global competition facing developing countries, there has been a strong pressure to reduce labour costs. The employment of 'flexible' labour has played an important part in this. It allows employment to be confined to limited periods of time determined by the labour demands of production and reduces the non-wage costs of employment, such as social insurance (Standing, 1989). The feminization of this type of labour has further allowed employers to pay lower wages where pay discrimination is still prevalent, with less resistance to poor conditions of employment by women workers who do not have a tradition of union organization. This cheap flexible labour force has formed part of the 'comparative advantage' of many developing countries in the global economy.

The competitive pressure to reduce employment costs has contributed to a 'downward spiral' in labour conditions in many developing countries (Sengenberger and Campbell, 1994). Low pay, long hours, unsafe and unhygienic working environment, lack of social protection and prohibiting labour organizations have come to mark the working lives of many employed in export production. In some countries, the use of child labour is not uncommon. Women in particular can face problems of discrimination, sexual harassment and invasive personal intrusion by employers. Poor labour standards are reinforced in the case of flexible workers, where legal protection is at its weakest. Insecurity of work and lack of organization among this group makes them the most vulnerable to abuse of their employment rights and subjugation to inferior working conditions. Given high female concentration relative to male among flexible labour, women in particular tend to suffer these types of employment problems.

Globalization has led to changes in the gender patterns of employment and increased feminization of the workforce, but the gender division of labour within the household has often not adapted to the incorporation of women into paid work. Most women continue to take primary responsibility for reproductive childcare and domestic work in addition to their paid employment. The fact that this is 'flexible' employment in some cases perpetuates the myth that women work for 'pin money', even in situations where they are primary income earners. With the reduction in state social provision under structural adjustment and economic liberalization, many women have also taken on increased responsibility for care of family members and community organization. As a consequence, globalization has reinforced the 'triple burden' of women (Elson, 1991). But some writers have also noted that despite these pressures, the increase in paid employment can also have empowering effects for women (Kabeer, 1994a). Their independence is enhanced as they now earn their own income and their negotiating position within the household can be improved. Paid employment also allows women to have greater social interaction outside the home. Although they do not have a tradition of union organization, working women can find new forms of organization and resistance (Rowbotham and Mitter, 1994). Globalization has thus had contradictory effects on women. They tend to be drawn into flexible employment where labour conditions are poorest, and they suffer the triple burden of paid, domestic and community work; yet there can also be empowering consequences, and globalization can thus throw up new opportunities for women workers (Afshar and Barrientos, 1999).

Many case studies of flexible labour and new forms of female employment can be found in manufacturing, particularly in EPZs. There is a concentration of female employment in parts of light industry, especially electronics, textiles and clothing, where women are often employed for their perceived 'nimble fingers' (Elson and Pearson, 1981; Kabeer, 1994b; Ward, 1990). Another area that is less well studied is the employment of women in what has been termed 'non-traditional agriculture', mainly the production for global export of high-value fresh horticultural products such as fruit, exotic vegetables and flowers. This is an area where globalization has clearly affected both employment and consumption. A decade ago, most people could afford to buy fresh produce and flowers only when they were in season locally, or on special occasions. As a result of advances in technology, transport, production and global supply arrangements, this produce is now in abundance on our supermarket shelves all year round at prices accessible to a larger proportion of households. The produce itself is homogeneous in terms of product specification (the varieties, size, shape and colour are continually the same), but it is sourced from around the world in different locations as the seasons change from one country to another.

Data on employment in this sector are unreliable, as much of it is seasonal or temporary work. Estimates indicate, however, that the percentage of female employment is high in many countries. For example, in Colombia, 80 per cent of workers in flower export production are women; in Ecuador, 69 per cent of NTAE employment is female; in Chile, 52 per cent of temporary fruit employment is female; and in South Africa, 53 per cent of all fruit employment is female (Barrientos *et al.*, 1999a; Kritzinger and Vorster, 1996; Thrupp, 1995). The high level of temporary employment in this type of production is partly dictated by the seasonal nature of the work. But in many countries there is a clear gender pattern of employment, with men being more concentrated into permanent jobs, and women into temporary work. This latter tends to be the most precarious employment, with no guarantee of work from season to season.[1] The types of problem faced by seasonal workers include low pay, variable pay rates, lack of employment contracts, long hours, discrimination, no unionization, lack of social insurance and poor working conditions (Barrientos *et al.*, 1999a,b). Many 'flexible' workers experience these problems but, in addition, workers in horticulture often suffer exposure to agrochemicals, which can affect their health and that of their children. Female employment is often most concentrated in packing sheds and greenhouses, where ventilation is poor and concentration of chemicals is higher (Thrupp, 1995).

Despite these problems, in some areas agribusiness has allowed rural women to take up paid employment, often for the first time. It allows them to earn an income in their own right and provide their own financial contribution to the household, over which they have control. Employment provides new opportunities for socialization with other workers and greater independence. As one fruit worker in Chile put it, 'We have always worked, now we are being paid for it'. Where this employment is seasonal, changes to women's position are only partial and they return to their primary role in the household the rest of the year. But despite the additional burdens paid work brings, research in Chile indicates that many women welcome it and gain a sense of empowerment from it (Barrientos *et al.*, 1999a).

Ethical trade and globalization

Horticulture is one example of a sector where globalization has stimulated an increase in flexible female labour and conditions of employment are poor. Many developing countries now compete on the basis of a cheap 'feminized' flexible labour force as part of their 'comparative advantage' in global export markets, contributing to a downward pressure on labour standards. A paradox of globalization, however, is that more recently there has been a trend towards 'ethical trade'. Ethical trade involves the voluntary application by large Northern companies of codes of conduct along their supply chains in developing countries, with the aim of ensuring minimum employment standards. These have been adopted by a number of leading brand name companies in North America and Europe, but are predominant in the areas of clothing, footwear, food and household goods. In all these sectors, there is a relatively high level of female employment and therefore there are important gender implications for codes of conduct.

The UK has been at the forefront in the development of ethical trade. In 1998, a number of companies joined together with NGOs and trade unions to form the Ethical Trading Initiative (ETI) with the support of the DFID. The main supermarkets and a number of leading clothes retailers are among those that have played an important role in advancing this initiative.[2] The aim of the ETI is to adopt a common approach to codes of conduct, in partnership with different stakeholders, and to avoid the problem of companies adopting a proliferation of diverse company codes, often for the same suppliers. The ETI formulated a baseline code of conduct, which all member companies aim to adopt as a minimum standard, although this does not preclude them from also applying an individual company code (Ferguson, 1998). The ETI baseline code is based on ILO core conventions, and covers the following:

○ freedom of association and collective bargaining
○ equal pay
○ no discrimination
○ work freely chosen
○ no child labour
○ living wage.

Suppliers are also expected to adhere to their own national law covering employment, or the baseline code, whichever provides a higher level of coverage (ETI, 1998). In principle, relevant suppliers are not expected to comply immediately with a code of conduct, but to work towards its implementation over an agreed period of time. The ETI set up three pilot projects in 1998, combining companies, NGOs and unions in an assessment of how procedures for the monitoring and verification of codes of conduct could best be developed. These pilots were in South Africa (wine), Zimbabwe (horticulture) and China (clothes), with further pilots planned from 1999. The process of implementing ethical trade is therefore still at a relatively early stage, but is likely to evolve over the next few years (ETI, 1999).

Ethical trade could, if it is effective, help to reverse (or at least limit) the downward spiral in labour conditions that have been so prevalent under globlization. The reasons behind the emergence of ethical trade are complex, but they are intimately linked with the process of globalization itself. An important aspect has been increasing NGO and consumer pressure on many Northern companies. Consumer consciousness has increased over recent years, initially in relation to environmental and more recently social conditions of production. NGOs in the North and South have become more coordinated through the use of the Internet and e-mail, and they have been able to focus consumer concern on these issues through their advocacy and campaign work. Globalization has also changed the nature of the companies themselves, and the way in which they operate their global sourcing policies, making them more vulnerable to scrutiny and pressure by NGOs. Large companies no longer source their goods in anonymous wholesale markets, but have increased the vertical integration of their global supply chains to control the quality and branding of the goods they sell. Integrated supply chains and global communication flows also help NGOs to acquire information, often because workers themselves in developing counties put the brand label on to the goods they produce, and can pass information about their conditions to local organizations linked to global NGO networks. Large northern companies, especially those selling brand name final consumer goods, are thus increasingly vulnerable to the emergence of stories of adverse employment conditions in their supply chains. Adopting ethical sourcing policies helps companies to avoid the risk of adverse publicity campaigns and press reports that might damage their corporate reputation in a competitive global market place.

Ethical trade is therefore a paradox of globalization. On the one hand globalization has led to a downward pressure on employment costs and labour conditions, encouraging the widespread use of flexible labour, much of it female, to meet the demands of global export production. On the other hand, globalization has also stimulated tendencies that have combined in the form of ethical trade to counteract this downward pressure. As a result, codes of conduct are being introduced to suppliers in developing countries, but given the flexible nature of most employment in those locations, there are questions as to whether ethical trade can genuinely address the employment needs of women and men employed in those export firms.

Flexible female labour and ethical trade

For many companies the implementation of ethical trade along their supply chains is relatively new, and its longer-term effects will take time to materialize. However, it is possible to assess the potential gender implications of ethical trade and the effect they might have on more marginalized forms of flexible employment, which have become an essential element in much global export production. This section focuses specifically on this issue in the context of employment in horticultural exports. It draws on examples from research that I have undertaken on codes of conduct, gender and horticulture in South Africa, with Liz Orton and Sharon McClenaghan of Christian Aid, and earlier work related to the same theme in Chile.[3] Here we shall consider the broader gender implications of ethical trade at two levels. First, given the nature of flexible employment, what are the immediate practical effects of codes of conduct likely to be for women workers who constitute a core part of flexible labour? Second, what are the broader potential benefits and limitations of codes of conduct in addressing gendered employment relations, and creating new opportunities for women to address their strategic needs and interests?

Molyneux has drawn out the distinction between practical and strategic gender interests. Practical gender interests are 'given inductively and arise from the concrete conditions of women's positioning within the gender division of labor ... Practical interests are usually a response to an immediate perceived need, and they do not generally entail a strategic goal such as women's emancipation or gender equality' (Molyneux, 1985: 233). In contrast, strategic gender interests 'are derived in the first instance deductively, that is from the analysis of women's subordination and from the formulation of an alternative, more satisfactory set of arrangements to those which exist' (Molyneux, 1985: 232). This approach provides a framework to examine gender and ethical trade. We shall first consider the extent to which codes of conduct are likely to improve the existing employment conditions of women, given the type of employment they currently occupy. These are issues relating to the practical or more immediate effect of codes. However, the conditions of employment women encounter relative to men are also linked to the nature of their employment and underlying gender social relations. We shall then consider the extent to which codes might help address these longer-term employment relations, and hence address more strategic gender interests.

Practical gender interests

From the outset, there are clear boundaries to ethical trade. It is important to delineate these in order to assess what could be expected from codes of conduct at a practical level. Codes of conduct apply to the conditions of employment only during the period an employee is in work. They are voluntarily adopted by companies in the North to apply along their supply chains, and producers in the South receive them as a condition of supply, but formally have the option of withdrawing from that supply agreement. They do not apply to all export producers and they do not cover domestic producers. Clearly, therefore, ethical trade is limited in the extent of its coverage, and those limitations are reinforced in the case of flexible labour. Permanent workers, who in the case of horticulture are mainly male, working for a relevant export producer will be covered by codes all year round during the length of employment. Workers in insecure seasonal employment, who are mainly female in horticulture, are covered only for the period they are employed by a producer applying codes, and not covered while employed in any other part of the export or domestic sector. By the nature of their employment, therefore, codes will give more comprehensive cover to men as the majority of the permanent labour force than to women, who are the majority of the temporary labour force.

Codes of conduct have not been designed to specifically address gender issues except at a formal level. Most codes of conduct based on ILO conventions (for example the ETI baseline code) include clauses on equal pay and non-discrimination (ETI, 1998). But companies implementing codes do not see it as their responsibility to address gendered patterns of employment, only overt cases of discrimination and unequal pay. The problem in horticulture, as in many other sectors, is that discrimination and unequal pay are often based on embedded gender social relations. Within horticultural employment, the fact that women are more often employed as seasonal labourers and men as permanent workers reflects an underlying pattern of gender subordination. Yet this pattern of employment is often unquestioned by both men and women employees. Women who are dependent on insecure temporary work for survival are also likely to think twice before they challenge an employer on grounds of discrimination and risk losing access to future flexible work. In the specific context of South Africa, many women living on-farm work as temporary labourers as an implicit condition of the employment of their male partner or relatives and do not have employment in their own independent right. Codes do not challenge these types of employment patterns. Linked to this, pay in horticulture is also often unequal (especially if comparison is made between the annual income of a permanent compared to temporary worker). But there is often a clear gender division of labour within employment. Men are given the more arduous tasks and work in the fields, while women do lighter tasks and work in the pack houses, and methods of payment (day rates or piece rates) often vary between the different tasks. Challenging inequality and determining equal pay for work of equal value is again very difficult in these circumstances. Therefore, formal clauses in codes are unlikely to go far enough in reducing unequal pay and subtle forms of discrimination based on embedded gender patterns of employment.

Research in South African horticulture clearly showed that employment conditions are worse for temporary workers, where female employment is concentrated. Permanent workers were more likely to receive a contract of employment, have higher pay, be trained in relation to health and safety, and receive non-pecuniary benefits such as housing, social insurance and pensions. Temporary workers, on the contrary, were less likely to be in receipt of these employment benefits. Where codes are able to improve working conditions and wipe out the worst excesses, they should benefit both permanent and temporary workers (Barrientos *et al.*, 1999b). Codes have a longer way to go in improving the conditions of temporary workers than of permanent workers, and unless they are extremely effective, or employers fully compliant, it is questionable whether the former will be brought up to the level of the latter.

The effectiveness of codes will depend largely on the monitoring and verification systems put in place to ensure their enforcement. Some companies implementing codes independently are using their own personnel to check that suppliers are implementing codes. These are usually buyers or technologists, who rarely have sufficient training or experience in employment regulation (especially in different countries) or gender issues of employment. They are outsiders, with a close relation to management, and are likely to find it difficult to relate to workers, who often have a different language and cultural background. Alternatively, some companies are using independent auditors to verify labour standards for them, such as those using the SA 8000 Standard developed by the Council on Economic Priorities. Professional auditors have better training and specialist knowledge, and often work with local labour organizations as part of their verification procedures. But they still have the handicap of being seen to represent management, even where they consult with local unions and NGOs. Spot checks are unlikely to pick up underlying problems associated with poor employment conditions, for example more subtle forms of embedded discrimination. Monitoring and verification of codes done by companies, or professional auditing bodies that represent them, risk only superficially extending beyond the tip of the employment hierarchy, examining mainly the conditions of permanent (male) workers and less those of temporary or casual women workers.

The ETI is taking a more participatory approach to implementing codes of conduct. The ETI baseline code was elaborated in collaboration with NGOs and unions in the UK, and pilot studies are being undertaken to examine different ways in which local stakeholders can be involved in monitoring and verification procedures in the South. These pilot studies are at an early stage, and clearly the context within different countries can vary quite markedly. However, this opens up the possibility of participation by labour and community organizations in the process, which are able to represent the interests of both female and male workers. Where their own labour organizations are involved, workers are likely to have more confidence and be less wary of the process. But there are still limitations, particularly in the representation of flexible workers and women. Agricultural workers in particular (both permanent and temporary) tend to have very low levels of unionization.[4] Where there is unionization, this often does not incorporate temporary workers, but mainly only permanent workers. Many local NGOs and trade unions often reflect traditional gender bias and are dominated by men, so their ability to reflect the interests of women are limited. While a participatory approach is to be welcomed, a risk remains that the interests of permanent workers will be more readily represented than those of flexible female workers.

Our study in South Africa illustrated the problems, but also potential advantages, of this approach to ethical trade. Within the paternalist traditions of agriculture, reinforced under the system of apartheid, the word of the farmer ruled within his domain, and workers had little or no recourse to any outside authority. Formally this situation has changed with the introduction since 1993 of new legislation covering farm workers, including the right to unionization. But enforcement mechanisms are very weak. Workers living on farms are isolated and difficult to organize, and embedded paternalist traditions persist, in which the rights of workers have little resonance, especially women seasonal workers who are subordinate within the farm hierarchy. In focus group interviews, many workers expressed a lack of belief that unions could benefit them, especially women who carried the dual burden of seasonal on-farm work and household responsibilities. A number of rural NGOs exist that support farmworkers, a few with a specific focus on women's needs, but they tend to be small and under-resourced. In reality, therefore, on many farms the authority of the farmer remains unchallenged and employment conditions poor. Ethical trade could help to alter this situation. Many growers supply UK supermarkets that are implementing codes of conduct, as they are an important market for them. These growers now have a commercial incentive to ensure minimum employment standards. Where unions and rural NGOs exist, they will have recourse to external commercial pressure as a means of ensuring workers' rights, especially if they have an input into the monitoring and verification of codes. Potentially, also, this may improve the benefits of organization to workers, including women if their needs are addressed, and enhance their representation within the process.

Despite the limitations to ethical trade, codes of conduct constitute a potentially progressive step that should be welcomed. If little more, they are a challenge to the prevailing culture, so that employers are no longer encouraged to compete solely on the basis of low labour costs and poor labour conditions. As such, codes should help to improve the most basic conditions of employment for all workers covered, including those in flexible employment, and provide a limit to the downward spiral in labour conditions, which are detrimental to workers. Ethical trade also enhances the potential for independent organization among workers, and if this is developed with a sensitivity to gender, it could also facilitate the organization of more marginalized women workers.

Strategic gender interests

Whether or not ethical trade can help to provide longer-term benefits for flexible labour and help to address underlying issues relating to gendered employment relations can be considered only at a more speculative level at this stage. Just as globalization is a contradictory process which has thrown up the paradox of ethical trade, so the gender implications of codes are likely to be complex, leading to unforeseen outcomes. From the above, we have already seen that codes are limited in their coverage. At the same time, ethical trade helps to open up new possibilities for organization among more marginalized workers, which has not existed before. Ethical trade could as a result contribute to a broader process of change under globalization, the outcome of which is yet to become clear.

Just as codes of conduct have not been designed to address gendered employment conditions, so they have also not been designed to alter or challenge gendered patterns of employment or underlying social relations. Codes are not intended to impact on the use of temporary labour and do not challenge flexible labour as a central component of the employment strategy of many export producers.[5] Nor are codes in any way designed to affect the gender division of labour or job segregation within employment. The concentration of women into flexible forms of employment, and their allocation to certain types of jobs, is unlikely to change as a result of codes of conduct per se. As we have seen above, research in South Africa has indicated that conditions are linked to the underlying gendered pattern of employment, and flexible labour tends to endure poorer conditions. In so far as the underlying pattern of employment persists, codes are inherently limited in their longer-term ability to address the fundamental employment needs of flexible female workers. It is likely their work will continue to be insecure, they will continue to have lower pay, they will continue to receive less training, and they will continue to receive fewer non-pecuniary and social benefits. Many women workers in flexible employment will continue to be in a disadvantaged position relative to more secure permanent workers.

Ethical trade also addresses only issues related to paid employment in its narrowest sense. It assumes a strict division between productive and unproductive work, and has no bearing on the latter. Unlike many men, women who enter paid work normally continue to bear the main burden of childcare and domestic responsibility. They are likely to be the primary carers within the household and will often have additional community responsibilities that contribute to household survival. For women trying to juggle these multiple roles with paid employment, there is no clear division between paid and unpaid work. No company code to my knowledge addresses these problems. Codes of conduct do not include provision of suitable childcare facilities or paid leave in the case of family sickness, and at best enforce only minimum statutory requirements on maternity leave. The ETI baseline code does include a clause on the provision of adequate living conditions where housing is provided as part of employment, but beyond that, employers are not expected to make other social or community provision to their employees.

Hence codes of conduct are inherently limited in the extent to which they can address the overall working needs (paid and unpaid) of women, and as such are unlikely to affect more strategic gender interests.

Despite these limitations, ethical trade does open up new opportunities for women that could help them to address their more fundamental needs. This is particularly so if the participatory approach to the monitoring and verification of codes of conduct being piloted by the ETI becomes established. A problem with participation noted above is that many labour organizations are traditionally weak in their representation of flexible, non-permanent workers, and women in particular. If ethical trade facilitates participation of local NGOs and community organizations in the process of monitoring and verification, this could stimulate the representation of women's interests through renovation of existing labour organizations or through new forms of organization. At one level, globalization and expansion of flexible labour has undermined the ability of labour to organize through traditional mechanisms of trade union bargaining. But at another level it has opened up opportunities for flexible workers, and especially women, to develop a new space through which they can represent their interests and needs. The extent to which this happens will depend partly on how ethical trade itself evolves. In this context, flexible labour is always at a disadvantage in relation to the more powerful commercial interests of employers in influencing the process. But it also depends on the extent to which women and local organizations are able to capture the opportunities that are opened up and make maximum use of the process of change to their benefit. This is likely to be different from location to location and from country to country, given the diversity of local circumstances. But one of the advantages of globalization is that local organizations are now able to integrate more easily into global networks of NGOs also involved in the process. They are able to gain support in their activities from Northern NGOs, which in turn are able to put pressure on Northern companies implementing ethical trade (for whom the risk of adverse publicity remains), and who have the ultimate corporate power to enforce codes of conduct on their suppliers.

As part of a process of globalization, therefore, ethical trade does open up opportunities that have not existed previously. In and of themselves, codes of conduct are clearly limited in the extent to which they can address practical and especially strategic gender interests of flexible labour drawn into the global export sector. But ethical trade has not come about in isolation. It is an integral part of a wider process of change under globalization that is both complex and contradictory. Within that, ethical trade does open new doors and create a new space for representing the interests of women workers, who in many cases have been drawn into the global export sector for the first time. Ethical trade on its own will not lead to fundamental change for women, but in conjunction with other aspects of social and political transformation under globalization, it has the potential to create new opportunities. How and the extent to which women are able to capture and build on those opportunities will depend on many factors. But if nothing else, ethical trade has helped to create a shift in culture. Poor employment conditions in exports, including those of flexible workers, need to be addressed, and the interests of those workers can no longer be automatically marginalized or ignored. This is a progressive shift providing a new momentum, which potentially could be harnessed in the interests of working women.

Conclusion

Twenty years ago it would have been hard to imagine that women in developing countries would be drawn into paid employment in export industries to the extent they have. Ten years ago it would have been hard to imagine that ethical trade would come to the fore and Northern companies would start insisting that those workers were ensured at least minimum employment conditions. Globalization has led to significant changes over the past two decades, especially for women who have been drawn into the process. Many of the effects of globalization have been negative: increased poverty, even with paid employment, the triple burden, increased insecurity to name a few. But there have also been unintended consequences and benefits for women, particularly increased independence, social interaction, and an ability to network and organize in ways that were not possible before.

Globalization, as we have seen, is a complex and contradictory process, and ethical trade is a paradox of globalization reflecting the contradictions. Two interconnected factors have been central to the emergence of ethical trade. While globalization has led to freer markets and freer trade, in reality changing commercial relations have meant that large Northern companies now have greater integration and control along their supply chains, enabling them to determine the production conditions of their suppliers. Integrated supply chains, however, leave these Northern companies more vulnerable to adverse publicity regarding employment conditions among their suppliers. This risk has been enforced by the expanding role of NGOs, filling the vacuum left by the reduction in government activity. NGOs have been able to harness global communications to build information networks and channel publicity in support of their campaigns. Northern companies seeking to reduce their vulnerability have independently adopted codes of conduct to ensure that minimum employment standards operate along their supply chains. In the case of the UK, ETI companies have sought to further reduce their vulnerability by coming together with NGOs, unions and other civil society organizations to develop codes on the basis of broader stakeholder participation. Ethical trade is therefore a product of globalization and freer markets, which paradoxically introduces a new element of regulation over labour standards through commercial and non-government mechanisms rather than more traditional government regulation.

Labour market deregulation and increased competition under globalization have both contributed to an increased use of 'flexible' labour and a downward spiral in labour standards over recent decades. This has meant that workers drawn into export employment have often endured insecurity of work, low pay and poor employment conditions. Where labour organization has been allowed, intimidation and fear of losing work have often prevented participation. Labour has been weak in the global export sectors, with flexible workers and women often at the greatest disadvantage. Developing countries in particular have used cheap labour costs as part of their 'comparative advantage' in export markets. Ethical trade represents a reversal of the downward spiral, it provides a floor to the continued worsening of employment conditions as central to global competition, at least among the suppliers to whom it applies. For workers in the relevant firms, their conditions are unlikely to deteriorate, and could possibly now improve.

A weakness of ethical trade, however, is that it is more likely to improve the working conditions of permanent workers than those of flexible workers who form an increasingly important component of export employment, and where there is a high concentration of women. This weakness stems from the limitations of codes of conduct themselves, and the fact that they address only the more transparent employment issues during the period a worker is in work. Using examples from horticultural employment – a relatively new area of expanding export production – we have seen that employment conditions are often worse for flexible or temporary workers. Workers in this group are also less likely to raise their labour concerns and are least organized to do so, given the insecurity of their employment. There is a risk, therefore, that ethical trade will improve conditions more readily among the labour hierarchy of permanent workers, predominantly male, but that it will less easily improve the conditions of flexible workers, where there is a higher concentration of women. Despite this, it is likely that codes of conduct will eradicate the worst excesses of labour abuse, and it does provide an opportunity to improve the general conditions of employment. Hence it has the potential to address the practical gender needs of flexible workers.

In terms of addressing underlying gendered employment relations, ethical trade is clearly limited. It is not the aim of codes of conduct to alter the division of labour within employment, and this division is usually highly gendered. The mere fact that women are concentrated in the flexible labour force reflects this. Many of the employment problems of women stem from the nature of their employment, and so long as their work remains insecure or temporary, it will continue to be difficult to improve their conditions. Further, the fact that codes of conduct are narrowly restricted to the conditions of paid employment and do not extend to childcare, social or community provision, means that the problems women have of combining paid employment with other working roles are also not addressed. On its own, therefore, ethical trade is likely to have little impact on the strategic gender needs of flexible workers, or to alter the underlying gender relations that frame the nature of their employment.

Ethical trade does, however, potentially create new opportunities for workers, and especially flexible labour, which has traditionally been marginalized. These opportunities are clearer in the case of the UK ETI, which has taken a participatory approach to the monitoring and verification of codes of conduct. If local NGOs and unions are genuinely incorporated into this process, it could open up the possibility for new forms of participation and organization among flexible workers at a local level. This could allow women to express their interests and needs through mechanisms that have not been available to them before. On its own, local community organization is often weak in the face of the commercial power of employers. But if local NGOs involved in ethical trade can link up to global networks and Northern NGOs, which are themselves an important force behind ethical trade, then they could exert pressure on employers through the supply chain and Northern companies, which originally introduced the code of conduct. The extent to which this happens will depend both on how monitoring and verification evolves, and whether women at a local level are able to organize and capture the opportunity open to them. This in turn will depend on local circumstances, which is likely to be variable from place to place. But the potential opportunities thrown up by ethical trade should not be overlooked.

Ethical trade is part of a complex process of globalization which, despite its negative effects, has also led to changes which might over time help to improve the lives of women workers. Whatever our views of globalization, the reality is that large numbers of women and men in developing countries are dependent today on employment in the global export sector, and there is little alternative for them. The conditions of employment are often poor, and in some circumstances abhorrent. Ethical trade provides the possibility of helping to improve their conditions of work and hence the quality of their daily lives. As such it should be welcomed as a beneficial step. But ethical trade cannot be viewed in isolation. It is part of a much broader process of social, political and economic change, the outcome of which we cannot predict. But where positive opportunities do arise, such as in the case of ethical trade, they should be developed and harnessed as best as possible in the interests of all workers employed in global export production.

10 Globalization and environmental change in Madagascar: the opportunities and challenges faced by Rio Tinto

PHILIP MULLIGAN

Introduction

THIS CHAPTER DEALS with the enormity of the relationship between globalization and environmental change by focussing in on a specific situation. It looks at the example of Rio Tinto's[1] proposed $400 million titanium dioxide[2] mining project in southeast Madagascar, which both epitomizes and illustrates the nature of the contemporary global political economy, and also neatly captures some of the dilemmas faced by developing countries with regard to environmental change.

The more prominent aspects of globalization are briefly highlighted to illustrate the links between the proposed mining venture and the wider global political economy. Giddens' early attempt at characterizing the condition of late modernity is worth noting. For example, he defines globalization as 'the intensification of worldwide social relations which link distant localities in such a way that local happenings are shaped by events occurring many miles away and vice versa' (Giddens, 1990: 64). A common theme among analysts has been the way revolutionary advances in transportation, communications and information technology have resulted in 'space-shrinking' (Dicken, 1992: 103), a phenomenon Robertson refers to as 'the compression of the world' (Robertson, 1992: 8).While it is axiomatic that globalization refers to a *global* process and condition, it has been observed by McGrew that globalization is highly uneven and highly differentiated in its impacts around the globe (McGrew *et al.*, 1992: 23). The differential impacts of globalization are clearly brought out through the case study, but to emphasize the point further, it is worth briefly illustrating the discrepancies with another example. If one thinks of environmental change, specifically 'global warming', it is ironic that dramatic increases in carbon emissions have been brought about by the increasingly globalized nature of economic activity, yet the very recognition of climate change as a global environmental problem, and the international agreements necessary to deal with it, have also been facilitated by processes of political globalization. Likewise, many of the economic 'benefits' that come with the use of fossil fuel are generally separated in time and place from the environmental cost of climate change. And when these costs become inescapable, it is, to use Bauman's evocative imagery, the 'tourists' as opposed to the 'vagabonds' who are able to meet the costs (Bauman, 1998). Globalization, then, can be said to increase the scope and intensity of global processes (McGrew *et al.*, 1992: 23) while dislocating costs and benefits both within and between communities. Nowhere is this encapsulated more explicitly than in the existence and operation of modern TNCs. Although globalization is not reducible to the activity of TNCs, the increased scope and intensity of the operations of TNCs has come to epitomize economic globalization for many writers (for example Lang and Hines, 1993; Hildyard *et al.*, 1996; Raghavan, 1996). The ability of TNCs to set and control conditions throughout the production chain has led Dicken to argue they are 'the most important single force creating global shifts in economic activity' (Dicken, 1992: 7–8), and there is growing concern over the increasingly unregulated power of TNCs. The sheer size of TNCs gives them enormous financial muscle without the constraint of democratic channels of accountability (see Korten, 1995). It has been estimated that, in 1988, there were 20 000 TNCs with total assets worth over $4 trillion (Dunning, 1993: 14) and that they now control up to 70 per cent of world trade (World Bank figures quoted in Lang and Hines, 1993: 34). In the early 1990s, there were only 60 countries with GNPs in excess of $10 billion, whereas there were more than twice that number of TNCs with annual sales greater than $10 billion (Sklair, 1994: 166–7). It is not just the number and size of TNCs that has raised concerns, however, but also their global reach. The global ascendancy of neo-liberal ideology has facilitated economic globalization by legitimizing the market deregulation, promoted through institutions such as the WTO. Not only has economic globalization been given the fillip of such structures, but the demise of institutions monitoring and regulating TNCs, such as the United Nations Centre on Transnational Corporations (UNCTC), has removed further constraints on investment (Greer and Bruno, 1996: 23). Critically, corporate lobby groups were successful in removing examination of the environmental impact of TNCs from the UNCED process in Rio (Hildyard, 1993: 28–9; Chatterjee and Finger, 1994). It is therefore claimed that TNCs are frequently more powerful than the states in which they operate (Waters, 1995: 33). '[G]iven the increasing economic power of these corporations and their ability to slip between the network of the sovereignty of individual states, there will continue to be concerns about their activities' (Luard, 1990: 151). The case study presented in this chapter is an attempt to examine how some of these concerns, particularly the link between TNCs and environmental change, is being played out in Madagascar.

Giddens' idea that globalization involves the linking of 'distant localities in such a way that local happenings are shaped by events occurring many miles away and vice versa' (Giddens, 1990: 64), is highly pertinent for an understanding of the impact TNCs are having in developing countries. The local economy of the proposed mining site in Madagascar, the people that live there and the biodiversity of the region are all now inextricably linked to the wider world. For example, investment decisions being made at board meetings in Canada, campaign rallies held by Friends of the Earth in London, shareholder actions in Australia, government designation of protected status to areas of similar mineral deposits in South Africa, the tailoring of consumer tastes for 'white' goods by advertising agencies in New York, the funding criteria being laid down by the World Bank in Washington and conservation priorities of WWF in Switzerland, all impact on Madagascar, just as all of these things are affected by what goes on in the region.

NGOs are increasingly emerging as significant actors in moderating the behaviour and impacts of TNCs. It can be argued that the role of NGOs in this process is more important now than it has ever been. However, NGOs are not just responding to new business practices stemming from globalization – they themselves have been as much affected by 'the intensification of worldwide social relations' (Giddens, 1990: 64). Global interconnections have allowed NGOs to expand their number, size and geographical coverage (Willetts, 1998: 207; Fabig and Boele, 1999). The growth of international communications and information technology has facilitated worldwide networking and alliances, which increasingly transcend geographical boundaries, broadening the power and influence of NGOs (Watts, 1998: 24). There are three crucial ways in which NGOs influence the activities of TNCs. First, through lobbying and encouraging others to lobby, they have brought pressure to bear on TNCs. Second, they have helped set and enforce regulations and standards which, at the risk of financial loss, TNCs are keen to aspire to. For example, WWF has worked with industry to develop the Forest Stewardship Council, which provides environmental labelling for timber. The ISO has, at the same time, broadened the scope of its certification, moving from a concern over product standards to process, management, environmental and now even social standards (Finger and Tamiotti, 1999). Third, NGOs have helped to generate consumer concern to the extent that it is now in a company's long-term competitive interests to act responsibly. TNCs are increasingly attempting to gain greater environmental kudos than their competitors by having their activities associated with responsible practice (Beloe, 1999).

The intensifying power of TNCs and increasing role of NGOs may have been facilitated by the compression of space and time, but it has been the key role of the global and electronic media that have helped place environmental and social issues firmly on the international political agenda. Modern communications now allow 'global events' to occur simultaneously anywhere in the world (Scholte 1996, 45-6), be this a 'Live Aid' concert to raise funds for drought-stricken African farmers or the harrowing images of East Asia's rainforests burning. As concerned publics seek 'causes' for these environmental disasters, TNCs feel they are increasingly operating in a 'global goldfish bowl' (Watts, 1998: 24) in which their operations in specific localities are being judged by a worldwide audience. All of this has meant that TNCs that operate in the global market 'need more and more to take account of opinions which are formed internationally' (Mitchell, 1998: 1). TNCs, therefore, are exhibiting their green credentials simultaneously to a broad audience internationally, nationally and locally. This is clearly shown in the case of Rio Tinto in Madagascar, where the world's largest mining company is seeking to shake off the negative publicity from past projects in an attempt to turn around its poor environmental reputation and become a world leader in corporate responsibility.

Businesses are starting to recognize that they need to respond to (or at least be seen to respond to) the 'triple bottom line' (Elkington, 1998) of not only meeting existing profit margins, but also environmental and social concerns. One key aspect of this ethical approach to business is the need to increasingly involve and engage with indigenous people when a company's activities change local environments. Even with the increasingly unregulated powers of TNCs noted above, this element is likely to become ever more important as NGOs and pressure groups expand the social norms of what is tolerable behaviour and help set higher moral standards for business practice.

For a range of reasons TNCs are now keen to present themselves as socially and environmentally responsible to a variety of actors at the international level. First, there are actual and potential investors, including shareholders, shareholding institutions, and multilateral and bilateral donor agencies. Second, it is often valuable to have the support for a project of intergovernmental organizations such as agencies of the UN. Third, NGOs with enormous influence within the global political arena are targeted for their support. Fourth, it is important for TNCs to present themselves and their products favourably to consumers. The last main actor at the international level is the media. In recent years, high-level bursts of negative media coverage have necessitated diversions from the pursuit of short-term profit by several TNCs (Gray, 1998: 75), a situation most would rather avoid. These factors have combined to engage TNCs with other interested actors in complex interactions, both directly and indirectly, across the global political system.

In addition to this, at the national level, TNCs must also gain the acceptance of states. While most states are keen to demand high environmental and social standards within their borders, at least rhetorically, the reality of escalating debts can make the imperative of attracting investment greater than that of stipulating (or enforcing) social and environmental regulations. The state is thus 'becoming increasingly subordinate to imperatives of the global marketplace' (Cerny, 1996), in which TNCs are dominant players. Being attractive to investment by such companies often means exploiting a key comparative advantage for developing countries over their Northern competitors: lower environmental standards.

At the local level too, actors such as local government, NGOs and the media must be reached, as the increasingly interconnected nature of global systems allows the rapid transfer of local issues to national and international arenas, and vice versa. It is increasingly important, therefore, for TNCs to engage with, involve and gain the consent of local people affected by their activities. Previously it was possible for TNCs to focus more on gaining state consents and attracting international finance than working with local people. Now, however, the climate is changing and TNCs are finding it ever more important to be seen to be working with the local communities where they operate. They can no longer ignore local values and impose changes on communities (Willetts, 1998: 225).

Examining the interaction between TNCs and NGOs, then, not only gives an insight into one of the main ways in which the global political economy connects distant localities with local happenings, but also brings to the fore the 'development' dilemmas many developing countries face with regard to environmental change. In the case of southeast Madagascar, biodiversity loss as a result of indigenous forest clearance is taking place. It is not the national government that has the funds, experience or even motivation to deal with such environmental change, but outside actors like TNCs and NGOs. Yet leaving the management of environmental change to external agencies raises a possible dilemma for nation states: either having 'eco-colonial' policies imposed or accepting the terms and alternative costs associated with the 'development' offered by TNCs.

The case study – Rio Tinto in Madagascar

Much of the material in this chapter is drawn from fieldwork conducted during 1997–98 in and around the village of Evatra, which is at the centre of a proposed mining site by Rio Tinto.[3] Examination of Rio Tinto's current mining venture gives us a chance to try to distinguish the opportunities and challenges for the practice of environmental politics that the globalization process throws up. It enables an assessment to be made of the company's attempts to gain legitimization for their activities (the 'opportunities' globalization presents), while also providing the occasion to suggest areas that need more attention (the 'challenges' involved).

Rio Tinto's environmental and social record has received much criticism in the past (Moody, 1990, 1996; FoE, 1995; PARTiZANS quarterly). As the biggest and most global mining company in the world, Rio Tinto is regularly engaged in controversial projects. Past criticism when working in environmentally sensitive areas and lands occupied by indigenous peoples has led the company to adopt a new strategy for its Madagascar project. Whereas the company in the past has been associated with attempts at lowering standards, here it is voluntarily seeking to set its own standards of environmental and social responsibility at a very high level. Acknowledging that business will lead the way in such ethical standard-setting only as long as profit margins allow, the question here is how reconcilable are concerns about the environment and social development, with utilitarian interests in maintaining long-run business viability and attaining more immediate public relations goals.

Madagascar is one of the world's poorest countries, with an external debt of approximately \$3.0 billion in 2000 (World Development Indicators Database, April 2002). The proposed project to mine titanium dioxide would be worth \$400 million over 40 years. There are clear benefits from the project, particularly: regional economic development, infrastructural improvements (such as a new port, road building, electrification and water supply), employment and social development initiatives. However, there are also a number of potential drawbacks. All large 'development' projects are associated with environmental change.[4] Of most significance with this project will be the loss of large areas of complex and delicate littoral forest ecosystem (with endemic species), and its replacement, post-extraction, with plantation species. The mining company maintains that forest loss is occurring naturally due to the 'unsustainable' practices of local inhabitants. They argue that it is better to have the 'managed' vegetation change they are proposing, with the additional benefit of mining revenues and a thoroughly researched replanting programme, than the current situation.

As well as changes in vegetation cover, there will also be impacts on the local economy. Setting aside the finite nature of mineral extraction, which makes it an inherently unsustainable activity, existing local economic activities may be undermined and the economic multiplier of the project may not be as great as these activities (particularly tourism and seafood operations). There will be significant changes to land use in and around the project area, most notably for the resident villagers who currently utilize many natural resources in the vicinity. Sacred lands, including cemeteries (which are highly significant within the context of Malagasy ancestral veneration), are likely to be affected by the venture. Although Rio Tinto has entered a partnership arrangement with the Malagasy government, questions remain to be answered about the extent of local involvement and consent.

The opportunities

The stretching and deepening of global processes (McGrew *et al.*, 1992: 23) is providing three opportunities for Rio Tinto to contribute in a positive way to environmental politics in southeast Madagascar. First, rather than waiting to respond to criticism about their project, Rio Tinto has, from an early stage, publicly acknowledged the environmental and social changes that mining in the area is likely to cause. In conjunction with this, it has accepted that responsibility for dealing with these changes, to a large extent, lies with them and as such it is trying to find appropriate solutions. A number of social and environmental satellite projects have been proposed to mitigate the negative impacts of the mining. Instead of operating in a secretive or even hostile manner, it is currently pursuing a strategy of engagement and open dialogue with various stakeholders and potential opponents. This is quite different from Rio Tinto's historical practices:

> Whereas in 1981 one RTZ [now Rio Tinto] director said he would 'crush Survival International like a fly' if the tribal peoples' support organisation did not call off its campaign against the Cerro Colorado mine in Panama, today the company invites its detractors to lunch. When Friends of the Earth in 1995 vehemently condemned RTZ's plan to exploit mineral sands in rainforests in south-east Madagascar, the environmental organisation was invited by company chairman Derek Birkin 'to be part of the process of appraising our plans, at some stage in the future' (Moody, 1996: 50).

Second, the company has incurred great effort and expense in recruiting various 'experts' to work on the project. The roll call of renowned academics and recognized specialists involved with the extensive Environmental Impact Assessment and current social study (involving a public consultation exercise) is impressive, and helps explain how the company has so far spent over $30 million on the project's development. A research station has been set up, which is at the cutting edge of knowledge building about the region's complex biodiversity. And while the company has carefully recruited appropriate personnel, it still recognizes the need to bring in outside expertise as and when necessary.

Third, the company is working in partnership with the government. Although the company has strategic interests in gaining state support,[5] by working with the government, Rio Tinto is demonstrating its broader commitment to the country, as opposed to trying to maximize short-term profits without regard for the local environment. An operating company has been established to run the project, in which the government holds a 20 per cent share. Rio Tinto is also encouraging government efforts to implement a regional development plan for the southeast of the country where the mining project would take place. The company is keen to emphasize that the ultimate decision as to whether the project can go ahead or not rests with the government. It also stresses the independence and high standards of various governmental organizations with responsibility for vetting the progress of the proposed project at each stage.

There are two fundamental ways in which Rio Tinto's efforts to take up some of the opportunities presented by the project are positive. First, it is commendable that Rio Tinto is *attempting* to act in a responsible way with regard to the environmental impact of its activities. Its acknowledgement of certain environmental changes associated with the project means that at least attempts are being made to minimize the negative impacts of such development on the environment and local people. The company is already engaged in a number of social development projects and has plans for more should the project commence. Through these initiatives, the sustainability of local livelihood systems is being encouraged and there is recognition by the company that the needs of the poorest must be addressed.

Second, the company is committed to the use of what it believes are appropriate methods and best practice in generating research concerning the management of the environmental impacts of the project. Its approach is cautious and the company has been careful not to raise expectations irresponsibly. It has spent over ten years so far producing baseline data and conducting surveys and feasibility studies. As well as bringing in outside experts where necessary, the company is committed to employing local people at all levels. The company is also trying to operate in a more transparent manner, with the research material it has commissioned being made available within the public domain.

The challenges

The challenges that the Rio Tinto project highlights for achieving genuine advances in the socially and environmentally responsible investment fall into three categories.

(i) Greenwash

When a company with an ethical record like Rio Tinto's seems to have undergone such an about turn, one is tempted to question its motivation. However, it is difficult to prove motivation, and different branches or departments within the company may hold multiple or even contradictory motives simultaneously. It is also worth noting that for the local people affected by the project the question of motivation is not necessarily an important one. Actions offer some indication of the company's intentions, however, and although Rio Tinto appears to have spent a considerable sum on laudable undertakings, $30 million over the past 12 years is negligible compared to annual sales, which in 1997 alone were $7.7 billion (TIS, 1999).

Taking a broader picture, it is useful to judge TNCs not only by the efforts they are making on the projects they themselves put forward as examples of best practice, but also to look at a wider spectrum of their activities. The 'greening' of one project may, intentionally or otherwise, divert attention from other less acceptable practices. In the case of Rio Tinto, opencast mining continues in Irian Jaya, where local people have not been consulted or compensated and sacred sites have been destroyed (WDM, 1999); uranium mining proceeds at Kintyre in Australia; and in Bougainville, mining has destroyed the environment while indigenous rights have been ignored (Rowell, 1996: 275). Taking a wider company perspective allows a more balanced assessment as to whether a project like the one in Madagascar is a 'flagship', setting standards for other business ventures to meet, or a 'smokescreen' behind which less acceptable activities hide. If these less acceptable activities exist, they can seriously undermine the credibility of positive efforts being made to manage environmental change elsewhere.

One indication of the extent to which the enlightened thinking of the subsidiary operating in Madagascar has permeated the rest of the company, will be whether it sets up structures to transplant what it learns in Madagascar to its existing and forthcoming projects elsewhere.

(ii) Participation

Two factors are significant here. The first concerns the meaningfulness of the participation that Rio Tinto is promulgating. While it is to be welcomed that the corporate sector is adopting participatory approaches in assessing the changes its projects will bring, local villagers (in almost every case) are ill informed about most aspects of the Rio Tinto mining venture to such an extent as to question how meaningful participation with the company has been. While this exercise may be comprehensive, extensive and even expensive, if it fails to recognize that most villagers would have difficulty in comprehending the scale of the project or the extent and ways in which their lives and the local environment are likely to be altered, it is also of limited value in terms of effective participation. For local consent to the project to be truly legitimate, it must be gained from people with a full understanding of what they are consenting to. This is necessary to avoid claims of 'teleguided' participation where people 'do not feel they are being forced into doing something, but are actually being led to take actions which are inspired or directed by centres outside their control' (Rahnema, 1996: 116). However, the difficulty for all external actors (not just the mining company) in trying to gain meaningful consent to and understanding of that which is outside the world view of the villagers should be recognized.

The second factor in relation to participation concerns land rights. The company does not recognize traditional local land claims, but instead upholds the government's assertion that all land without legal title belongs to the state. It is hardly surprising that virtually no villagers are in possession of legal title to the land they use, nor do villages collectively hold legal title to their traditional commons. In not recognizing local ownership of ancestral lands, the mining company does not have to give the participation of local people as much importance as it does to the 'owners' of the land.

(iii) Subtle corporate strategy

The remaining challenges concern the more subtle mechanisms and techniques that are being utilized by the company in its attempt to gain legitimacy for its actions. First, through use of 'experts' and 'expert knowledge', the company is able to claim an intellectual monopoly over debates concerning the project. The company, by establishing certain forms of knowledge as valid, is able to marginalize in the debate those groups incapable of participating in these forms of discourse.

Second, by emphasizing the abundant nature of processed titanium dioxide in everyday products that most people (in the North) use (such as toothpaste, paper, plastic, paint, etc.), the company implicates consumers in the environmental and social costs of production. Attributing blame to consumers in this case is somewhat unfair, however, as people are generally unaware that they are using the product and are not given a choice of alternatives. They are also unaware, in most cases, of the social and environmental changes and costs associated with its production.

Third, company research has called into question the current sustainability of local livelihoods as population growth impacts on already increasing rates of forest destruction. Constructing local livelihoods as unsustainable helps to justify the case for the mine as an economic alternative for the region. What is problematic here is that these claims of local unsustainability are made by a company that has historically derived most of its money in environmentally unsustainable ways.

Finally, one should be aware of Rio Tinto's dominance in setting the agenda of the proposed project and governing its operation. There is a danger that the company will become implementer and assessor of the project. The whole process of environmental and social impact studies is designed to co-opt people into a process of approval. Outcomes are validated by a process whose terms are set by the company. If the process was not being driven by the company, then instead of the current focus on how the project can best be carried out, there may be more attention to asking if the project should be done at all. By widening the menu of choices, a more meaningful degree of consultation will have been achieved.

In a world where states are less willing or able to regulate TNCs, new forms of governance are expected of TNCs in conjunction with environmental NGOs (Newell, 2000). This leaves the question of who governs the governors as yet unanswered and can inevitably lead to local conflicts of interest when TNCs act as states within states or as de facto states.

Policy implications

A number of policy implications stem from the case study. While they are specific to the example in question, the broad themes may be transferable to other similar situations where large development projects are proposed by TNCs in environmentally sensitive areas.

1. In order to gain meaningful consent, the project's pros *and cons* should be discussed with the local people, along with the ways in which their environment is likely to change, in a way that is comprehensible to them. This may require some education as to what the project actually involves, what alternatives exist and how existing economic practices will probably be affected. Scope should be made for allowing members of the community to define for themselves what their priorities are in relation to the project.

2. Independent auditing and monitoring throughout the different stages of the venture is necessary. This could be done either by independent consultants or by the company in conjunction with those affected by the project, with appropriate NGO contributions. To maintain the credibility of the project and those involved with it, it needs to be made clear that when experts are consulted it is for knowledge and advice rather than validation. Giving consultants freedom to pursue and publish their enquiries and allowing them to retain copyright of material produced could help facilitate this. One possible strategy to help maintain the independence of monitors, advisors and researchers would be to pay for them from a 'blind fund' of monies given to a holding body, possibly in conjunction with other companies that have similar interests. Alternatively, 'blind funds' could be established with particular institutions, rather than companies funding specific people at institutions to carry out individual pieces of research.

3. The company is encouraged to offer some recognition of the collective land claims being made by indigenous groups, as expounded in the draft Declaration of the United Nations Working Group on Indigenous Peoples (UN, 1992). These land rights would include the rights to subsurface mineral deposits (see Donigi, 1994, on the legal case for this). This recognition could be in the form of a lease or profit share arrangement with the village, giving the villagers a stake in the mining project. It could be clearly stated and agreed by all sides what the project entails and what the villagers can expect. A limited 'get out clause' if the villagers became unhappy with the project would act as an incentive for the mining company to act responsibly. 'Strict civil liability agreements' may serve this purpose (Greer and Bruno, 1996: 254–6). These agreements would have to be sensitive to where the villagers' interests fit into the wider economic needs of the region. This would avoid the risk of one village being able to unreasonably hold up the economic development of the whole region.

4. On an ideological level, the success of TNCs can be attributed to the way in which they blur the distinction between their own private and national state interests (Lang and Hines, 1993: 33). In this light, the power of Rio Tinto to influence the formation of the regional development plan in their favour

must be recognized: 'RTZ, its subsidiaries and its partners maintain an extraordinary capacity to influence domestic power brokers in the regions where they operate' (Moody, 1996: 48). The independence of the regional plan must be maintained, including the assessment of the proposal and fair consideration of alternatives to the mining project. The lower levels of financial and cultural capital that proponents of alternative development plans may have need to be recognized and taken into consideration. Any plan for the region must be focused around the long-term interests of both the people and the environment of the area. The finite nature of the mineral deposits would need to be duly acknowledged in this. Strategies to deal with changes to the region that are likely to result from the establishment and conclusion of the project would thus be put in place.

5. In specific relation to upholding the interests of the poor, responsibility falls on both Rio Tinto and the NGO/development community. The mining company must continue to make efforts to include the poor in all aspects of the project, in meaningful and appropriate ways. As well as pursuing its mining interests, Rio Tinto can try to maintain concurrent indigenous livelihoods systems, supporting them where possible or necessary. The development community, including NGOs, may be encouraged to cautiously welcome the climate of conciliation and cooperation that it would appear Rio Tinto is trying to engender. By actively engaging with the company, and sharing knowledge and expertise, many of the challenges that the project presents could be addressed with more favourable results for the environment and the poorest members of society, than if previously entrenched positions of scepticism and hostility are returned to.

Conclusions

Before a judgement can fully be formed about the mining project in this case study, a number of factors should be borne in mind. These include the potential economic value of the project to the region and local community, a sense of what it is reasonable to expect companies to do and the repercussions of non-investment by Rio Tinto or any other mining company. It has to be remembered that TNCs are profit-seeking organizations and cannot be expected to adopt the same concerns as NGOs or the people affected by their development projects.

The case study is useful in indicating some of the wider implications that exist for the relationship between globalization and development by focussing on TNCs as the harbingers of change. As such, globalization can be seen as something of a 'self-fulfilling prophecy'. It is partially responsible for establishing conditions that necessitate globalized solutions. The mining project is seen by many as 'necessary' for addressing unemployment, rejuvenating derelict infrastructure, servicing international debt and other such conditions, which are themselves the result of what McGrew describes as the 'highly uneven and highly differentiated' impacts of globalization across different societies (McGrew *et al.*, 1992: 23). The case study also illustrates how globalization offers opportunities as well as costs. The economy of southeast Madagascar is very depressed and the mining project does represent an opportunity for much-needed poverty alleviation. And it is the nature of the global political economy, with its ideology of consumerism, its networks of communications, its systems of transportation, its technologies of production and its concentration of finance in vast TNCs that allows remote mineral deposits to be located and exploited. The fact that TNCs are also being kept in check by 'global and integrated responses by NGOs' to the increasing interconnection of social and environmental issues can also be seen as an opportunity that globalization facilitates.

Large-scale projects like the proposed mining venture are increasingly inevitable given the nature of the global political economy. As such, the development community should work *with* TNCs to try to reduce adverse impacts and get as many of their social and environmental concerns as possible on the agenda. In doing so, a 'better' outcome is hoped for than one where TNCs are left to their own devices, and although it is too early to judge, Rio Tinto's current efforts indicate that there is some potential for reform. This will not, however, appease critics who argue that big development projects like the proposed mining venture are fundamentally flawed and are unlikely to have positive outcomes for their host communities, especially the poorest in society, such as indigenous peoples and for the environment.

This case study illustrates that globalization is both a cause of poverty and a potential way of alleviating it. On the one hand, the actions of TNCs within the wider global political economy have contributed significantly to the dire economic situation Madagascar finds itself in, with all the associated pressures on the poor and the environment. On the other hand, it is mainly TNCs that have both the money for the large-scale development and the need to maintain their reputations, which makes them susceptible to calls for corporate responsibility. Most TNCs, however, have a long way to go before the potential they offer as agents of positive economic, social and environmental change is realized. Many still appear to be interested only in the economic 'bottom line' and where they are taking steps towards meeting broader concerns, it is generally because they are being pushed rather than taking the lead themselves.

In terms of the dialogue about the environmental impact of Rio Tinto's project case examined here, it remains to be seen how meaningful the current process turns out to be. There is a strong case for independent assessment during and after the project to help establish this. This is because the impotence of the state and its weak financial position call into question its ability to be able to do this effectively, and the capacity of TNCs to regulate themselves has yet to be established. Nevertheless, what is clear is that companies are increasingly subject to new pressures. The challenge, in a wider context, is to develop best practice models of NGO–TNC engagement centred on the needs of affected communities and the environment.

11 Managing multinationals: the governance of investment for the environment

PETER NEWELL

Introduction: the regulation of TNCs and the environment[1]

TRANSNATIONAL COMPANIES ARE increasingly critical players in development. For some, TNCs are key actors in delivering sustainable development, exporting best practice and initiating great improvements in technology (Schmidheiny, 1992). For others, the mobility of capital and the internationalization of production that make international investment possible, give companies unprecedented freedoms to locate their businesses where it is most profitable to do so, often at the expense of communities and their environment (Madeley, 1999). Of particular concern is the fact that developing countries often experience greater economic and political volatility, which means that foreign investors tend to engage in ventures that will yield a high rate of return over a short period, often resulting in environmental devastation and social dislocation (Sauermann, 1985–86).

Evidence about the relationship between FDI and regulation is mixed, and can be used to sustain competing claims of an upgrading effect and a downgrading effect depending on the sector and region being looked at and the type of standard under investigation (whether it is labour or environmental, for example). It is possible to find examples both of a 'race to the bottom', and of FDI having an upgrading effect (Vogel 1997, World Bank 2000). Others have found that more significant than the lowering of standards may be the stalling of the introduction of new environmental regulations, what is sometimes termed 'regulatory chill'. Whichever view is taken, there can be little doubt that TNCs are increasingly central to environmental decision making and resource use behaviour. This is because of the importance of their investment decisions for the development paths pursued by countries, the environmental impact of transporting goods around the world and the environmental impact of their production processes. Recognizing this role is key to understanding contemporary interest in approaches to the regulation of TNCs.

This chapter looks first at the failure of attempts to regulate TNCs at the national and international level by states and international organizations, before considering two approaches to the regulation of TNCs' investment practices adopted by NGOs and community organizations. These are, first, 'civil regulation',[2] a term used to describe a broad range of strategies increasingly adopted by civil society organizations aimed at holding companies to account for their environmental responsibilities, and second, transnational litigation against companies accused of negligence in one of their overseas operations. Both approaches provide interesting insights into the sources and possibilities of non-state regulation in a context of globalization and contribute to our understanding of the prospects of embedding economic activities in social frameworks supportive of development goals.

It is argued that these strategies respond to a perceived 'governance deficit', in that the global power of TNCs is not adequately matched by existing regulatory instruments. It is the limited scope of existing regulation of the environmental impact of companies' activities that forms the background to attempts by environmental NGOs to create the forms of 'civil regulation' discussed below. They have sought to develop their own mechanisms of corporate accountability by forging alliances with consumers, institutional investors and companies themselves. In the case of foreign direct liability (FDL), it is often the absence or breakdown of effective regulation that makes litigation necessary for communities blighted by industrial hazards. Both sets of strategies have the potential to contribute to the regulation of the environmental impact of the activities of TNCs.

The aim of this chapter, therefore, is to explore the possibilities and limitations of these different approaches to corporate regulation as mechanisms for promoting responsible investment strategies and deterring social and environmentally destructive practices. Such an exercise helps us to determine the potential for developing mutually supportive packages of multilevel, formal and informal initiatives on corporate responsibility for development.

Power without responsibility? The limits of existing regulation

The globalization of production and finance have increased policy and academic attention to the role of regulation in promoting responsible business investment at the national and international levels and between public and private partners (Picciotto and Mayne, 1999). This interest focuses on the role of environmental and social obligations within international investment treaties such as the proposed Multilateral Agreement on Investment (MAI) (Ayine and Werksman, 1999), as well as informal 'private' and non-state practices of regulation manifested in codes of conduct and 'stewardship regimes' negotiated between businesses and NGOs (Newell, 2000).

Contemporary interest in regulation is born of concerns about the continued absence of effective regulation of TNCs at the international level. Critics point to the fact that there is a lack of recognition in international environmental agreements of the role of TNCs in causing social and environmental problems. The issue of TNC regulation was dropped from the UNCED agenda, and while Agenda 21 includes recommendations that affect TNCs it does not take the form of a code of conduct. A code of conduct to regulate the activities of TNCs has been on the international agenda since the 1970s. The UN Centre on Transnational Corporations (UNCTC) was set up in 1973, largely at the request of developing country governments amid concern about the power of TNCs, but was unable to conclude negotiations on a code of conduct. This failure is explained by conflicts of interest between developed and developing countries and the opposition of the USA, in particular, and in 1993 the UNCTC was restructured to become the Commission on International Investment and Transnational Corporations, housed within UNCTAD. Guidelines and standards promoted by bodies such as the ILO[3] and the OECD are not widely known and therefore rarely used, are entirely voluntary and without sanction, and are outdated, compared even with companies' own codes of conduct (McLaren, 2000). Instead, the importance of these agreements may be that they act as benchmarks for other regulatory initiatives and private codes (Seyfang, 1999). In addition, as Muchlinksi notes, 'Although the OECD guidelines are non-binding, they do represent a consensus on what constitutes good corporate behaviour in an increasingly global economy. Furthermore, they are clear that home countries of MNEs have a moral duty to ensure that the standards contained in the guidelines are maintained worldwide' (Muchlinksi, 2001: 39).[4]

While innovative and ambitious, national and regional attempts to advance the legal debate about the obligations of TNCs when they invest overseas have also not progressed very far. The Howitt Resolution,[5] which seeks to set standards that EU companies would have to adopt wherever they operate, has been adopted by the European Parliament but is unlikely to progress much further. Political opposition and the principle-driven nature of the resolution will make it difficult to implement its terms concretely (Ward, 2000). Similarly, despite some support for a Bill on the overseas conduct of companies domiciled in Australia, the range of responsibilities it covers and the sanctions it seeks to impose on companies that violate its terms, mean that it will not be passed in the short term (Australian Senate, 2000).[6] At best then, these instruments provide evidence of the (contested) expectations state actors have regarding the conduct of TNCs.

Of particular concern is the perceived imbalance between the rights and responsibilities of TNCs. The history of business regulation reveals an imbalance between the promotion and protection of investor rights over investor responsibilities (Muchlinski, 1999), regulation *for* business rather than regulation *of* business. The attempt to create an MAI and the WTO's TRIPS agreement are examples of regulation *for* business aimed at facilitating investment opportunities and creating protection for investments. The TRIPS agreement is part of a broader power shift in which regional trade organizations, such as the North American Free Trade Agreement (NAFTA), also permit companies to challenge governments and local authorities about restrictions on their activities (Rowen, 1998).

While national regulation and public international law approaches to regulating TNCs help to create frameworks of expectation about the responsibilities of companies to the communities in which they invest, it is clear that they provide a weak level of protection for those most vulnerable to irresponsible investment practices, given their non-binding nature and lack of enforcement in most cases.

Civil regulation: from confrontation to collaboration[7]

It is against this background of weak instruments and failed initiatives at the international level that NGOs have begun to target TNCs with increasing frequency and vigour in recent years. Rather than providing a coherent alternative approach to social regulation, the forms of civil regulation described below amount to a patchwork of activities and campaigns aimed at challenging the environmental impact of TNCs' operations. Civil regulation creates new fora for dialogue and new sets of 'carrots' and 'sticks' to encourage compliance with environmental standards that go further than state-based regulation, but at the same time supplement its weaknesses. In this sense, as Wapner notes, 'The governing capability of global civil society complements but does not replace that of the state system' (Wapner, 1997: 67). Taken together, they constitute 'moves', in a Polanyian sense, to re-embed the market within a framework of social norms and expectations about the responsibility that corporations have in relation to the communities in which they invest.[8]

A combination of critical and liberal strategies (Newell, 2001a) working with and against companies have been forged, which draw on NGOs' assets and bargaining leverage to generate new mechanisms of accountability for the conduct of corporations. At the more liberal end of the spectrum, a range of strategies has been adopted aimed at working with businesses to generate reform. Cooperative agreement and the use of the market are what set these approaches apart from the critical strategies discussed later.

Consumer pressure provides one such channel for holding companies to account; the use of market to express political will and the harnessing of consumer power to the goal of corporate reform. Such pressure embodies both a 'carrot' and a 'stick' for industries targeted by this action. Consumers can both express their support for a business practice considered to be desirable by buying organic produce or fair trade goods, for example, and thereby create a market for it, or they can penalize a company by boycotting products produced in an environmentally damaging way. Examples of campaigns that were successful in changing company behaviour in this way are the CFC (chlorofluorocarbon) boycott directed towards manufacturers of those chemicals (Wapner, 1995) and the boycott of petrol produced by the company Shell over its disposal of the Brent Spar oil rig in the North Sea (Dickson and McCulloch, 1996).

Codes of conduct provide another increasingly popular mechanism for engaging corporations in a discussion about their responsibilities. In 1989, a coalition of environmental, investor and church interests known as the Coalition for Environmentally Responsible Economies (CERES) met in New York to introduce a ten-point environmental code of conduct for corporations. The aim was to provide criteria for auditing the environmental performance of large domestic and multinational industries. The code called on companies to minimize the release of pollutants, conserve non-renewable resources, use sustainable energy sources and use environmental commitment as a factor in appointing members to the board of directors. The principles are known as the *Valdez Principles* (named after the Exxon Valdez disaster in 1989) and have been used by groups such as Friends of the Earth to enlist corporations to pledge compliance. Companies endorsing the CERES principles are required to report annually on their implementation of the principles. The principles have been used to foster shareholder pressure on companies to improve their environmental performance, to help investors decide on socially responsible investments, and as a code with which to praise or criticize corporate behaviour (Wapner, 1995). Wapner argues, 'The CERES Principles represent a new set of institutional constraints on companies and thus another instance of going outside the states system to institutionalise guidelines for widespread and transnational behaviour' (Wapner, 1997: 82).

The principles open up new channels of reform and avenues of pressure on company conduct. However, while they provide a useful lobbying tool that environmental groups can use to pressure companies to remain faithful to their promises, companies have been able to use them as a way of avoiding government regulation.[9] In addition, codes of conduct provide few channels for verification of compliance with their terms. More generally, codes of conduct are often designed without the participation of those they are intended to benefit and so often fail to have the desired impact because they are not sufficiently targeted to their needs (Barrientos and Orton, 1999). There is also concern that codes of conduct undermine the need for legally binding and state-enforced regulation of MNC investment practices (Kearney, 1999).

Stewardship regimes, which bring together environmental groups, companies and other interested parties to formulate accreditation procedures to identify good corporate conduct, have also begun to develop in recent years. These are more formalized and institutionalized than codes of conduct. They provide an ongoing arena in which dialogue and review take place. The Forestry Stewardship Council (FSC) provides an interesting example of this form of civil regulation.

The background to the FSC's creation was WWF-UK's decision to pursue an alternative strategy in its campaign for sustainable forestry; a direct response to the 'lack of commitment and progress being observed at the international policy level' (Murphy and Bendell, 1997: 105). Manufacturers' misuse of claims about forestry management led to pressure for the establishment of a standard-setting body with a system for verifying product claims. Hence the FSC was established in 1993. The founding group consisted of environmental NGOs, forest industry representatives, community forest groups and forest product certification organizations. The FSC set up an independent forest accreditation programme to alleviate consumer confusion about environmentally friendly wood products. Members of the FSC also agree to nine principles of forestry management. An FSC logo denotes that the product was sourced from an independently certified forest according to FSC principles. There has been a proliferation of such schemes elsewhere in the world, with NGOs initiating buyer groups and FSC working groups. In each case, 'a lack of effective government action was a significant factor in making environmental groups turn to the industry itself' (Murphy and Bendell, 1997: 130).

Each of these strategies, in different ways, provides both positive inducements for reform and rewards for action taken in terms of positive profile and even certification of approval in the case of the FSC. Their aim, therefore, is to promote best practice. As well as guiding and changing behaviour, regulation, if it is to be effective, also has to deter and to provide penalties for non-compliance. This is where critical strategies, described below, play a role. Groups pursuing these strategies are more willing to confront a company about its activities and make damaging public claims about them. The issue is not worked out in closed-door meetings between business and NGOs, but in the public arena (through the media or at garage forecourts) aimed at exposing and punishing environmental (and other) abuses. Nevertheless, in as far as the company responds to the criticisms, reforms its behaviour in light of the confrontation, or adopts new working practices, new forms of social regulation are produced.

One example of this has been the growth of organizations devoted towards the surveillance of the activities of TNCs. They expose companies involved in acts of environmental degradation and disseminate that knowledge to other activists. There are umbrella groups such as 'Corporate Watch' in the UK and 'Multinationals Resource Center' in the USA, as well as sector specific monitors such as 'OilWatch', which has offices in a number of developing countries in which oil companies operate, and company specific groups such as PARTiZANs (RTZ) and Bayerwatch (Bayer). Based on the premise that what companies say about their own activities is not to be trusted, and that government surveillance of their operations is limited, TNC monitors seek to deter companies from violating their legal and perceived social obligations by threatening exposure and the activation of campaigns against them.

In recent years, particularly in the USA and UK, there has also been a growth in what has been referred to as 'shareholder activism', whereby environmental groups buy a small number of shares in a company as a way of obtaining access to the annual general meeting (AGM) and to a forum in which they can influence company decision making. Oil, mining and road-building companies have been principal targets of this strategy. The sponsorship of resolutions at company meetings is aimed at overturning management decisions or at the adoption of a social responsibility measure (Marinetto, 1999). They play on the 'hassle factor', forcing corporations to devote a disproportionate share of their resources to defend a small part of their global operations (Rodman, 1997, 1998).

Shell Transport and Trading, the UK arm of Shell International, had an embarrassing confrontation with institutional shareholders in April–May 1997 over its environmental (and human rights) record in Nigeria. A group of shareholders holding just 1 per cent of the company called on the company to improve accountability by establishing new procedures for dealing with environmental and human rights issues (Lewis, 1997). The resolution called for a named member of Shell's committee of managing directors to take charge of environmental and corporate responsibility policies and for an external audit of those policies. The resolution, supported by groups such as WWF and Amnesty International, called on Shell to publish, before the end of the year, a report on its controversial activities in the Niger delta. In March 1997, in an attempt to pre-empt the shareholder motion, Shell revamped its Statement of General Business Principles to include human rights and sustainable development and published its first report on worldwide health, safety and environmental activities in an attempt to 'ward off further trouble' (Caulkin, 1997).

Limits of civil regulation

The literature on civil regulation suggests that the pressures it creates do have the effect of creating checks and balances on the activities of TNCs (Newell, 2000; Bendell, 2000; Murphy and Bendell, 1997). They have the effect of encouraging private actors to justify their actions to broader public constituencies of shareholders, consumers and civil society at large. The pursuit of profit alone increasingly requires justification. In this sense, the politics that the groups practise contribute towards a new framework of ethics about how companies should view their responsibilities to the communities in which they invest and their impact on the environment.

Clearly, however, civil regulation does not amount to an adequate or appropriate replacement for regulation at the state or international level. The NGOs engaging with the corporate sector in this way have neither the mandate nor the legitimacy to represent broader publics. Allowing the small section of society that NGOs represent to define the public interest in corporate regulation is highly problematic. Some strategies depend on large-scale popular support in order to make an impact. Boycotts in particu-

lar, if they are to be successful, have to be undertaken by a significant number of people in different markets if TNCs are to take them seriously.[10]
Private collaborations between NGOs and companies, on the other hand, are
not open to wider participation and scrutiny and are more likely to fuel concerns about representation.

At the moment, civil regulation is ad hoc and limited in geographical scope,
as well as focused on particular TNCs. To be effective, the boycotts have to be
adopted in those markets of greatest importance to the TNC. Fortunately for
the environmental movement, many of these TNCs that have been the target
of consumer action have been dependent for their profit margins on success
in markets in the West, where organized mobilization around companies'
environmental responsibilities is currently strongest. Often, however, there
are fewer checks and balances in place to restrain perceived 'deviant behaviour' in the developing world, and if the pressures for reform originate from
outside the host country, from Western NGOs, they can be portrayed as
interference.

As an effective form of regulation, it is also clear that many TNCs are relatively insulated from NGO campaigns, often those whose activities have the
greatest environmental impact. Rodman shows in his discussion of NGO
pressure on TNCs investing in Burma that the oil companies have been 'the
most impervious to non-governmental pressures' (Rodman, 1997: 29). The
conflict over Shell's operations in Nigeria also demonstrated the failure of
activists to exact a price high enough to elicit compliance with their demands
(Rodman, 1997: 36). Shell's access to technology, expertise and distribution
networks cannot easily be replaced by companies from other regions, encouraging the host nation to provide extra inducements to ensure the company
stays. Campaigns likely to be most successful are those targeted against particular projects which are of negligible value to the overall operations of the
company, so that fear of loss of profits and damage to reputation in other
(more important) markets make the targeted operation a liability. Only those
TNCs vulnerable to NGO pressure, and where consumer preference really
matters, are being affected by these strategies. In this sense, the scope of the
surveillance is restricted to 'easy' targets.

Litigation against TNCs[11]

Given the limitations of both international law and civil regulation as instruments of corporate social regulation, there is a pressing need to look at what
role litigation can play in defending the poor where companies are exposing
people to environmental risks. For while international law may set standards
and generate expectations, and civil negotiation supplies additional incentives and disincentives to conform to these and go beyond them, when
companies consciously violate standards or act negligently, litigation has a

role to play. Moreover, a number of recent high-profile cases of transnational environmental litigation (foreign direct liability, FDL) suggest that holding parent companies to account for the conduct of their subsidiaries, wherever they may operate, provides a potentially vital channel for ensuring that TNCs do not exploit lower environmental standards and poor enforcement regimes at the expense of workers and their environment. It offers a possible vehicle for internationalizing standards of protection.

FDL claims refer to two approaches to holding companies legally accountable in their home jurisdiction for negative environmental or health and safety impacts, or complicity in human rights abuses in developing countries where they operate (Ward, 2000: 2). First, appeals have been made to use the *Alien Tort Claims Act* of 1789 in the US, which gives district courts the power to hear civil claims from foreign citizens for injuries caused by action 'in violation of the law of nations or a treaty of the United States'. Actions for compensation are based on allegations of corporate complicity in violations of human rights or principles of international environmental law. Examples include litigation against Texaco over environmental damage in Ecuador (Wray, 2000), and Shell, in relation to human rights abuses in Nigeria (Ward, 2000). Key to the successful use of the *Alien Tort Claims Act* is demonstrating that through a 'symbiotic' relationship with the state, a company is culpable for a violation of international law. The case brought against Unocal for the use of forced labour on its gas pipeline project in Burma, for example, had to demonstrate evidence of clear complicity with the state's use of forced labour.

A second type of case has also been brought against parent companies in the UK, Australia and Canada, claiming that they have a responsibility to ensure that home country standards of care apply to subsidiaries, wherever they may be based.[12] A few landmark settlements have been won in this regard, setting important legal precedents. In the Thor case (*Sithole and Others v Thor Chemicals Holdings Ltd*), 20 workers who suffered potentially lethal mercury poisoning in a factory in South Africa won substantial damages (£1.3 million) from the UK parent company because of negligent design, transfer and supervision of an intrinsically hazardous process. In a case brought against Cape plc by workers at their asbestos plant in South Africa (*Lubbe et al v Cape plc*) for negligence, the issue was not that the company had breached British or South African law, but that knowing the harmful effects of asbestos (given the levels accepted in Britain), the company adopted lower standards in South Africa.

The benefits of bringing such cases include the possibility of generating positive reforms in systems of public regulation. For example, Sripada (1989) argues that despite the failings of the case brought against Union Carbide for the Bhopal gas leak disaster in terms of the way it was handled by the Indian government and the amount of compensation that was settled upon, the Bhopal incident has prompted action by governments and corporations.

Following the case, TNCs everywhere have been under greater popular and government pressure to disclose information regarding environmental impact and safety and to put in place more comprehensive risk assessment and avoidance measures. Governments, in turn, have responded by promulgating new environmental legislation or by making existing legislation more stringent. Even if not successful in adequately compensating the victims of corporate negligence, therefore, the act of bringing cases against TNCs can prompt positive reforms.

On the other hand, there are many limitations to using litigation as a strategy for holding companies to account. Legal strategies often reduce complex social problems to questions of monetary compensation. The legal illiteracy of the poor alienates potential users of the law, and poorer communities often express distrust and suspicion towards the legal system and the lawyers whom they feel often exploit the plight of the poor for their own ends. In the aftermath of the Bhopal gas leak, US lawyers descended on the slum dwellings of the city looking for plaintiffs to bring a case against Union Carbide (on the condition that the lawyer received a substantial sum of any award by the Court). This incident, in particular, has heightened calls for a code of conduct among the legal profession to avoid future irresponsible practice along these lines (Anderson and Ahmed, 1996).

In addition, a key problem in bringing legal suits for negligence on health and environmental grounds, is identifying cause–effect relationships between manifested effects and particular pollutants, as well as deciphering direct from indirect effects. Common law traditions, in particular, establish high requirements for scientific evidence. The technical nature of the industrial processes and the fact that the burden of proof rests on the plaintiff to establish that an environmental standard has been violated, by recourse to independent and reliable technical and scientific data, excludes all but the most wealthy or technically competent.[13] Added to this are concerns about the level of funds required to sponsor such cases and to cover the payment of fees to the defendant in the event that the case is unsuccessful. Intimidation by governments and companies against communities considering bringing cases has also been a key deterrent, especially where governments have often created strong incentives for companies to locate there. George Frynas's work on Shell in Nigeria (1998, 1999), for example, shows how threats to the personal security of potential plaintiffs have deterred them from bringing cases against the company in seeking compensation for damage to their lands and subsequent loss of livelihood earnings.

Community legal actions are often rejected on the grounds that they do not represent the specific grievances of individuals involved in the case. In Ecuador, for example, unlike the 'class action' system in the USA, courts abide strictly by the principle of direct interest in a case. Activist Norman Wray, engaged in a case against Texaco, sums up the situation thus: 'in practice if the trial goes on in Ecuador, the 30 000 people that constitute this class action suit, have to sue individually ... This will provoke chaos in the civil court of Lago Agrio' (Wray, 2000: 6). India, on the other hand, has an innovative system of public interest litigation in which organizations and individuals who are not part of the affected class can nevertheless represent them (Cottrell, 1992; Anderson and Ahmed, 1996). Nontheless, in mass tort cases, where large sections of a poor community have been affected by a damaging company investment, issues of who is entitled to speak on behalf of the victims serve to stall or slow the legal process.

The common law legal doctrine of *forum non conveniens* has been the principal means by which transnational cases against companies have been stalled. While the choice of forum is normally the prerogative of the plaintiff, the defendant can invoke the principle to claim that the proposed forum is inconvenient if there is another 'clearly and distinctly more appropriate forum' where justice between the parties will be done. Plaintiffs often argue that, rather than deterring plaintiffs from 'forum-shopping' in order to access higher levels of compensation, this doctrine allows companies to engage in 'reverse forum-shopping' to evade their obligations in their home country. World Development Movement (WDM) argues, 'such shopping around [*by plaintiffs*] is not the reason people from developing countries bring cases to Britain or the U.S. For most of them, it is their only hope of obtaining justice. The choice is not therefore between different levels of compensation, but between justice and no justice at all' (WDM, 1998: 7). Issues raised above, such as fear of persecution, delays in local courts and lack of funding, are more probable reasons for foreign plaintiffs pursuing cases in Northern courts.

The underdevelopment of the legal personality of corporations means that different components of TNCs are legally accountable only to the laws of the country in which they are operating. This makes it necessary for campaigners involved in transnational litigation to 'pierce the corporate veil' in demonstrating a clear chain of command between the headquarters of a company and its subsidiaries. Difficult in any tort case, it becomes very difficult indeed when parent companies often claim they are merely stock or shareholders and that they are only connected for book-keeping purposes. Where a plant design or technology has been designed and exported by the parent company for use in a subsidiary country, in the knowledge of the potential dangers associated with its use, the connections are easier to establish (as in the *Thor* case discussed above). Nevertheless, it is difficult for plaintiffs themselves to identify units within the company that were chiefly responsible for making key decisions. The Indian government made this point to the US Court hearing the Bhopal case: 'Persons harmed by the acts of a multinational corporation are not in a position to isolate which unit of the enterprise caused the harm, yet it is evident that the multinational enterprise that caused the harm is liable for such harm. The multinational must necessarily assume this responsibility for it alone has the resources to discover and guard against hazards and to provide warnings of potential hazards' (Baxi and Paul, 1986).

As a strategy for addressing the immediate needs of communities affected by damaging investments, litigation is often viewed as a last resort option because of the slowness,[14] complexity and costs of the process, and the uncertain nature of the outcomes. There are no clear precedents in this area as none of the cases to date has been pursued successfully to completion. Most cases are either pending, have been rejected, or are currently stalled in the legal machinery. For many of the reasons outlined above, pursuing cases against TNCs through foreign courts is not a realistic strategy for most communities. We should also not lose sight of the fact that working with TNCs to avoid these problems in the first place, undertaking impact assessments, agreeing standards or negotiating conditions on investments may avoid the need for these cases. Many companies, concerned for their reputation, will respond to such an approach. The problem comes with 'rogue' companies – those intent on exploiting lower standards in countries where governments are either unwilling or unable to ensure that adequate safeguards are put in place. This is where a legal approach may be necessary. The suitability of litigation will rest on the type of change being sought: prevention, exposure, or compensation. Determining this helps us to consider the point at which legal remedies stop being useful, and informal patterns of soft or civil regulation become important or perform useful supplementary functions.

At the moment, the popularity of *forum non conveniens* as grounds for not hearing cases in foreign courts, the difficulty of using the *Alien Tort Claim Act* and, in many cases, the impenetrability of the corporate veil, means that companies looking to exploit lower environmental and social standards in developing countries can often do so without fear of meaningful legal redress. Multipronged, multilevel legal and non-legal strategies combining formal and informal mechanisms that reinforce a system of obligations for TNCs are needed to reverse this situation. From a development perspective, in which socially and environmentally responsible business practice is the goal, achieving a 'deterrent effect' is critical, whereby companies build safeguards into their operations for fear of the penalties they may accrue for acting irresponsibly. This was an issue raised in the Bhopal case, for example, where a call was made for damages 'sufficient to deter' Union Carbide and all TNCs 'involved in similar business activities' from 'wilful, malicious and wanton disregard of the rights and safety of the citizens of India' (Baxi and Dhandra, 1990). As well as securing short-term compensation, this surely has to be the aim of litigation – not just making companies liable for their activities wherever they happen to be based, but ensuring that weaker systems of governance or enforcement in developing countries, which expose the poor and their environment to risks that would not be acceptable in the North, are not a legitimate basis for comparative commercial advantage.

Conclusion

This chapter has attempted to provide a critical assessment of the benefits and limitations of three types of approach to corporate regulation. Starting with traditional mechanisms of formal regulation of corporate activity, it was argued that most initiatives at the international level, and by individual countries to create legislation regulating the conduct of their TNCs overseas, are either severely limited or have not progressed very far. Instead, it was suggested, there is an imbalance between the rights and responsibilities of TNCs that provides the impetus for the alternative strategies that are discussed in this chapter. These included civil society-based approaches to business regulation, aimed, in different ways, at holding companies to account for their social and environmental responsibilities by mobilizing the public and their consumer power towards that end. It was suggested that while such strategies usefully generate new expectations about the responsibilities of corporations when they invest in developing countries, and do appear to engage many larger companies concerned for their brand names, they provide only a limited means of surveillance, such that the worst polluters and violators often escape attention. Finally, the role of transnational litigation was discussed as a further means by which checks and balances on the impacts of investment can be created. It was argued that while important precedents have been set, and changes brought about through out-of-court settlements or indirect pressures on other companies to change their behaviour, litigation is a limited strategy for the poor in most settings. For this reason, combinations of formal and informal approaches are likely to be necessary depending on the goal of the action.

Interestingly, a combination of the limitations of civil regulation and transnational litigation, as well as their growing popularity, may generate demands from the public and industry themselves for new international and national binding standards. The limited applicability of foreign direct liability in many legal systems and the confusion surrounding many non-state labelling and certification schemes has heightened the need for public regulation. In the legal area, there have been moves, for example, to harmonize jurisdictions and to advance negotiations towards a multilateral convention on civil jurisdiction and judgements under the auspices of the Hague Conference on Private International Law (Muchlinski, 2001). There have also been calls for a corporate accountability convention (FOEI, 2002). The appeal of public regulation is its ability to provide the consistency, transparency and enforceability that many civil regulation approaches lack. The history of weak public regulation of the corporate sector suggests, nevertheless, that it is no panacea. More likely is that we shall be faced with a dense and interrelated set of regulatory approaches, both formal and informal, existing at multiple levels from the international down to the local level. The challenge is to ensure that the combinations of measures adopted are responsive to the needs of the poor, who are most vulnerable to destructive investments.

Notes

Introduction

1 This echoed the commitments made in the 1997 White Paper on development: 'We want to see a global society in which people everywhere are entitled to live in peace and security with their families and neighbours, and enjoy in full their civil and political rights. We want to see economic endeavour hand-in-hand with accountable government, the rule of law and a strong civil society.'

2 Giddens in his Reith Lectures and Held *et al.* in their book *Global Transformations* make the following distinction between the various positions on the nature of globalization: (i) The hyper-globalizers who see globalization as a process driven by capitalism. Both liberal and neo-Marxist scholars argue from this position, though of course, within very different analytical and normative frameworks. (ii) The sceptics – who deny any structural break with the past globalizations and argue that indeed globalization of the economy is less secure today than it was in the earlier phases, with regional blocs emerging as counterfoils to globalization. (iii) The transformationalists who characterize contemporary globalization, which is conceived of as a transformative force responsible for a massive 'shake-out' of societies and economies, as the central driving force behind socioeconomic changes that in turn underpin globalization.

3 This section draws on Rai, S. (1998) Engendered development in a global age? CSGR, Working Paper 20.

4 World exports rose from US$ 61 billion in 1950 to US$ 3447 billion in 1990 (Khor, 2000).

5 World Bank internal memo from Lawrence Summers, 12 December 1991, reproduced at http://www.counterpunch.org/summers.html

6 The poorest quintile of the world accounts for just 1 per cent of world exports and of foreign direct investment (Nayyer, 2000).

7 This section draws from Newell, P., Globalisation and the environment: exploring the connections, *IDS Bulletin*, vol. 30(3), 1999.

8 It has been estimated for example that the NAFTA agreement will lead to a sevenfold increase in cross-border trucking (Goldsmith, 1997).

9 For arguments for and against this see *Global Environmental Politics*, vol. 1(1), 2001, especially the contributions by Newell, Whalley and Zissimos and Biermann.

Chapter 1

1 This chapter draws on Dauvergne, P. (1999) *The Environment in Crisis: Asia and donors after the 1997 financial crisis*, The Australian Agency for International Development of the Department of Foreign Affairs and Trade (AusAID), Canberra. The views in this article are the author's alone.

2 For a range of useful definitions of globalization, see Giddens (1990); Holm and Sørensen (1995); and Hirst and Thompson (1996). For a discussion of the globalization of environmentalism, see Dauvergne (1998b).

Chapter 4

1 The authors belong to the Research and Information System for the Non-Aligned and Other Developing Countries, New Delhi, India. The views expressed here are the authors' own and do not reflect those of the organization to which they belong.
2 See for instance, Brandao, A. and Marlin, W. (1993) Implications of Agricultural Trade Liberalisation for Developing Countries, World Bank Working Paper, No. WPS 11/6.
3 The Cairns Group members are countries that have major interests in agricultural exports: Argentina, Bolivia, Brazil, Canada, Chile, Colombia, Costa Rica, Fiji, Guatemala, Indonesia, Malaysia, New Zealand, Paraguay, Philippines, South Africa, Thailand and Uruguay.
4 Bound rates of duties are the maximum levels of duties that WTO members have agreed to impose on imports.
5 The use of the term European Community reflects WTO usage.
6 The USA, Japan, Canada and the EC make up the Quad.

Chapter 5

1 This chapter was completed in March 2000.
2 See www.ecology.or.jp/isoworld/english/analy14k.htm
3 Such a de facto consequence is, however, in direct contradiction with Article 12.3 of the TBT Agreement, which indicates that contracting parties, in the process of standards and technical regulations making, must take into account the specific needs of developing members, so that these standards and technical regulations do not create unnecessary barriers to exports of developing country members.

Chapter 6

1 In the literature the words are usually capitalized and often limited to their initials KM.
2 I refer here to a variety of perspectives to reflect the problem inherent in speaking of 'feminism' without referring to the historical and geographical specificity of feminist ideas and practices, as well as to the consequences of the dominance of a Western tradition.
3 The chapter represents my own individual opinions, and does not reflect Oxfam's policy or formal understanding of the issues covered.
4 De Waal's analysis concerns NGOs working in emergencies, but the argument can be applied more broadly.
5 'Institutional learning' indicates the processes and the 'learning organization' structures through which organizations learn from their own experience (Malhotra, 1996).
6 Dasgupta (1993), on the contrary, believes that knowledge only resembles a public good. This is exactly because it is jointly usable, but at the same time it is possible to exclude some people from its benefit, for example by the private rights granted by patents and copyrights.

Chapter 7

1 This definitional problem is perhaps most significant when considering SMEs that dominate smaller markets. Fujita, for example, describes 32 per cent of SMEs making foreign direct investments in developing countries as doing so only in

markets in which they enjoy oligopolistic control (Fujita, 1995b: 251). Yet this form of market share would, in many definitions, exclude firms from being defined as 'small' or 'medium-sized' (e.g. Bolton, 1971; EU Commission).
2 On Italy see Weiss (1988).
3 Gorman was one of the key figures to split the Conservative Party under John Major and has persistently represented the traditional and non-modern in British politics, as demonstrated by her ardent Euroscepticism.
4 Other research has since shown that: only a few SMEs contribute to most of the growth; that many small firm start-ups force others out of business in low entry barrier businesses (the 'crowded platform' effect) (Atkinson and Storey, 1993); that SMEs also contribute to many lost jobs (Wagner, 1995); and that SMEs are not very good at predicting how much employment they are likely to create (Ashworth *et al.*, 1998).
5 Indeed, so important was this model of economic organization that it was seen to herald a 'new competition' (Best, 1990).
6 For an elaboration of the concept of embeddedness see Granovetter (1986) and Polanyi (1980).
7 For more information see DTI (1992).
8 For surveys see SME Observatory Reports (an annual publication compiled by EIM, Zoetmeer for the Commission of the EU), Sengenberger *et al.* (1990) and Bagnasco and Sabel (1995).

Chapter 8

1 Now published – see Joekes and Weston (1994).
2 Several of the papers prepared for regional meetings are available in published form. See: UNIFEM (1996); Wee (1998); and Cardero *et al.* (2000).
3 This is commonly known as the Michael Jordan syndrome – Jordan gets paid more in one year just for advertising Nike shoes than does the entire Southeast Asian workforce involved in making them!
4 For some specific statistics on home-based workers see Chen *et al.* (1999). A major first step in developing strategies to assist homeworkers is to be able to accurately count their numbers. Work has started on this through Women in Informal Employment: Globalizating and Organizing (WIEGO) – an international coalition which provides research and policy support to associations of homeworkers.
5 For more information on HomeNet see: www.gn.org/homenet
6 For more information on StreetNet see: www.streetnet.org.za
7 See, for example, Gibb (1997). UNIFEM has also supported the creation of TRADEFEM, which posts information on gender and trade/globalization. See: www.unifem.undp.org/trade
8 For a list of WIEGO members and information about its programmes, see: www.wiego.org

Chapter 9

1 This is less so in South Africa, where most women live on-farm with their male partner or relative, but their employment is dependent on his. Although this sector is often called 'non-traditional agricultural exports', this type of export has long taken place in South Africa, and the term is not applicable to this country. Nevertheless, there are many similarities between it and other countries, which have more recently entered this sector, to which the term does apply.
2 Companies participating in the ETI include: Anchor Seafood, ASDA, CSW, J Sainsbury, Levi Strauss, Littlewoods, Marks and Spencer, Monsoon, Pentland Group, Premier Brands, Somerfield Stores, Tea Sourcing Partnership, Tesco and The Body Shop (ETI Information Sheet. 1999).
3 The details of each case study are examined elsewhere (see Barrientos *et al.*, 1999a, b, 2000).
4 In South Africa and Chile, the estimated level of union membership among horticultural workers ranges between 2 and 8 per cent. Therefore, over 90 per cent of horticultural workers in both countries are not unionized.
5 The ETI base code does relate to continuous employment, but this is where temporary contacts are used to cover permanent workers.

Chapter 10

1 As QIT, the company proposing the mining venture, is a wholly owned subsidiary of Rio Tinto, the parent company is generally referred to throughout this chapter.
2 Titanium dioxide is used mainly as an industrial whitener.
3 For further details of the village and elaboration of the type of research methods employed see the article dealing with tourism and land rights (Mulligan, 1999).
4 The 'environment' in 'environmental change' is used here in a broad sense to cover the total environment of social as well as biological actors and processes.
5 For example, it was necessary to create new legislation allowing the project to proceed, and the company requires substantial government spending on regional infrastructure for the project to remain financially feasible.

Chapter 11

1 I use the term 'transnational companies' here to denote the fact that control and decision making are often concentrated within the Western branches of these companies. Given that power, resources and authority are not diffused throughout the organizations, the term 'multi' exaggerates the global scope of the company (see Gill and Law, 1988).
2 These ideas have been developed by both Newell (2000) and Bendell (2000).
3 The 1977 ILO Tripartite declaration of principles concerning Multinational Enterprises and Social Policy, for example, is voluntary, contains no reference to environmental protection and has dealt with only seven complaints against TNCs in its history.
4 Paragraph 2 of the concepts and principles in the revised guidelines, 27 June 2000, states 'governments adhering to the Guidelines encourage the enterprises operating on their territories to observe the Guidelines wherever they operate, while taking into account the circumstances of each host country'.
5 European Parliament Resolution on the creation of a Code of Conduct for European MNCs Operating Abroad.

6 There have also been moves within developing countries themselves to recognize the right of citizens to hold TNCs accountable for personal and environmental injuries committed abroad. The NGO coalition AIDA, in Costa Rica, is calling for a bill 'that would officially recognize the right of Costa Rican citizens to bring suits abroad against foreign corporations for environmental and other damages caused in Costa Rica' (cited in Ward, 2000: 23).

7 This section draws on Newell (2001a).

8 Mittelman suggests the use of the term 'move' rather than movement to describe similar 'micro-counter-globalizing tendencies' to recognize the proto forms of such activities before the transformative potential of a 'true' Polanyian counter-force can be ascribed to them (Mittelman, 1998: 867).

9 For example, Humphreys (1997) highlights the case of the Sun company (a petroleum refining company), that has used its endorsement of the Valdez Principles to gain credibility when lobbying against environmental legislation in Congress.

10 The limited impact, to date, of the campaign against Exxon's refusal to acknowledge the need for international action on climate change may be due to the Europe-centred nature of the boycott against the oil giant.

11 The discussion is developed more fully in Newell (2001b).

12 Such cases have been brought against Cambior (over its gold mine in Guyana), BHP (over pollution in Papua New Guinea), Rio Tinto (over its uranium mine operations in Namibia), Thor chemicals (over mercury poisoning of its workers in South Africa) and Cape (also over its operations in South Africa).

13 As Frynas (1999: 124) argues, 'The oil industry normally has a superior knowledge compared to individual litigants. Consequently, it may often be difficult for the plaintiff to argue that the oil company was unreasonably negligent or did not adopt accepted standards during its operations'.

14 Often up to two years for preliminary appeals, two years substantive trial and two years appellate proceedings.

References

Introduction

Acharya, S. and Acharya N. (1995) Structural adjustment and small producers: Reflections from case studies, *Economic and Political Weekly*, Bombay, 7 January.

Agarwal, B. (1997) Editorial: Re-sounding the Alert – Gender, Resources and Community Action, *World Development* vol. 25(9): 1373–80.

Albrow, M. (1996) *The Global Age*, Polity Press, Cambridge.

Barber, B. (1996) *Jihad and McWorld*, Ballantine Books, New York.

Bendell, J. (Ed.) (2000) *Terms of Endearment: business, NGOs and sustainable development*, Greenleaf Publishers, Sheffield.

Braithwaite, J. and Drahos, P. (2000) *Global Business Regulation*, Cambridge University Press, Cambridge.

Charmes, J. (1998) Women Working in the Informal Sector in Africa: new methods and new data, WIEGO (www.wiego.org/papers/1informal).

Clapp, J. (1997) Threats to the environment in an era of globalization: an end to state sovereignty? in Schrecker, T. (Ed.) *Surviving Globalism: the social and environmental challenge*, Macmillan, London.

Cosbey, A. (2000) The Sustainable Development Effects of the WTO TRIPS Agreement: a focus on developing countries, www.wtowatch.org/library/admin/uploaded files/Sustainable_Development Effects_of_the_WTO_TRI.htm

Cox, R. with Sinclair T.J. (1996) *Approaches to World Order*, Cambridge University Press, Cambridge.

DAW (1999) *World Survey on the Role of Women in Development*, United Nations, New York.

Doremus, P., Keller, L., Pauly, L. and Reich, S. (1998) *The Myth of the Global Corporation*, Princeton University Press, Princeton.

DFID (2000) *Eliminating World Poverty: making globalization work for the poor*, White Paper, DFID, London.

Elson, D. (1995) *Male Bias in Development*, Manchester University Press, Manchester.

Enloe, C. (1989) *Bananas, Beaches and Bases, Making Feminist Sense of International Politics*, Pandora Press, London.

Fabig, H. and Boele, R., (1999) The changing nature of NGO activity in a globalising world: Pushing the corporate responsibility agenda, *IDS Bulletin*, vol. 30(3).

Fukuyama, F. (1993) *End of History and the Last Man*, Free Press, New York.

Giddens, A. (1990) *Consequences of Modernity*, Polity Press, Cambridge.

Gill, S. (1993) *Gramsci, Historical Materialism and International Relations*, Cambridge University Press, Cambridge.

Gill, S. (1995) Theorising the interregnum: the double movement and global politics in the 1990s, in Hettne, B. (Ed.) *International Political Economy: understanding global disorder*, Zed Books, London.

Glover, D. (1999) Defending communities: local exchange trading systems from an environmental perspective, *IDS Bulletin*, vol. 30(3): 75–82.

Goldsmith, E. (1997) Can the environment survive the global economy?, *The Ecologist*, vol. 27(6): 242–9.

Grant, W., Matthews, D. and Newell, P. (2000) *The Effectiveness of EU Environmental Policy*, Macmillan, Basingstoke.

Gray, J. (1998) *False Dawn, The Delusions of Global Capitalism*, Granta Books, London.

Held, D., McGrew, A., Goldblatt, D. and Perraton, J. (1999) *Global Transformations*, Polity Press, Cambridge.

Hirst, P. and Thompson, G. (1996) *Globalisation in Question*, Polity Press, London.

Hoogvelt, A. (1997) *Globalisation and the PostColonial World: the new political economy of development*, Macmillan, Basingstoke.

Huntington, S. (1996) *The Clash of Civilisations and the Remaking of World Order*, Simon and Schuster, New York.

IDS Bulletin (Newell, P., Ed.) Globalisation and the governance of the environment, vol. 30(3), IDS, Brighton.

Khor, M. (2000) Globalization and the South: some critical issues, Discussion Paper No. 147, UNCTAD, April.

Korten, D. (1995) *When Corporations Rule the World*, Earthscan, London.

Marchand, M. and Sissons Runyan, A. (2000) *Gender and Global Restructuring*, Routledge, London.

Martinez-Alier, J. (1997) The merchandising of biodiversity, in *Varieties of Environmentalism: essays from north and south*, Earthscan, London, pp. 109–27.

Miller, M. (2001) Tradegy for the commons: the enclosure and commodification of knowledge, in Stevis, D. and Assetto, V. (Eds) *The International Political Economy of the Environment*, Lynne Rienner, Boulder, CO and London, pp. 111–35.

Mittelman, J.H. (1998) Globalisation and environmental resistance politics, *Third World Quarterly*, vol. 19(5): 847–72

Nayyer, D. (2000) Globalization and Development Strategies, paper prepared for High-level Round Table on Trade and Development, Directions for the Twenty-first Century, Bangkok, 12 February.

Newell, P. (2000) Environmental NGOs and Globalisation: the governance of TNCs, Cohen, R. and Rai, S. (Eds) *Global Social Movements*, Athlone Press, London, pp. 117–34.

Newell, P. (2001) Global challenges to the future state, *Seminar*, vol. 503, July, New Delhi.

Newell, P. and MacKenzie, R. (2000) The Cartagena Protocol on Biosafety: legal and political dimensions, *Global Environmental Change*, vol. 10: 313-317.

OECD (1997) *Globalisation and Small and Medium Enterprises*, vol. 1, OECD, Paris.

Oxfam, Agricultural Trade and the Livelihoods of Small Farmers, discussion paper for DFID towards development of a White Paper on globalization, Oxfam GB, March 2000.

Peterson, V.S. (2000) Analytical advances to address new dynamics, in Tetreault, M.A., Denemark, R.A., Burch, K. and Thomas, K.P. (Eds) *New Odysseys in International Political Economy*, Routledge, London.

Peterson, V.S. (2002) Rewriting (Global) Political Economy a Reproductive, Productive and Virtual (Foucaldian) Economics. *International Feminist Journal of Politics* vol. 4(1): 1–30.

Picciotto, K. (1996) Fragmented States and International Rules of Law, Inaugural lecture, Lancaster University, 31 March.

Picciotto, S. and Mayne, R. (1999) *Regulating International Business: beyond liberalization*, Macmillan, Basingstoke.

Polanyi, K.(1980) *The Great Transformation: the political and economic origins of our time*, Beacon Press, Boston, MA.

Rai, S. (1998) Engendered Development in a Global Age?' CSGR Working Paper 20.

Saurin, J. (1996) International relations, social ecology and the globalisation of environmental change, in Vogler J. and Imber, M. (Eds) *The Environment and International Relations*, Routledge, London, pp.77–99.

Scholte, J.A. (2000) *Globalisation: a critical introduction*, Macmillan, Basingstoke.

Sen, A., Global Doubts, Commencement Day Address, Harvard University, 8 June 2000 (www.commencement.harvard.edu/sen.html).

Shiva, V. and Holla-Bhar, R. (1996) Piracy by patent: the case of the neem tree, in Mander, J. and Goldsmith, E. (Eds) *The Case Against the Global Economy*, Sierra Club Books, San Francisco.

Smillie, I. (2000) *Mastering the Machine Revisited*, ITDG Publishing, London.

Strange, S. (1996) *The Retreat of the State*, Cambridge University Press, Cambridge.

Truong, Than Dam (1999) The Underbelly of the Tiger: Gender and the demystification of the Asian miracle, Working Papers Series 269, Institute of Social Studies, The Hague.

Vogel, D. (1997) Trading up and governing across: transnational governance and environmental protection, *Journal of European Public Policy*, vol. 4(4): 556–71.

Weiss, L. (1998) *The Myth of the Powerless State*, Polity Press, Cambridge.

World Bank (1997) *The State in a Changing World*, World Development Report, Washington, DC.

World Bank (2000) *World Development Report*.

Chapter 1

Afsah, S. (1998) Impact of financial crisis on industrial growth and environmental performance in Indonesia, July (www.worldbank.org/nipr/work_paper/shakeb/index.htm).

Agence France-Presse via Pacific Islands Report (1998) Solomon Islands to end unsustainable use of forests, 27 October.

Akella, A.S. (1999) *The East Asian financial crisis: evolution and environmental implications for Indonesia*, Macroeconomics for Sustainable Development Program Office, World Wide Fund for Nature, Jakarta.

*Antara (*1998a) Indonesia may become world's biggest exporter, 26 October.

Antara (1998b) Agribusiness playing important role in boosting R's exports, 27 October.

Asia Environmental Trading (1998) *Asian Environmental Review*, September.

Asian Development Bank (1997) *Emerging Asia: changes and challenges*, Asian Development Bank, Manila.

Asian Development Bank (www.asiandevbank.org/megacity/summary.htm).

Baillie, T. (1998) Indonesian women and the Asian crisis, A Study for the Gender and Education Group, Canberra, AusAID, July.

Bello, W. (1998) The end of a 'miracle': speculation, foreign capital dependence and the collapse of the Southeast Asian economies, *Multinational Monitor*, vol 19(1&2), (www.essential.org/monitor/mm1998/mm9801.05.html).

Capistrano, A.D. and Kiker, C.F. (1995) Macro-scale economic influences on tropical forest depletion, *Ecological Economics*, vol 14(1): 21–9.

Casson, A. (1999) The hesitant boom: Indonesia's oil palm sub-sector in an era of economic crisis and political change, November, Program on the Underlying Causes of Deforestation, Bogor Indonesia, Centre for International Forestry Research (www.cgiar.org/cifor/).

Central Bank of Solomon Islands (CBSI) (1998) *1997 Annual Report*, CBSI, Honiara.

CIFOR News (1998) Center for International Forestry Research, No 20, September.

Clapp, J. (1998) Hazardous waste and human security in Southeast Asia: local–global linkages and responses, draft paper for the Development and Security in Southeast Asia (DSSEA) Project, Conference in Manila, the Philippines, 15–19 December.

Cubol, E. (1998) Development, security, and industrial pollution in the Philippines, draft paper for the Development and Security in Southeast Asia (DSSEA) Project, Conference in Manila, the Philippines, 15–19 December.

Dauvergne, P. (1998a) Burning down Indonesia: the politics of forest fires, *The Asia-*

Pacific Magazine, No. 11: 34–37.

Dauvergne, P. (1998b) Globalisation and deforestation in the Asia-Pacific, *Environmental Politics*, vol. 7(4): 113–34.

Down to Earth (1998) Bank report exposes chaos at Central Kalimantan mega-project, *Down to Earth*, No. 39, November.

Fabig, H., and Boele, R. (1999) The changing nature of NGO activity in a globalising world: pushing the corporate responsibility movement, *IDS Bulletin*, vol. 30(3): 58–67.

Feridhanusetyawan, T. (1999) Security implication of the economic crisis for Indonesian workers, a draft paper for the Development and Security in Southeast Asia (DSSEA) Project, presented at Emerging Southeast Asian Identities in an Era of Volatile Globalization, Joint NWRCSEAS & CCSEAS Conference, Vancouver, Canada, 23 October.

Gates, C.L. (1998) The East Asian crisis: causes and dynamics, *Development Bulletin*, vol. 46 (Winter), pp.7–10.

Giddens, A. (1990) *The Consequences of Modernity*, Stanford University Press, Stanford, CA.

Greenlees, D. (2000) Forest bandits, *The Australian*, 22-3 July, p.26.

Griffith-Jones, S., with Cailloux, J. and Pfaffenzeller, S. (1998) The East Asian financial crisis: a reflection on its causes, consequences and policy implications, Institute of Development Studies Discussion Paper 367. (www.ids.susx.ac.uk/ids/publicat/dp367.html).

Hirst, P. and Thompson, G. (1996) *Globalization in Question: the international economy and the possibilities of governance*. Polity Press, Cambridge.

Holm, H., and Sørensen, G. (1995) *Whose World Order? Uneven globalization and the end of the Cold War*, Westview Press, Boulder, CO.

Indonesian Observer, Illegal Fish Exports Top Rp33 Trillion, 5 September 2000.

Intal, P. Jr. and Medalla, E. (1998) The East Asian crisis and Philippine sustainable development', Plenary Paper, Economy and Environment Program For Southeast Asia, prepared for the Forum on the Asian Financial Crisis and Sustainable Development at the Sixth Session of the United Nations Commission on Sustainable Development, New York, 22 April.

International Tropical Timber Organization (ITTO) (2000) *Annual Review and Assessment of the World Timber Situation: 1999,* ITTO, Yokohama.

Jakarta Post (1996) Integrate a 'green GDP' into development: scholar, 26 December.

Jakarta Post (1999) Palm oil industry needs Rp 20t in investments, 25 November.

Jakarta Post (2000a) Investment in forestry, plantations at zero level, 10 May.

Jakarta Post (2000b) KL firms allegedly involved in illegal timber trade, 20 May.

Krugman, P., See various articles at http://web.mit.edu/krugman

Lamb, D. (1998) Indochina finds its not immune to Asia crisis, *Los Angeles Times*, 15 February.

McBeth, J. (2000) Undercut: Illegal mining has reached unprecedented levels, harming legitimate companies and putting the economy and environment at risk, *Far Eastern Economic Review*, 13 July.

Potter, L., and Lee, J. (1998) Tree planting in Indonesia: Trends, impacts and directions, CIFOR Occasional Paper No. 18 (www.cgiar.org/cifor/publications/new-pub.html).

Reuters (2000) Tension in RI deters palm oil investors, 24 May.

Roubini, N., What caused Asia's economic and currency crisis and its global contagion? (www.stern.nyu.edu/~nroubini/asia/AsiaHomepage.html#social).

Salim, E. (1998) Environment key to sustaining recovery in Asian economies, *South China Morning Post*, 18 March.

Star [The] (1998) Villagers worry about river pollution, 16 October.

Sunderlin, W. D. (1998) Between danger and opportunity: Indonesia's forests in an era of economic crisis and political change, 11 September (www.cgiar.org/cifor/).

Sunderlin, W.D. (1999) The effects of economic crisis and political change on Indonesia's forest sector, 1997–99, 15 November (www.cgiar.org/cifor/).

Tangprasert, P. and Ratchasima, N. (1999) Jobless farmers issue dire threat, *Bangkok Post*, 25 January.

Tickell, O. (1999) Forest crisis in Indonesia, *Timber & Wood Products International*, August.

Wall Street Journal, Poverty stricken Indonesians turn to native animals to survive, November 1998.

Williams, L. (1998) Starving children a lost generation, *Sydney Morning Herald*, 20 October.

World Bank (1998) Environment in crisis: a step back or a new way forward? *East Asia: the road to recovery*, Chapter 6, World Bank, Washington, DC.

World Bank (1999) *Environmental Implications of the Economic Crisis and Adjustment in East-Asia*, Discussion Paper Series No. 01, East Asia Environment and Social Development Unit, Washington, DC.

Yamin, K. (1998) Environment bulletin – Indonesia: crisis yields 'green' gains, InterPress Service, 5 September.

Yoga, S.S. (1998) An open aid to destruction, *Star Publications*, 17 November.

Chapter 2

Acharya, R. (1996) Intellectual property rights and information technology: the impact of the Uruguay Round on developing countries, *Information and Communication Law*, vol. 3(2).

Appleton, H. (Ed.) (1995), *Do It Herself*, Intermediate Technology Publications, London.

Block, F. (1990) *Postindustrial Possibilities: A critique of economic discourse*, University of California Press, Berkeley, CA.

Braudel, F. (1985) *La Dynamique Du Capitalisme*, Flammarion, Paris.

Cosbey, A. (2000) The Sustainable Development Effects of the WTO TRIPS Agreement: a focus on developing countries, www.wtowatch.org/library/admin/uploaded files/Sustainable_Development Effects_of_the_WTO_TRI.htm

Dasgupta, B. (1999) Patent lies and latent danger, *Economic and Political Weekly*, April 17–24.

DAW (1999) World Survey on the Role of Women in Development, United Nations, New York.

Deardoff, A.V. (1993) Should patents be extended to all developing countries? in Stern, R.M. (Ed.) *The Multilateral Trading System: Analysis and options for change*, Harvester, Wheatsheaf, New York.

Fuller, E. (1955) *Tinkers and Genius*, Hastings House, New York.

GAIA and Genetic Resources Action International (GRAIn) (1998) *Global Trade and Biodiversity in Conflict*, 1 April, London.

Hoggard, S. (1994) Politics and institutions in the World Bank's East Asia, in Fishlow, A. *et al.* (Eds) *Miracle or Design: lessons from the East Asian experience*, Overseas Development Council, Policy Essay No. 11, Washington, D.C.

Keyala, B.K. (1998) *TRIPS Agreement on Patent Laws: impact on pharmaceuticals and health for all*, Centre for the Study of Global Trade System and Development, New Delhi.

Ling, L.H.M. (1997) The other side of globalization: hypermasculine developmentalism in East Asia, paper presented at the International Studies Association Meeting, Toronto, 18–22 March.

Mukund, K. (1999) Women's property rights in South India, *Economic and Political Weekly,* Mumbai, May 29–June 4.

Nayyar, D. (Ed.) (1997) *Trade and Industrialisation*, Oxford University Press, New Delhi.

New Scientist (1984) The innovative woman, *New Scientist*, 24 May.

Oman, C. (1994) *Globalisation and Regionalisation: the challenge for developing for countries*, Development Centre Studies, OECD, Paris.

Page, S., Davenport, M. and Hewitt, A. (1991) *The GATT Uruguay Round: effects on developing countries*, Overseas Development Institute, London.

Palmer, I. (1992) Gender equity and economic efficiency in adjustment programmes, in Afshar, H. and Dennis, C. (Eds), *Women and Adjustment Policies in the Third World*, St Martin's Press, New York.

Polanyi, K. (1980) *The Great Transformation: the political and economic origins of our time*, Beacon Press, Boston, MA.

Ramachandra, A. (1977) Self-reliance in technology and the patent system, in WIPO, *World Symposium of the Patent System in Developing Countries*, No. 638(E), Geneva.

Sell, S.K. (1998) *Power and Ideas: North South politics of intellectual property and anti-trust*, State University of New York, New York.

Sell, S.K. (2001) Intellectual Property Rights After TRIPS: promotion and protest, paper presented at the International Studies Association Annual Meeting, Chicago, February.

Shiva, V. and Holla-Bhar R. (1996) Piracy by patent: the case of the neem tree, in Mander, J. and Goldsmith, E. (Eds) *The Case Against Global Economy*, Sierra Club Books, San Francisco.

Shiva, V. (1988) *Staying Alive : women, ecology and development*, Zed Books, London.

Shiva, V. (2000) Poverty and Globalisation, Reith Lectures http://news.bbc.co.uk/reith_2000.

Stanley, A. (1998) Women hold up two-thirds of the sky, in Hopkins, P.D. (Ed.) (1998) *Sex Machine, Readings in Culture, Gender and Technology*, Indiana University Press, Bloomington & Indianapolis.

Stanley, A. (2000) Inventors, *Routledge Encyclopedia of Women's Studies*, Routledge, New York.

Stewart, F. (1993) Biases in Global Markets: can the focus of inequity and marginalisation be modified? Paper submitted to the North-South Round Table Meeting, 1–13 September 1993, Bretton Woods, New Hampshire, USA.

Swanson, T. (1997) *Global Action for Bio-Diversity – an international framework for implementing the convention on biological diversity*, Earthscan, Cambridge.

UNCTAD (1996) *Globalisation and Liberalisation: effects of international economic relations on poverty*, Geneva.

UNDP (1990) *Human Development Report*, Oxford University Press, New York.

UNIFEM (1999) *Women Making a Difference in Science and Technology – Case Studies*, UN, New York.

Vaistos, C. (1972) Patents Revisited: their function in developing countries, *Journal of Development Studies*, 9 October.

Vidal, J. (1999) The Seens of Wrath, *The Guardian Weekend*, 19 June.

Vivian, J. (1995) *Adjustment and Social Sector Restructuring*, Frank Cass, London.

White, G. (1993) Towards a Political Analysis of Markets, *IDS Bulletin* vol. 24(3): 4–11.

WIPO (1998) *World Symposium of the Patent System in Developing Countries*, No. 638(E), Geneva. www.undp.org/unifem/ec_tech.htm

Chapter 3

Committee of Donor Agencies for Small Enterprise Development (1998) *Business*

Development Services for SMEs: preliminary guidelines for donor-funded interventions (Summary Report), ILO.

Dawson, J. and Oyeyinka, B. (1993) Structural adjustment and the urban informal sector in Nigeria, *World Employment Programme Research Working Paper 65*, ILO Geneva.

Dawson, J. with Jeans, A. (1997) *Looking Beyond Credit: business development services and the promotion of innovation among small producers*, IT Publications, London.

King, K. (1997) Growing Up but Will the Informal Sector Mature? *Appropriate Technology* vol. 24(1), June.

Meagher, K. and Yunusa, M.B. (1992) Limits to Labour Absorption: conceptual and historical background to adjustment in Nigeria's urban informal sector, UNRISD Discussion Paper 28, Geneva.

Schmitz, H. (1982) Growth constraints on small-scale manufacturing in developing countries: a critical review, *World Development*, vol. 10(6), Washington.

Steel, W. and Webster, L. (1991) *Small Enterprises to Adjustment*, World Bank.

Tendler, J. and Amorin, M.A. (1996) Small firms and their helpers: lessons on demand, *World Development*, vol. 24(3): 407–26.

Chapter 5

Alger, C. (Ed.) (1998) *The future of the United Nations System: potential for the twenty-first century*, United Nations University Press, Tokyo.

Asher, M. and Gupta, A. (1998) *Environment and the Developing World. Principles, policies and management*, Wiley & Sons, Chichester, Sussex.

Brennan, D.F. (1997) Trade and environmental goals at a crossroads: challenges for global treaties and national environmental regulation, *International Environment Reporter*, BNA, vol. 20(3), p.133.

Cavanagh, J. *et al.* (Eds) (1994) *Beyond Bretton Woods. Alternatives to global economic order*, Zed Books, London.

Charnovitz, S. (1993) Environmental harmonization and trade policy, in Zaelke, D., Orbuch, P. and Housman, R.F. (Eds) *Trade and the Environment. Law, economics, and policy*, Island Press, Washington, D.C., pp.267–86.

Charnovitz, S. (1997) The World Trade Organization and the environment, *Yearbook of International Environmental Law*, vol. 8, pp.98–116.

Clapp, J. (1998) The privatization of global environmental governance: ISO 14000 and the developing world, *Global Governance*, vol. 4, pp.295–316.

Cohen, J. (1998) More than 4,000 companies certified under ISO 14001; Japan, Europe lead way, *International Environment Reporter*, BNA, vol. 21(13), p.650.

Favre, C.J. (1998) Aspects of ISO's cooperation with the World Trade Organization (WTO), *ISO Bulletin*, vol. 29(12), p.2.

Finger, M. (1991) The military, the nation-state and the environment, *The Ecologist*, vol. 21(5): 220–5.

Finger, M. (1998) Néolibéralisme contre nouvelle gestion publique, *Nouveau Cahiers de l'IUED*, Geneva, No. 8, pp.5776.

Finger, M. and Kilcoyne, J. (1997) Why transnational corporations are organizing to 'Save the global environment', *The Ecologist*, vol. 27(4): 138–42.

Fredericks, I. and McCallum, D. (1995) International Standards for Environmental Management Systems: ISO 14000, www.mgmt14k.com/ems.html

Gleizes, F. (1998) Voluntary EMS standards will not replace government regulation, seminar concludes, *International Environment Reporter*, BNA, vol. 21(10): 460.

Hauselmann, P. (1998) WWF's experience in following ISO's work on environmental management, PPCG special session on ISO Environmental Management Standards and implications for policy making, 4 May, Paris, OECD, unpublished.

Hutchinson, G.A. (1998) If you give to those in need, it will be returned to you manifold, *ISO Bulletin*, October.

International Environment Reporter (1998) China: adherence to ISO 14000 standards to be monitored by auditors' board, *International Environment Reporter*, BNA, vol. 21(1): 17.

International Environment Reporter (1999), Developing countries said to be increasingly viewing environment rules as protectionist, *International Environment Reporter*, BNA, vol. 22(16): 652.

Krueger, A. (Ed.) (1998) *The WTO as an International Organization*, The University of Chicago Press, Chicago.

Krut, R. and Gleckman, H. (1998) *ISO 14001. A missed opportunity for sustainable industrial development*, Earthscan, London.

Murray, P.C. (1997) The International Environmental Management Standard, ISO 14000: a non-tariff barrier or a step to an emerging global environmental policy?, *University of Pennsylvania Journal of International Economic Law*, vol. 18(2), pp.577–615.

Pinckard, E. (1997) SO 14000, *Colorado Journal of International Environmental Law and Policy*, vol. 8(2): 423–50.

Roht-Arriaza, N. (1995a) Shifting the point of regulation: the International Organization for Standardization and global law-making on trade and the environment, *Ecology Law Quarterly*, vol. 22(3): 479–539.

Roht-Arriaza, N. (1995b) Private voluntary standard-setting, the International Organization for Standardization, and international environmental law-making, *Yearbook of International Environmental Law*, vol. 6, pp.107–63.

Rotherham, T. (1998) The ISO 14001 Environmental Management System standard, *Bridges*, March, p.9.

Schwamm, H. (1997) World trade needs worldwide standards, *ISO Bulletin*, vol. 28(9), pp.12–28.

South Centre (1997) *For a Strong and Democratic United Nations. A South perspective on UN reform*, Zed Books, London.

Speer, L.J. (1997) From command-and-control to self-regulation: the role of environmental management systems, *International Environment Reporter*, BNA, vol. 20(5), p.227.

Tamiotti, L. and Finger, M. (2001) Environmental Organizations: Changing Roles and Functions in Global Politics, *Global Environmental Politics*, vol. 1(1): 56–76.

Timoshenko, A.S. (1992) Ecological security: response to global challenges, in Brown Weiss, E. (Ed.) *Environmental Change and International Law: new challenges and dimensions*, United Nations University Press, Tokyo.

Tobon, F. (1999) Twinning and sharing between partners at a similar stage of development, *ISO Bulletin*, August.

UNCTAD (1996a) *Self-regulation of Environmental Management. An analysis of guidelines set by world industry associations for their member firms*, United Nations, New York and Geneva.

UNCTAD (1996b) ISO 14001: International Environmental Management Systems standards, five key questions for developing country officials, draft report, Geneva.

UNCTAD (1997) *Report of the expert meeting on possible trade and investment impacts of environmental management standards, particularly the ISO 14000 series, on developing countries, and opportunities and needs in this context*, Geneva, TD/B/COM.1, TD/B/COM.1/EM.4/3.

Chapter 6

Abell, A. (1998) So you want to be a CKO too … ? *Library Association*, vol. 1(8).

Albrow, M. (1990) Introduction, in Albrow, M. and Kind, E. (Eds) *Globalisation, Knowledge and Society: Readings from International Sociology*, Sage Publications, London.

Alvarez, F. (1998) Knowledge Management at the World Bank. A report of a visit 9.11.1998, Oxfam, Oxford.

Alvarez, F. (1999) *Oxfam Interventions and People's Knowledge: the case of hurricanes Mitch and George in CAMEXCAR and floods in East Asia*, Oxfam, Oxford.

Bebbington, A. (1994) Theory and relevance of indigenous knowledge: knowledge, agency and organization, in Booth, D. (Ed.) *Rethinking Social Development*, Longman Scientific and Technical, Harlow.

Beijerse, R.P. (1999) Questions in knowledge management: defining and conceptualising a phenomenon, Journal of Knowledge Management, vol. 3(2), pp.94–109.

Cameron, D., Frazer, L., Harvey, P., Rampton, M.B.H. and Richardson, K. (1992) *Language: issues of power and method*, Routledge, London.

Chambers, R. (1992) Rural Appraisal: rapid, relaxed and participatory, University of Sussex, IDS Discussion Paper 311.

Clark, J. (1997) The state, popular participation and the voluntary sector, in Hulme, D. and Edwards, M. (Eds) *NGOs, States and Donors: too close for comfort?*, Save the Children and Macmillan Press, London.

Crush, J. (1995) *Power of Development*, Routledge, London.

Dasgupta, P. (1993) *An Inquiry into Wellbeing and Destitution*, Clarendon Press, Oxford.

Davenport, T. and Marchand, D. (1999) Is KM just good information management? *Financial Times*, 8 March, pp.2–3.

Davies, S. (1994) Information, knowledge and power, *IDS Bulletin*, vol. 25(2), pp.1–13.

Despres, C. and Chauvel, D. (1999) How to map knowledge management, *Financial Times*, 8 March 8, pp.4–5.

De Waal, A. (1997) *Famine Crimes: politics and the disaster relief industry in Africa*, African Rights and James Curry, Oxford.

Eade, D. and Williams, S. (1995) *The Oxfam Handbook of Development and Relief*, Oxfam, Oxford.

Guardian (2000) Disillusion 2001? Jubilee 2000 must not be betrayed, *Guardian*, 21 July.

Hallam, E. and Walker, M. (1998) Why get involved in the Internet?, in Grimwood-Jones, D. and Simmons, S. (Eds) *Information Management in The Voluntary Sector*, ASLIB, London.

Harding, S. (1991) *Whose Science?Whose Knowledge?*, Open University Press, Milton Keynes.

Holden, C.M. (1993) An investigation into the substantive basis of participatory rural appraisal, MA Dissertation, School of Development Studies, East Anglia.

Howes, M. and Roche, C. (1996) How NGOs learn: the case of Oxfam UK, paper presented at the DSA Conference.

Long, N. and Villareal, M. (1993) Exploring development interfaces: from the transfer of knowledge to the transformation of meaning, in Schuurman, F. (Ed.) *Beyond the Impasse: new directions in development Theory*, Zed Books, London.

Jorgensen, L. (1996) What are NGOs doing in civil society?, in Clayton, E. (Ed.) *NGOs, Civil Society and the State: building democracy in transitional societies*, INTRAC Publications, Oxford.

Made, P.A. (2000) Globalization and gender training for the media: challenges and lessons learned, *Gender and Development*, vol. 8(1), pp.10–20.

Malhotra, Y. (1996) Organizational learning and learning organizations: an overview, (www.brint.com/papers/orglrng.htm).

McGrew, A. (2000) Sustainable globalization?The global politics of development and exclusion in the new world order, in Allen, T. and Thomas, A. (Eds) *Poverty and Development into the 21st Century*, Oxford University Press, Oxford.

Neefjees, K. (1994) *PRA and Planning for Sustainable Development: a report on workshop in Muong Kuong District, Vietnam*, Oxfam, Oxford.

Oxfam (1998) *Setting Course for the Twenty First Century*, Oxfam Strategic Review 1998.

Panos (1999) Information, Knowledge and Development, *Debate and Development* October, Panos, London.

Pearson, R. (2000) Moving the goalposts: gender and globalisation in the twenty-first century, *Gender and Development*, vol, 8(1), pp.10–20.

Pinder (1999) Whose terms? Observations on 'development management' in an English city, *Development in Practice*, vol. 9(1–2): 151–9.

Rahnema, M. (1992) Participation, in Sachs, W. (Ed.) *The Development Dictionary: a guide to knowledge as power*, Zed Books, London.

Rai, S.M. (2002) *Gender and the Political Economy of Development*. Polity Press, Cambridge.

Roche, C. (1995) Institutional learning in Oxfam: some thoughts, internal memo, Oxfam, Oxford.

Roman, S. and Edwards, C. (1998) Knowledge Management, LIAC (98) 2nd Meeting, Paper 3

Selener, D., Endara, N. and Carvajal, J. (1999) *Participatory Rural Appraisal and Planning Workbook*, International Institute of Rural Reconstruction, Cavite, Philippines.

Shiva, S. (1988) *Staying Alive*, Zed Books, London.

Shiva, V. (2000) Respect for the Earth, Reith Lecture no. 5.

Siochru, S. (1999) *Contribution to Development Project Knowledge Network*, Nexus Research, Dublin

Stanley, L. and Wise, S. (1990) Method, methodology and epistemology in feminist research processes. in Stanley, L., *Feminist Praxis: research, theory and epistemology in feminist sociology*, Routledge, London.

Webb, S.P. (1998) *Knowledge Management: linchpin of change*, ASLIB, London.

Wilson, G. (1999) Local knowledge and changing technologies, in Skelton, T. and Allen, T. (Eds) *Culture and Global Change*, Routledge, London.

World Bank (1999) *Knowledge for Development 1998/99*, Oxford University Press, Oxford.

Youngs, G. and Sreberny, A. (1999) Women and new ICTs, *The Network Newsletter*, The British Council, no. 18, April, pp.1–3.

Chapter 7

Ashworth, J., Johnson, P. and Conway, C. How good are small firms at predicting employment?, *Small Business Economics*, vol. 10, 1998, pp.379–87.

Atkinson, J. and Storey, D. (1993) *Employment, Small Firms and the Labour Market*, Routledge, London.

Autio, E. (1997) 'Atomistic' and 'systemic' approaches to research on new, technology-based firms: a literature survey, *Small Business Economics*, vol. 9, pp.195–209.

Bagnasco, A. and Sabel, C. (1995) *Small and Medium Sized Enterprise*, Pinter, London.

Best, M. (1990) *The New Competition*, Oxford University Press, Oxford.

Berger, S. and Dore, R. (Eds) (1998) *National Diversity and Global Capitalism*, Cornell, Ithaca, NY.

Birch, D.L. (1979) *The job generation process*, MIT Press, Cambridge, MA.

Bolton, J. (1971) *Chairman Report of the Commission of Inquiry on Small Firms,* Command 4811, HMSO, London.

Boyer, R. and Drache, D. (1996) *States Against Markets – the limits of globalization,* Routledge, London.

Buckley, P.J. (1989) Foreign direct investment by small and medium sized enterprises: the theoretical background, *Small Business Economics,* vol. 1(2), pp.89–100.

Dannreuther, C. and Lekhi, R. (1999) Globalisation and the political economy of risk, paper presented at the International Studies Association, Washington.

Dicken, P. (1998) *Global Shift,* 3rd edn, Paul Chapman Press, London.

Diwan, R. (1989) Small business and the economics of flexible manufacturing. *Small Business Review,* vol. 1: 101–9.

DTI (1985) *Burdens on Business: report of the scrutiny of administrative and legislative requirements,* HMSO, London.

DTI (1992) *Checking the Cost to Business: a guide to Compliance Cost Assessment,* HMSO, London.

Ferner, A. and Hyman, R. (1992) *Industrial Relations in the New Europe,* Blackwell, Oxford.

Froud, J. and Ogus, A. (1996) 'Rational' social regulation and compliance cost assessment, *Public Administration,* vol. 74, pp.221–37.

Fujita, M. (1995a) Small and medium sized transnational corporations: trends and patterns of foreign direct investment, *Small Business Economics,* vol. 7, pp.183–204.

Fujita, M. (1995b) Small and medium sized transnational corporations: salient features, *Small Business Economics,* vol. 7, pp.251–71.

Fukuyama, F. (1992) *The End of History and the Last Man,* Free Press, New York.

Granovetter, M. (1986) Economic action and social structure: the problem of embeddedness, *American Journal of Sociology,* vol. 91(3), pp.481–510.

Hall, P. (1993) Policy paradigms, social learning and the state. The case of economics policy-making in Britain, *Comparative Politics,* vol. 25(3), pp.275–96.

Henrekson, M. and Johansson, D. (1999) Institutional effects on the evolution of the size distribution of firms, *Small Business Economics,* vol. 12, 1999, pp.11–23.

Hirst, P. and Thompson, G. (1996) *Globalisation In Question,* Polity Press, Cambridge.

Hood, C. (1991) A public management for all seasons, *Public Administration,* vol. 69(1), Spring, pp.3–19.

Julien, P-A. (1993) Small business as a research subject: some reflections on knowledge of small businesses and its effects on economic theory, *Small Business Economics,* vol. 5, pp.157–66.

Keeble, D., Lawson, C., Lawton Smith, H., Moore, B. and Wilkinson, F. (1998) Internationalisation processes, networking and local embeddedness in technology-intensive small firms, *Small Business Economics,* vol, 11, pp. 327–42.

Majone, G. (1994) The rise of the regulatory state, *Western European Politics,* vol. 17(3), August, pp. 77–101.

Majone, G. (1996) *Regulating Europe,* Routledge, London.

Marglin, S. and Schor, J. (1990) *The Golden Age of Capitalism: reinterpreting the postwar experience,* Clarendon Press, Oxford.

McHugh, J. (1986) The self-employed and the small independent entrepreneur, in Curran, J., Stanworth, J. and Watkins, D. (Eds) *The Survival of the Small Firm,* Gower, Aldershot.

de la Mothe, J. and Pacquet, G. (1994) National innovation systems, 'real economies' and instituted processes, *Small Business Review,* pp.100–11.

Nugent, N. (Ed.) (1979) *Respectable Rebels: middle class campaigns in Britain in the 1970s,* Hodder and Stoughton, London.

OECD (1997) *Globalization and Small and Medium Sized Enterprises (SMEs),* vol.1 (synthesis report), OECD, Paris.

Omhae, K. (1990) *The Borderless World*, Fontana, New York.
Petrella, R. (1996) 'Globalisation and Internationalisation: the dynamics of the emerging world order, in Boyer and Drache (1996) *States Against Markets – the limits of globalization*, Routledge, London.
Piore, M.J. and Sabel, C. (1986) *The Second Industrial Divide*, Basic Books, New York.
Polanyi, K. (1980) *The Great Transformation: the political and economic origins of our time*, Beacon Press, Boston, MA.
Robertson, R. (1992) Social theory, cultural relativity and the problem of globality, in King. A. (Ed.) *Culture, Globalization and the World-System*, Macmillan, Basingstoke.
Sengenberger, W., Loveman, G. and Piore, M. (1990) *The Re-emergence of the Small and Medium Sized Enterprise*, International Labour Organisation, Geneva.
Schonfield, A. (1965) *Modern Capitalism: the changing balance of public and private power*, Oxford University Press, London.
Wagner, J. (1995) Firm size and job creation in Germany, *Small Business Economics*, vol. 7, pp.469–74.
Watson, M. (1999) Globalisation and the development of the British political economy, in Marsh, D. *et al.* (Eds) *Postwar British Politics in Perspective*, Polity, Cambridge.
Weiss, L. (1988) *Creating Capitalism – the state and small business since 1945*, Blackwell, Oxford.

Chapter 8

Barndt, D. (1999) *Women Working the NAFTA Food Chain, Women, Food and Globalization*, Second Story Press, Toronto.
Barrientos, S., Bee, A., Matear, A. and Vogel, I. (1999) *Women and Agribusiness: working miracles in the Chilean fruit export sector*, Macmillan, Basingstoke.
Bekure, Z. *et al.* (1997) *Local to Global: the international market for shea butter*, UNIFEM, New York.
Bhattachararya, D. (1999) The post-MFA challenges to the Bangladesh textile and clothing sector, in *UNCTAD, Trade, Sustainable Development and Gender*, United Nations, New York and Geneva.
Cardero, M.E., Barron, A. and Gomez Luna, M.E. (2000) *NAFTA's Impact on the Female Work Force in Mexico*, UNIFEM, Mexico.
Carr, M. (1998) Gender implications of globalization (with special reference to the Asian financial crisis), paper presented to a roundtable during International Women's Week, sponsored by the Women in Development and Gender Equity Division, Policy Branch, CIDA Canada.
Carr, M., Chen, M.A. and Tate, J. (2000) Globalization and homebased workers, *Feminist Economics*, vol. 6(3), pp.123–142.
Chen, M., Sebstad J. and O'Connel, L. (1999) Counting the invisible workforce: the case of homebased workers, *World Development*, vol. 27(3).
DAW (1999) *World Survey on the Role of Women in Development*, United Nations, New York.
Division for the Advancement of Women (DAW) (1999) *World Survey on the Role of Women in Development: globalization, gender and work*, United Nations, New York.
Dolan, C., Humphrey, J. and Harris-Pascal, C. (1999) Horticulture Commodity Chains: the impact of the UK market on the African fresh vegetable industry, IDS Working Paper 96.
FAO (1995) *Trade Restrictions Affecting International Trade in Non-wood Forest Products*, FAO, Rome.
FIAS (1998) Foreign Direct Investment and Poverty Alleviation: background paper by C. Aaron and T. Andaya, HIID.

Fontana, M., Joekes S. and Masika, R. (1998) *Global Trader Expansion and Liberalization: gender issues and impacts*, DFID, London.

Gereffi, G., and Korzeniewicz, M. (Eds) (1994) *Commodity Chains and Global Capitalism*, Praeger, Westport.

Ghiara, R. (1999) The impact of trade liberalization on female wages in Mexico, *Development Policy Review*, vol. 17(2).

Gibb, H. (1997) *Gender Front and Centre: an APEC primer*, North South Institute, Ottawa.

International Union for Conservation of Nature (IUCN) (1999) *Big Fish, Small Fry* (video).

Joekes, S. (1995) *Trade-related Employment for Women in Industry and Services in Developing Countries*, UNRISD, Geneva.

Joekes, S. (1999) A gender-analytical perspective on trade and sustainable development, in *UNCTAD, Trade, Sustainable Development and Gender*, United Nations, New York and Geneva.

Joekes, S. and Weston A. (1994) *Women and the New Trade Agenda*, UNIFEM, New York.

Kabeer, N. (1995) Necessity, sufficient or irrelevant? Women, wages and intrahousehold power relations in Bangladesh, IDS Working Paper No. 25, Brighton.

Kaihuzi, M. (1999) LDCs in a globalizing world: a strategy for gender and balanced sustainable development, in *UNCTAD, Trade, Sustainable Development and Gender*, United Nations, New York and Geneva.

Kapila, S. (1999) Internal Report, IDRC, Nairobi.

Ongile, G. (1999) *Gender and Agricultural Supply Responses to Strucutural Adjustment Progammes: a case study of small holder tea producers in Kericho*, Kenya. Nordiska Afrikainstitutet, Research report No. 109, Uppsala.

Overseas Development Institute (ODI) (1997) Direct Foreign Investment in developing countries. ODI Briefing Paper, London.

Provost, S. (1995) *Etude de la Filiere Karite au Burkina Faso*, CECI, Montreal.

Rodrik, D. (1997) *Has Globalization Gone Too Far?* Institute for International Economics, Washington, D.C.

Schoettle, E.S.B. and Grant, K.L. (1998) *Globalization and Information Technologies*, The Rockerfeller Foundation, New York.

Singh, A. and Zimmit, A. (1999) International capital flows: identifying the gender dimension, prepared for the workshop Gender, Macroeconomics and Globalization, hosted by UNDP, 25–26 March, New York.

Skinner, C. (1999) *Local Government in Transition – a gendered analysis of trends in urban policy and practice regarding street trading in five South African cities*, School of Development Studies, University of Natal, Research Report (18).

Stark, A. and de Vylder, S. (1998) *Mainstreaming Gender in Namibia's National Budget*, Department of Women's Affairs, Namibia/SIDA Stockholm.

TCFUA (1995) *The Hidden Cost of Fashion*, report on the National Outword Information Campaign, TCFUA, Sydney, Australia.

TCFUA (1996) *People Behind Profit*, TCFUA, Sydney, Australia.

UNIFEM (1996) *Global Trading Practices and Poverty Alleviation in South Asia: regional perspectives on women and trade*, UNIFEM, New Delhi.

USAID Office of Women in Development (1999) *Saving the Seeds of Opportunity: women in agribusiness*, Information Bulletin No. 7, USAID, Washington D.C.

Wee, V. (Ed.) (1998) *Trade Liberalization: challenges and opportunities for women in SouthEast Asia*, UNIFEM and Engender, Singapore.

WIEGO (1999a) Social Protection Programme, Overview Paper.

WIEGO/IDRC (1999b) Women and Non-Timber Forest Products, paper prepared for WIEGO Annual Meeting held in Ottawa.

Chapter 9

Afshar, H. and Barrientos, S. (1999) *Women, Globalization and Fragmentation*, Macmillan, Basingstoke.

Barrientos, S., Bee, A., Matear, A., Vogel, I. (1999a) *Women and Agribusiness, Working Miracles in the Chilean Fruit Export Sector*, Macmillan, Basingstoke.

Barrientos, S., McClenaghan, S. and Orton, L. (1999b) *Gender and Codes of Conduct: a case study from horticulture in South Africa*, Christian Aid, London.

Barrientos, S., McClenaghan, S. and Orton, L. (2000) Ethical trade and South African deciduous fruit exports – addressing gender sensitivity, *European Journal of Development Research*, vol. 12(1): 140–58.

Blowfield, M. (1999) Ethical trade: a review of developments and issues, *Third World Quarterly*, vol. 20(4): 753–70.

Elson, D. (1991) *Male Bias in the Development Process*, Manchester University Press, Manchester.

Elson, D. and Pearson, R. (1981) Nimble fingers make cheap workers, an analysis of women's employment in Third World export manufacturing, *Feminist Review*, Spring, pp.87–107.

ETI (1998) *Purposes, Principles, Program – membership information*, Ethical Trading Initiative, London.

ETI (1999) *'Learning From Doing' Review, a report on company progress in implementing ethical sourcing policies and practices*, Ethical Trading Initiative, London.

Ferguson, C. (1998) *A Review of Company Codes of Conduct*, Department for International Development, London.

Hakim, C. (1987) Trends in the flexible workforce, *Employment Gazette*, November, pp.549–60.

Kabeer, N. (1994a) *Reversed Realities, Gender Hierarchies in Development Thought*, Verso, London.

Kabeer, N. (1994b) Women's labour in the Bangladesh garment industry: choices and constraints, in Fawzi El-Solh, C. and Mabro, J. (Eds) *Muslim Women's Choices, Religious Belief and Social Reality*, Berg, Oxford.

Kritzinger, A. and Vorster, J. (1996) Women farm workers on South African deciduous fruit farms: gender relations and the structuring of work, *Journal of Rural Studies*, vol. 12(4): pp.339–51.

Molyneux, M. (1985) Mobilization without emancipation? Women's interests, the state and revolution in Nicaragua, *Feminist Studies*, vol. 11(2): pp.227–54.

Rowbotham, S. and Mitter, S. (1994) *Dignity and Daily Bread, New Forms of Economic Organising among Poor Women in the Third World and First*, Routledge, London.

Sengenberger, W. and Campbell, D. (Eds) (1994) *International Labour Standards and Economic Interdependence*, International Labour Organisation, Geneva.

Standing, G. (1989) Global feminization through flexible labour. *World Development*, vol. 17(7): 1077–95.

Standing, G. (1999) Global feminisation through flexible labour: a theme revisited, *World Development*, vol. 27(3): 583–602.

Thrupp, L. (1995) *Bittersweet Harvests for Global Supermarkets, Challenges in Latin America's Agricultural Export Boom*, World Resources Institute, Washington D.C.

Ward, K. (Ed.) (1990) *Women Workers and Global Restructuring*, ILR Press, Cornell University.

Chapter 10

Bauman, Z. (1998) *Globalization: the human consequences*, Polity Press, Cambridge.

Beloe, S. (1999) Corporations: plus ça change?, *IDS Bulletin*, vol. 30(3): 43–9.

Cerny, P. (1996) What next for the State?, in Kofman, E. and Young, G. (Eds) *Globalization: theory and practice*, Pinter, London.

Chatterjee, P. and Finger, M. (1994) *The Earth Brokers*, Routledge, London.

Dicken, P. (1992), *Global Shift: the internationalization of economic activity*, Paul Chapman, London.

Donigi, P. (1994) *Indigenous or Aboriginal Rights to Property: a Papua New Guinea perspective*, Cornell University Press, London.

Dunning, J. (1993) *Multinational Enterprises in a Global Economy*, Addison-Wesley, Wokingham.

Elkington, J. (1998) The 'triple bottom line' for twenty-first century business, in Mitchell, J. (Ed.) *Companies in a World of Conflict*, Earthscan, London.

Fabig, H. and Boele, R. (1999) The changing nature of NGO activity in a globalising world: pushing the corporate responsibility agenda, *IDS Bulletin*, vol. 30(3), 58–67.

Finger, M. and Tamiotti, L. (1999) New global regulatory mechanisms and the environment: the emerging linkage between the WTO and the ISO, *IDS Bulletin*, vol. 30(3), 8–15.

FoE (1995) *Mineral Sands Mining Project in Madagascar*, Friends of the Earth, London.

Giddens, A. (1990) *The Consequences of Modernity*, Polity Press, Cambridge.

Gray, J. (1998) *False Dawn: the delusions of global capitalism*, Granta Books, London.

Greer, J. and Bruno, K. (1996) *Greenwash: the reality behind corporate environmentalism*, Apex Press, New York.

Hildyard, N. (1993) Foxes in charge of the chickens, in Sachs, W. (Ed.) *Global Ecology*, Zed Books, London.

Hildyard, N., Hines, C. *et al.* (1996) Who competes? Changing landscapes of corporate control, *The Ecologist*, vol. 26(4).

Korten, D. (1995) *When Corporations Rule the World*, Earthscan, London.

Lang, T. and Hines, C. (1993) *The New Protectionism: protecting the future against free trade*, Earthscan, London.

Luard, E. (1990) *The Globalization of Politics*, Macmillan, London.

McGrew, A.G., Lewis, P.G. *et al.* (Eds) (1992) *Global Politics: globalization and the nation state*, Polity, Cambridge.

Mitchell, J. (1998) Editor's overview, in Mitchell, J. (Ed.) *Companies in a World of Conflict*, Earthscan, London.

Moody, R. (1990) Rio Tinto Zinc: the British mining monster, *Multinational Monitor*, April.

Moody, R. (1996) Mining the world: the global reach of Rio Tinto Zinc, *The Ecologist*, vol. 26(2).

Mulligan, P., The marginalisation of indigenous peoples from tribal lands in southeast Madagascar, *Journal of International Development*, vol. 11 (Development Studies Associations Conference Special Addition), 1999, 649–59.

Newell, P. (2000) Environmental NGOs, TNCs and the question of governance, in Cohen, R. and Rai, S. (Eds) *Global Social Movements*, Athlone Press, London.

PARTiZANS (quarterly) Parting Company, People Against Rio Tinto Zinc And Subsidiaries, London.

Raghavan, C. (1996) What is globalization? *Third World Resurgence*, vol. 74.

Rahnema, M. (1996) Participation, in Sachs, W. (Ed.) *The Development Dictionary*, Zed Books, London.

Robertson, R. (1992) *Globalization: social theory and global culture*, Sage, London.

Rowell, A. (1996) *Green Backlash*, Routledge, London.

Scholte, J.A. (1996) Beyond the buzzword: towards a critical theory of globalization, in Kofman, E. and Youngs, G. (Eds) *Globalization: theory and practice*, Pinter, London, pp.43–57.

Sklair, L. (1994) Capitalism and development in global perspective, in Sklair L (Ed.) *Capitalism and Development*, Routledge, London, pp.165–85.

TIS (1999) The Industry Standard: Company profile – Rio Tinto PLC, www.cgrg.ohio-state.edu/interface/W96/page.html, 5 October.

UN (1992) Draft Universal Declaration of Indigenous Rights, United Nations, New York.

Waters, M. (1995) *Globalization*, Routledge, London.

Watts, P. (1998) The international petroleum industry: economic actor or social activist?, in Mitchell, J. (Ed.) *Companies in a World of Conflict*, Earthscan, London.

WDM (1999) World Development Movement, www.oneworld.org/wdm/action/mining/htm, 24 March.

Willetts, P. (1998) Political globalization and the impact of NGOs upon transnational companies, in Mitchell, J. (Ed.) *Companies in the World of Conflict*, Earthscan, London, pp.195–227.

World Development Indicators Database (2002), www.worldbank.org/data/wdi/2002/

Chapter 11

Anderson, M. and Ahmed, A. (1996) Assessing environmental damage under Indian law, REICIEL 5/4, pp.335–41.

Australian Senate (2000) Corporate code of conduct bill: A bill for an act to impose standards on the conduct of Australian corporations which undertake business activities in other countries and for related purposed, drafted by Senator Bourne.

Ayine, D. and Werksman, J. (1999) Implications of the MAI for use of natural resources and land', in Picciotto, S. and Mayne, R., *Regulating International Business: beyond liberalization*, Macmillan, Basingstoke, pp.126–42.

Barrientos, S. and Orton, L. (1999) *Gender and Codes of Conduct: a case study from horticulture in South Africa*, Christian Aid, London.

Baxi, U. and Paul T. (1986) *Mass Disasters and Multinational Liability: The Bhopal Case*, Indian Law Institute, New Delhi.

Baxi, U. and Dhandra, A. (1990) *Valiant Victims and Lethal Litigation*, Indian Law Institute, New Delhi.

Bendell, J. (Ed.) (2000) *Terms of Endearment: business, NGOs and sustainable development*, Greenleaf Publishers, Sheffield.

Caulkin, S. (1997) Amnesty and WWF take a crack at Shell, *Observer*, 11 May.

Cottrell, J. (1992) Courts and accountability: public interest litigation in the Indian high courts, *Third World Legal Studies*, pp. 199–213.

DFID (2000) *Eliminating World Poverty: making globalisation work for the poor*, White Paper on International Development, December.

Dickson, L. and McCulloch, A. (1996) Shell, the Brent Spar and Greenpeace: a doomed tryst?, *Environmental Politics*, vol. 5(1), pp.122–9.

Friends of the Earth International (FOEI) (2002) Towards binding corporate accountability, Draft FOEI paper for the WSSD, http://www.foei.org/campaigns/R10_10/prepcom.html

Frynas, G. (1998) Political instability and business: focus on Shell in Nigeria, *Third World Quarterly*, vol. 19(3), pp.457–78.

Frynas, G. (1999) Legal change in Africa: evidence from oil-related litigation in Nigeria, *Journal of African Law*, vol. 43, pp.121–50.

Gill, S. and Law, D. (1988) *The Global Political Economy*, Harvester/Wheatsheaf, Herts.

Humphreys, D. (1997) Environmental accountability and transnational corporations, paper presented to the International Academic Conference on Environmental Justice: Global ethics for the 21st century, University of Melbourne, Australia, 1–3 October.

Kearney, N. (1999) Corporate codes of conduct: the privatised application of labour standards, in Picciotto, S. and Mayne, R., *Regulating International Business: beyond liberalization*, Macmillan, Basingstoke, pp.205–21.

Lewis, W. (1997) Shell to face shareholder vote on ethics, *Financial Times*, 12 April.

Madeley, J. (1999) *Big Business, Poor People*, Zed Books, London.

Marinetto, M., The shareholders strike back – issues in the research of shareholder, *Activism Environmental Politics*, vol. 7(3), 1999, pp.125–33.

McLaren, D. (2000) *The OECD's revised 'Guidelines for Multinational Enterprises: a step towards corporate accountability?'*, Friends of the Earth, London.

Mittelman, J. (1998) Globalisation and environmental resistance politics, *Third World Quarterly*, vol. 19(5), pp.847–72.

Muchlinksi, P. (1999) A brief history of business regulation, in Picciotto, S. and Mayne, R. (Eds) *Regulating International Business: beyond liberalization*, Macmillan, Basingstoke.

Muchlinski, P. (2001) Corporations in international litigation: problems of jurisdiction and the United Kingdom asbestos cases, *International and Comparative Law Quarterly*, vol. 50.

Murphy, D. and Bendell, J. (1997) *In the Company of Partners*, Policy Press, Bristol, pp.105–30.

Newell, P. (2000) Environmental NGOs and globalisation: the governance of TNCs, in Cohen, R. and Rai, S. (Eds) *Global Social Movements*, Athlone Press, London, pp.117–34.

Newell, P. (2001a) Environmental NGOs, TNCs and the question of governance, in Stevis, D. and Assetto, V. (Eds) *The International Political Economy of the Environment: Critical Perspectives*, Lynne Riener, Boulder, CO, and London.

Newell, P. (2001b) Access to environmental justice? Litigation against TNCs in the South, *IDS Bulletin*, vol. 32(1).

Picciotto, S. and Mayne, R. (1999) *Regulating International Business: beyond liberalization*, Macmillan, Basingstoke.

Rodman, K. (1997) Think globally, sanction locally: non-state actors, multinational corporations and human rights, paper at Warwick University Conference on Non-state Actors and Authority in the Global System, 31 October–1 November, pp.29–36.

Rodman, K. (1998) Think globally, punish locally: non-state actors, MNCs and human rights sanctions, *Ethics and International Affairs*, vol. 12.

Rowen, A. (1998) Meet the new world government, *The Guardian*, 13 February.

Sauermann, D. (1985–86) The regulation of multinational corporations and Third World countries, 11 *South African Yearbook of International Law* 55.

Schmidheiny, S. (1992) *Changing Course: a global business perspective on development and the environment*, MIT Press, Cambridge, MA.

Seyfang, G. (1999) Private sector self-regulation for social research Programme, DFID/UEA.

Sripada, S. (1989) The multinational corporations and environmental Issues, *Journal of the Indian Law Institute*, vol. 31(4): 534–52.

Vogel, D. (1997) Trading up and governing across: transnational governance and environmental protection, *Journal of European Public Policy*, vol. 4.

Wapner, P. (1995) *Environmental Activism and World Civic Politics*, SUNY, New York.

Wapner, P. (1997) Governance in global civil society, in Oran Young, Oran, R. (Ed.) *Global Governance*, MIT Press, Cambridge, MA, pp.67.

Ward, H. (2000) Foreign direct liability: exploring the issues, FDL Workshop background paper, RIIA.

World Bank (2000) Is globalisation causing a race to the bottom in environmental standards?, Briefing paper, PREM Economic Policy Group and Development Economics Group.

World Development Movement (WDM) (1998) Law unto themselves: holding multi-nationals to account, Discussion paper, September, pp.5–7.

Wray, N. (2000) Texaco document, Center for Economic and Social Rights.

Index